CULTURAL CRISIS
AND LIBRARIES
IN THE
THIRD WORLD

CULTURAL CRISIS
AND LIBRARIES
IN THE
THIRD WORLD

Ronald Charles Benge

CLIVE BINGLEY
LONDON

LINNET BOOKS
HAMDEN · CONN

First published 1979 by Clive Bingley Ltd
1-19 New Oxford Street, London WC1, UK
Simultaneously published in the USA by
Linnet Books, an imprint of the Shoe String Press Inc
995 Sherman Avenue, Hamden, Conn 06514
Set in 10 on 12 point Press Roman by Allset
Printed and bound in the UK by Redwood Burn Ltd
Trowbridge and Esher
Copyright © Ronald Charles Benge
All rights reserved
Bingley ISBN: 0-85157-281-2
Linnet ISBN: 0-208-01668-6

Library of Congress Cataloging in Publication Data

Benge, Ronald C
    Cultural crisis and libraries in the Third World.

    Includes bibliographical references.
    1. Underdeveloped areas.   2. Underdeveloped areas—
Education.   3. Underdeveloped areas—Mass media.
4. Underdeveloped areas—Libraries.   I. Title.
HN980.B46   309.1'172'4   79-12929
ISBN 0-208-01668-6

CONTENTS

Dedicated to students and colleagues
at Ahmadu Bello University,
Zaria, Nigeria, 1973-79

PART I

DEVELOPMENT

INTRODUCTION

This work is an examination of themes which have been present in my other books; in particular it is a kind of sequel to *Libraries and cultural change* which was mainly concerned with Britain.

Anyone who writes about developing countries is faced with inherent difficulties. The most persistent of these is that doubts recur as to the possibility of generalising about millions of people whose lives have only one common element: the pattern called underdevelopment. Much of my working life has been spent in West Africa and my outlook has therefore been conditioned by that experience. It follows that this contribution may be more relevant to that part of the world than to others.

There are certain obvious historical factors which make the African situation unique. Compared with India or Latin America, the technological and cultural impact of the modernisation process in most African countries has been both sudden and recent. As Hunter has noted, 'Thus in modernising Africa it was not only that the impact of twentieth century technology and institutions was far sharper: it was not only that the period of forced adjustment was far shorter. There is a third factor: ideas of democracy and socialism had been implanted throughout the world, a wholly new concept of political, economic and social growth.' (1) It follows that I have been particularly concerned with a decolonising process which has taken place only within the last twenty years and a modernisation which is almost wholly of the twentieth century. These are extreme circumstances which have especially influenced Nigerian development. For reasons which need not concern us here, the characteristics of underdevelopment exist there in an acute form and it is this which makes a consideration of Nigerian conditions relevant for other countries where the same processes can be found operating in a more subdued fashion. (There is the further fact that one out of every four Africans is a Nigerian.)

Having noted that Africa has its own circumstances, it remains true that the symptoms of underdevelopment are universal and can be identified. Many authorities have observed that there are certain striking common features even with countries which have quite different backgrounds. Gunnar Myrdal, who has been called the 'Adam Smith of poverty' states with regard to education: 'The historical background and many other conditioning factors are very different in Latin America, in West Asia and in North Africa and the considerable similarities in educational situation are for this reason surprising. The one unifying common trait is the political domination by a small upper class.' With regard to development generally he concludes: 'A cursory study of the literature . . . confirms the impression that *almost everywhere there are broadly similar problems*' (2)

In certain respects the African situation is more hopeful than in countries where underdevelopment has a longer history. Obdurate political and social obstacles to change which are prevalent in the Middle East, in most parts of non-communist Asia and in Latin America are not present in Africa. I refer to such manifestations as rigid and vicious class or caste systems, restricted ownership of land, obscurantist religious institutions, severe overpopulation and the existence of ancient cultural traditions which cannot be modified without enormous social convulsions. The *possibilities* in Africa are therefore more open and variable: it is, in consequence, admissable to discuss them in the belief that they may have some relevance for all developing countries.

The scope of this enquiry is cultural in the restricted and more old-fashioned sense. We cannot be concerned with culture as a way of life since sociological investigations have to relate to specific circumstances. I am not therefore dealing primarily with material development but with what has been called the world of symbolic meanings. Most of the literature on development has naturally been concerned with the need for economic growth and little attention has been paid to an analysis of the cultural transfers which it is usually considered eventually follow material change. Anthropologists have dealt with cultural diffusion in the broad sense but the psychological characteristics of transitional society have more often been the concern of novelists, dramatists and poets. I have concentrated then, not on the traditional past nor on current economic changes, but on the diffusion of ideas especially as they are reflected in common attitudes rather than in intellectual systems. These cloudy matters relate to the sociology of knowledge and in much of what I have set down I am conscious of speculation. These chapters

10

are therefore necessarily *explorations* and owe more to my experience than to documentary sources.

However, it is not possible to explore the process of cultural change (where mystifications abound) without dealing first with the general nature of development. I have found that students find it difficult to know what development is and they are in good company. (A response which I obtained from one group was that in Africa it consists of the replacement of white experts with black ones of the same kind—a very perceptive answer since that is what has mainly happened so far.) Because of this difficulty I have considered it necessary to discuss the general nature of development in the first part of this work.

Brief reference is required to the vexed problem of terminology. It is a universal experience in this field that none of the terms dealing with development are satisfactory since they all have inadmissable implications. The temptation is to use quotation marks every time works like 'modernisation' or 'developing' have to be used; this is not practical and would result in a rash of spots. What I have done, therefore, is to use the terms without every time indicating that they are either inaccurate or dishonest.

Next there is the question of readership. Not for the first time I have been faced with problems arising from the fact that I am trying to communicate with several sorts of people. They include librarians and students of library studies with particular reference to students in the Third World, since the work was prompted by their needs in the first place. Immediately conflicts arise, since what is painfully obvious to people in one set of circumstances may have to be spelt out for those in another. In addition to the librarians, I always hope for a wider readership since I feel that these matters should be of central concern to anybody especially at the present time. Because of this multiple aim I have not considered the implications for librarianship until the last three chapters.

There remains the question of bias: I have tried to make my own views apparent throughout and all that I need mention here is that the approach is personal. One would not wish to be anything else.

REFERENCES
1 Hunter, Guy: *The best of both worlds?*, OUP, 1967, p5.
2 Myrdal, Gunnar: *The challenge of world poverty*, Pelican, 1971, p207.

1

DOCTRINES OF DEVELOPMENT

When, one after another, the newly independent countries were admitted to the United Nations, the new concept of universal development had also arrived. Humanity, it was alleged, was on the march. Alfred, Lord Tennyson, sitting amidst the clamour of Victorian industrialism, had (in *Locksley Hall*) 'dipt into the future' and foreseen it all: 'Let the great world spin forever down the ringing grooves of change', and even more to the point, 'Better fifty years of Europe than a cycle of Cathay'. Ultimately would come the Parliament of Man and the Federation of the World. So it was that the new industrial civilisation of Europe was to be exported until it spread over the globe.

At first, in the 1950s and 60s, development was thought of mainly in economic terms, with particular reference to Gross National Product (GNP). This was natural because it was assumed, not without reason, that economic growth would lead to all other forms of development. The United Nations even announced that the 1960s were to be a decade of development, particularly via various schemes for foreign aid and international assistance. It was seriously supposed that economic development could not only be planned but predicted. There was the assumption that the new societies would develop according to the same economic laws which had operated in the West in the past.

Capital investment
A prominent advisor of new governments was the West Indian economist Mr (now Sir) Arthur Lewis. In connection with Trinidad and Jamaica he had claimed that foreign investment for indigenous industries would in the long run produce profits, savings and reinvestment which would ultimately lead to industrial growth. The same analysis had been made for other new countries, but, except where there have been special circumstances, this growth has not materialised. Local or national investment has not reached a sufficient level to constitute an economic breakthrough.

13

The new elites are not reproductions of nineteenth century European capitalists; they are primarily consumers concerned not with the future, but with their profits here and now. As Fanon notes, 'In underdeveloped countries, we have seen that no true bourgeoisie exists; there is only a sort of little greedy caste, avid and voracious, with the mind of a huckster . . . This get-rich-quick middle class shows itself incapable of great ideas of inventiveness. It remembers what it has read in European textbooks and imperceptibly it becomes not even the replica of Europe but its caricature.' (1) The moral indignation is perhaps a little overdone here, since, as we shall see, this 'caste' or elite has no obvious possibility of becoming a 'replica' of European society if only for historical reasons. In Nigeria, for example, most of the new rich do not invest in long-term productive ventures, but put their money into real estate. They do not have the confidence to take risks involved in long-term investment. Who is to say they are wrong?

By the end of the 1960s it became clear that development problems were more complex than some economists had supposed. In this context the classic example was the economic 'failure' of Nkrumah's Ghana.

Social justice
At the same time, it was becoming apparent that if some form of economic growth resulted in an *intensification* of certain characteristic features of underdeveloped societies, such as the huge gap between the new rich and the masses, or between the towns and the countryside, then the concept of development would have to be extended to include social justice. If the vast majority of the people (usually about 80 per cent) remain unaffected, or, because of inflation, become worse off than before, how can the word development mean anything at all? Again, this egalitarian aspect had been neglected at first, because although in the West, *eg* Britain, the industrial revolution had promoted terrible social injustice to *begin with*, the accumulated wealth eventually raised the standard of living of the people generally. (That a class system has remained is not in this context relevant.) But in the new areas of development, this spreading of wealth does not take place, or does so only to a slight degree, so that if 'development' is to mean anything, the economists have to start again. As one authority has said:

'It was the first period of disillusion: too many armies, too much bureaucratic parasitism, too much unequal distribution and not enough production, too much concentration on display projects and neglect of infrastructure, too much articulation of conflicts between communities,

14

in short too much politics for the elites, not enough authentic participation for the masses.' (2)

It is appropriate to note here that much of this 'disillusion' happened
(mostly to outside or expatriate academics) because their illustions were
surprising—or, at least, they *now* seem surprising—in the first place. For
example, the crucial item in the above catalogue of woes is 'the authentic
participation of the masses'. With the notable exception of China's
unique circumstances and the important eruptions of peasant revolts
throughout history, how many examples do we have of peasant 'participation', authentic or otherwise? Because of this we shall be dealing with
the 'culture of silence' diagnosed by Paulo Freire and the continued
presence of Fanon's 'wretched of the earth'.

Stages of growth
An economic principle which is now largely discredited still has reper-
cussions in many fields. This is that societies must develop in the same
way as other societies have developed in the past. There are, of course,
grandiose schemes of historical determination which have invoked historical laws or patterns of decline and fall—Hegel, Marx, Spengler and Toyn-
bee all produced their grand designs. But what we seem to have with
these theorists is not a vision of history, but merely a *methodology*,
which has to start with a model in order to function at all. So, for
example, Lerner once stated, 'The Western model of modernisation
exhibits certain components and sequences whose relevance is global . . .
indeed, the Western model is virtually an inevitable baseline for . . . development because there is no other model which can serve this purpose'. (3)

The only models available, then, either had to be found in an alien
past or in somebody's head. Both types have been used and both have
been found wanting. There is sometimes an implication that if the newly
developing countries have not corresponded to these models, they have
somehow failed. But the tests have been invented by outside academic
observers. To clarify this, it might help if we tabulate some of the obvious differences between the situation of the Third World countries
now as compared with 'Western' development in the past. These are
the differences which, however obvious, are often ignored.

1 In Europe the industrial revolution was preceded by an agricultural
revolution. It was possible for the rural sector to be absorbed into the
new economy, so that the 'dual economy' so characteristic of development today was avoided.

15

2 Most European countries were the beneficiaries of an imperialist economic system and Britain was the first workshop of the world. The new countries must either continue to receive their goods from these workshops and themselves remain producers of primary products, or they must build their own workshops for their own production in a highly competitive world economy.

3 The new countries are part of a world-wide economic structure within which they are obliged to operate. In this respect they are not in control of their own destinies; this is the reality of neo-colonialism.

4 In Europe and the USA, technological innovation was indigenous; it did not have to be 'transferred', but grew out of its own environment.

5 The European states, at the time of the industrial revolution, were not 'traditional' societies, but already nation-states with a long intellectual history and a background of scientific enquiry.

The above are only some of the differences, and others will emerge as we proceed. They are stressed because it is these new circumstances which do not permit the societies we are discussing to pass through the comparative stages hypothesised. Exactly what form their development will take therefore remains to be shown, and there is no reason why whatever patterns emerge which should be identical with past or present patterns in other countries.

Modernisation

Related to the linear 'stages of development' view of events was a concept called 'modernisation', largely produced by the knowledge industry in the United States. The term has been used to replace others which can be regarded as offensive or inadequate; these include 'urbanisation', 'civilisation', 'Europeanisation' and 'Westernisation'. The antecedents of modernisation theories are to be found in the social anthropology of the nineteenth century, when it was customary to distinguish between traditional and modern attitudes. The traditional outlook was designated pre-scientific or pre-logical and it was believed that this type of thinking was non-linear in the sense that it is devoid of causality. Another common doctrine was that 'primitive' people could not conceive of any other view of the world than the one they had absorbed from their tribal community. Emphasis was also put on attitudes to time. Non-literate people tend to hold concepts of time which puzzle outside observers. It appears to them that time is two-dimensional, with a long past, a present, and a future which is unreal because events that lie in it have not taken place. Modern production processes based on punctuality

16

and an extreme concentration on linear time are disrupted by these attitudes.

Much of this analysis had required modification and it has long been
apparent that more careful interpretations must be made. It became
necessary to define the nature of modernity with greater precision. If
the new countries were to plan their future they would surely need to
know what was traditional, what was modern, and also what was *transitional*, the condition in which they were alleged to be. Accordingly,
concepts of modernity were worked out, and indicators or yardsticks
were provided so that assessments of progress or its absence could be
made. The following are the usual prescriptions. It will be noted that
they are primarily *psychological*, that is to say, it is claimed that certain
attitudes are regarded as prerequisites for modernisation.

1 In a modern society, as distinct from one that is not, people (or
some of them) are receptive to change, innovation, new ideas and new
experience. They also have an ability to *empathise* with the attitudes of
others—they can imagine circumstances other than those in which they
find themselves.

2 In order to become modern, people must have an ability to con-
template the future and the present rather than the past. This is associated with an ability to sacrifice present interests in order to provide for
the future. It will be apparent that this can only proceed from some
kind of confidence that the future will exist and can be planned for.

3 The non-traditional person becomes aware of the wider world, and
the mass media of communication can play a major role in this process.

4 A modern environment is responsive to calculation, organisation
and control. The time factor is also relevant, since prediction is involved
rather than the arcane mysteries of prophecy.

5 It is claimed that modern societies are based on 'trust', and that
people have faith in the role of government. It is also implied that where
trust exists it is possible for individuals to tell the truth.

6 Modern societies are *secular* in the sense that they have a faith in
science and technology and a 'rational' view of life. This emphasis on
rationality follows the thought of the master (Weber) who interpreted
modernism mainly as the growth of rationality in the world.

7 Some sociologists have seen the development of *bureaucracy* as
an essential indicator of modernity. Again the association with rationality is apparent, since bureaucrats are entirely concerned with proper
procedures; societies where bureaucratic methods are 'improper', or
where they do not work, are therefore not modern.

17

8 An important ethical component of modernity is a belief in the need for social justice and individual dignity. Human rights, including those of women and ethnic minorities, have also been stressed.

9 Most of these psychological traits imply the development of individualism. It is claimed that modern social structures have provided for the socialisation of highly individualised persons. Indeed it has been suggested that the theme of individual autonomy is the most important element in modernity. It is true that transitional people—those people whose attitudes are in the stage between traditional and modern ways of looking at the world—find it difficult to be autonomous in this sense and most of them would not wish to be. It is, of course, an aspect of developed capitalist society which is most often deplored.

The above mentioned are the most usual attributes which are put forward but others have been added from time to time, such as independence from the family, a feeling of loyalty to the nation rather than to the group, and even a feeling that life in general is pleasant!

What is the layman supposed to make of these indicators? Perhaps a start could be made by asking oneself how many of these attitudes does one hold? In such a test most of us would fail on one or another count. We are, therefore, obliged to conclude that even in self-styled modern societies there must be a large number of non-modern individuals, particularly those who are not educated or who are outside the mainstream of culture. We must also conclude that if we count all these indicators, hardly any societies are wholly modern. For example, the human rights requirement along will rule out most of them. With regard to some of the specific indicators (as distinct from all of them), formidable objections can also be raised. Some of them are as follows:

1 Even in the nineteenth century it was apparent that there were different *modes* of thought—not just degrees of thinking, so that many anthropologists began to realise that a 'scientific' way of thinking is not so much superior to as different from traditional thought. Furthermore, the scientific mode *should not be the only one*, which is what is apparently implied by modernisation. If a belief in technology is to lead to 'one-dimensional' man and a loss of the ability to use other modes of perception, is modernisation then desirable? (The theorists seem to assume that modernity is superior, although this point is not always explicitly made.)

2 The concepts are centri-cultural or ethnocentric insofar as they assume that attitudes which are typical of some industrial societies (usually the USA) *at a particular time* are what constitutes modernity, towards which goal the rest of mankind should march.

18

3 The indicators are therefore related to time and place, and to the bias of the would-be modernisers. Amongst the characteristics mentioned are several which many modern citizens of America or Europe would reject out of hand. The reaction of the counter-culture to technological civilisation is well documented and widespread. Not only this, but Daniel Bell and others with their concept of post-industrial society have made an impressive case to show that this kind of modernity is no longer modern even in its countries of origin, and was characteristic only of western capitalist development *in the past*.

4 The suggestion that modern individuals are rational rests on a simplistic view of human psychology, in the sense that it implies that people do not hold views which are inconsistent with each other, whereas it is well known that intelligent people are quite capable of holding contradictory views at the same time. Many scientists (for example Newton) have held religious views which would normally be regarded as wholly unscientific. As we shall see, most people in transitional societies have to live in this way; they instinctively understand that there are different kinds of truth and various modes of perception, and these can be kept separate.

5 There is a confusion in the literature on development because sometimes these indicators are listed as being typical of existing modern societies, and at other times they have been regarded as *pre-requisites* for development. When the latter view is held, it is possible to apply the indicators to institutions in developing societies to see whether they are on the way to modernity or not. Needless to say most of them are not.

6 As Freire so often proclaims, 'mere modernity' is not necessarily development, and whatever else the indicators may reveal, they do not suggest a programme of action. If we ask, 'What must we do to become modern?', they cannot tell us.

7 Developing countries are clearly not modern in this sense, and they can no longer be called traditional. For convenience therefore we call them 'transitional', but there is an inadmissible assumption in this usage since what is implied is a movement *towards* something which is thought of as modernity. Is it not possible to stay in a state of transition forever?

Are we then to reject the entire concept of modernity out of hand as being wholly unhelpful? Some sociologists have done so. For example, Caroline Hutton and Robin Cohen point out: 'Sociologists have taken the contrasts between "traditional" and "modern" for so long that they frequently assume these types to be self-evident . . . Nowhere, perhaps, have these types done so much damage as when they have been applied to African situations. The European experience of industrialisation and

19

the growth of capitalism is simply irrelevant to the current experience of African society . . . The terms "traditional" and "modern" do not have empirical bases in African contexts.' (4)

I think we can accept that statement, but I feel obliged to continue to use these terms for convenience, provided that we do not take them too literally. C E Black states, 'The advantage of a term such as "modernisation" is not only that it has a broader scope than "Westernisation", "Europeanisation", "industrialisation" or even "progress", but also that it is *less encumbered with accretions of meaning*' (5) (my italics). One might conclude from such a statement that it has no meaning at all, and at a deeper level than the familiar parlance of the professional developers it probably has not. The real situation is best described as a combination of concurrent processes which can be conveniently called modernisation, counter-modernisation and de-modernisation. It is surely significant that in the fly leaf of a copy of Black's work in the Ahmadu Bello University Library, Zaria, Nigeria, a student has written (perhaps as an instinctive reaction): 'Are we modernising or de-modernising? We are doing both Mr Man'.

The work ethic
The societies under review will never 'go anywhere', it is alleged, because the people do not work, will not work and have never worked hard enough to create a modern society. *Work* has been regarded as the key to the industrial successes of the advanced countries. Weber linked this belief in the importance of labour to the rise of protestantism which therefore made capitalism possible—thus the protestant ethic which inspired so much self-sacrifice and so many business empires. This doctrine is well known; what is perhaps less familiar is that Weber saw the connection as being with protestantism alone, and regarded other religions as an obstacle to such progress: 'For the various popular religions of Asia, in contrast to ascetic protestantism, the world remained a great enchanted garden in which the practical way to orient oneself or to find security in this world, or the next, was to revere or coerce spirits, and seek salvation through ritualistic, idolatrous or sacramental procedures. No path led from the magical religiosity of the non-intellectual classes of Asia to a rational methodical control of life. Nor . . . from the world accommodation of Confucianism, from the world rejection of Buddhism, from the world conquest of Islam or from the messianic expectations and economic pariah law of Judaism.' (6)

This was, of course, written some time ago and in the passage quoted, Weber does not mention catholicism or other versions of Christianity.

20

It is of interest that some writers have found the origins of the work ethic in the organisational rules and methods of the pre-reformation Benedictine monasteries, where work was a religious duty. Librarians will remember the important role of these institutions in the history of their profession—libraries have always been built up by human termites.

But we can now see that, with regard to protestantism, this position is wholly untenable, and that in other circumstances and societies the work ethic may take root within different religious traditions, even if they have to be bent or modified. I believe that the popular doctrine about developing countries is also inadmissible. It is quite true that, for various historical and social reasons, people in post-traditional societies in Africa or the West Indies have not 'worked' in the manner required for development. One used to hear similar arguments about the working classes in Britain, and we need not look far for the reasons why. For example, there is little point in peasants working harder to produce more crops for the market when they are going to be no better off, or may be even worse off than before though the intervention of speculators or 'middlemen'. Yet the doctrine that people in the Third World *cannot* absorb the work ethic survives: 'A widespread prejudice in the West maintains that non-Western cultures discourage work, and even produce individuals with an inherent incapacity for it. *The data do not support this*' (7) (my italics). The authors go on to say that 'the real problem of modernisation in the area of production is not to get people to work, but to get them to work in a particular way'.

Without pursuing this point further it should be obvious enough that in unjust societies, where work does not produce equivalent rewards, and where such rewards as do derive may come for quite other reasons, there is little incentive to work hard—it may be more important to 'know the right people', and so on. Under such circumstances only some form of slavery such as existed in former times could produce the required results. Slavery is omitted from our list of modernising indicators. The conclusion must be that no amount of exhortation or pressure will change these attitudes so as long as societies remain malign, corrupt and unconcerned.

Innovation

One of the indicators of modernisation listed above is the need to be open to new ideas and practices—what development literature usually calls 'innovation'. There is a widely-held notion that the main obstacle to development is the resistance of traditional attitudes, particularly

21

those of the peasants of the world—millions of them. The history of innovation in backward regions is most instructive.

Many experimental ventures in social development have been, and are still promoted by aid-bearing or international agencies, mostly concerned with agriculture—which is the key to all development. It could be said that this kind of 'development', *ie* one confined to particular projects, often as 'pilot' projects, is a continuation of the type of community development pursued by the British and others in colonial times. I refer to these earlier ventures because there are significant parallels, one of which is the element of outside aid or influence. What is also intersting (at least in former British colonies) is the *novelty* of these ventures. For example, referring to colonial rule about 1950, Sir B Sharwood-Smith, a former Governor of Northern Nigeria, has said, 'What we wished to find out was, in brief, what made the province tick economically, and what could be done to strengthen and expand the economy. But *no one, it seemed, had ever tackled the subject in Nigeria before*' (8) (my italics). This is an extraordinary admission, and indicates the limited nature of community development—that it was entirely confined to individual villages. There is also another prophetic remark: 'I had always been convinced that our first duty lay with the illiterate peasantry of the countryside who formed the mass of the population. Unless we could drastically change their present circumstances and outlook, we should be delivering them hog-tied by ignorance and poverty into the hands of whoever cared to exploit them when the time for self-government arrived.'

That, of course, is exactly what happened, but the historical responsibility for this state of affairs must surely be shared by the colonial masters who had never, by Sherwood-Smith's admission, previously thought about the matter. Whatever has happened to the peasantry since, it remains true that instead of being victims of exploitation, they are regularly labelled as the main obstacle to progress because of their resistance to change.

Much of the theory and practice of development was and is concerned with individual projects in particular areas, and very often foreign aid has been involved. This activity, immensely valuable as it has been in specific fields (for example the so-called 'Green revolution' in parts of Asia) falls short of what we mean by development as national planning. Indeed, the 'Green revolution' is especially relevant to this argument, since the value of the scientific breakthrough which occurred when new breeds of rice were obtained, has been nullified by social factors such

22

as the rapacity of landlords and middlemen, and the inability of the farmers to afford necessary fertilisers. Underdevelopment remains because the total environment was not considered.

It is noteworthy that some successes—for instance, the much-quoted Gezira cotton-growing scheme in the Sudan, dating from the 1920s—have taken place because there existed a consideration for the environment as a whole, and because a large amount of foreign, in this case colonial, aid was provided. (The scheme was launched to assist the British cotton industry.) Elsewhere, as in Nigeria at the present time, there are several agricultural schemes which have benefited from the mistakes of the past.

Here, however, we are concerned with the theory of development, and the point is that mostly the ideas were impractical because they ignored the society where they were to be applied. Many ventures foundered on this rock, and the ignorance of the 'innovators' about local conditions was often blamed on the intransigence of the peasantry who failed to 'co-operate'. In most cases, from a long-term production point-of-view, the peasants were right. Where projects have taken account of all or most of the relevant environmental factors, individual projects have worked, since peasants are perfectly capable of following their own true interests.

Valuable as some of these projects have been, not least with regard to their possible duplication elsewhere, they do not add up to national development. They are pointers or pilot projects, and in many cases the presence of foreign subsidisation means that reproduction of such activity on a national scale remains improbable.

In spite of all this, the relevant factor is that the evidence shows that people, like people anywhere, *are* capable of change, and it is not necessary to concentrate first on changing their attitudes. Social activity brings its own change in perception and consciousness. Anybody with experience of war or revolution or any sudden change knows that crisis-situations result in *new people*—dormant potentialities come to the fore. But the circumstances must be appropriate, which in most countries they have not been.

Perhaps even more telling instances of the difficulties inherent in innovation can be found in the vital area of public health. It is a commonplace that medical advances have reduced the high death-rate in poor countries (thus producing or contributing to the 'overpopulation' problem). It is also well know that public health—that is, the prevention of disease—has not kept pace with the scientific advances which have (largely) been made in the laboratories of the developed world. But

23

provision for public health, as distinct from the curing of disease by drugs, or even prevention by immunisation, has to be an indigenous *social* endeavour: no 'transfer' can be made here. The social obstacles remain and the innovators tend to stress ignorance as one of the most important. This is often true, but it is an over-estimated factor. Millions of people are chronically sick or die because they drink infected water. (The hoary doctrine that the 'natives' are constitutionally immune is a convenient myth.) So the innovators say, 'This is because these ignorant people won't boil the water'. Yet the truth is that most of them live in social circumstances where it is almost impossible to boil water; they would boil it quite happily all day long if they had enough fuel to boil it with, or somewhere to store it when boiled.

Urbanisation and population
The population expansion is most apparent in the 'exploding cities' of the Third World. Not until one has witnessed human conditions in some of these new shanty-towns can one understand what underdevelopment is about. In 1900, there were in the world eleven cities with a population of more than one million; now, there are nearly 200, and by 1984, it is estimated, there will be 300. This rate of increase is of course higher than the much-quoted figure for total increase in world population— 2,000m in 1930 to 4,000m in 1976.

This wholly new form of urban growth is a consequence of the increasing impoverishment of rural areas, and this in turn is a sympton of underdevelopment. Once we appreciate that 'overpopulation', in whatever form, is a symptom and not a *cause* of poverty, we can understand why delegates from poor countries at international conferences become so annoyed when the emphasis is placed, not on remedies for poverty, but on a cure for overpopulation in the form of birth-control. This is why the Chinese and other Third World delegates at such conferences have condemned this approach to world economic development as impractical and dishonest. This political line has not prevented the Chinese from going a long way towards solving their own population-growth problem—perhaps the most under-publicised part of their achievements. In the case of India, where the problem is so extreme, former Prime Minister Mrs Gandhi and her advisers knew only too well that birth-control *by itself* would not eliminate poverty, yet they went ahead with their coercive policies, and the final consequence was the downfall of her government.

Some commentators have compared this drastic programme with Stalin's much more ruthlessly enforced collectivisation of the peasants in the 1930s. The analogy is misleading in one respect, which is that however inhuman the Russian policies were, they were dealing with one of the basic causes of underdevelopment and the programme, at whatever cost, survived. (To say that it 'succeeded' would beg too many questions.)

To return to the new cities, it is significant that in recent years the remedies proposed at international gatherings no longer concentrate on the total development problem, but have dealt with what might be done to ameliorate conditions. If large-scale programmes had become too remote from reality, then at least attention should be paid to immediate practical possibilities—reform on a modest scale rather than revolution, which was seen to be receding into the future.

Accordingly, at the UN-sponsored 'Habitat' Conference on Human Settlements in Vancouver in 1976, many delegates suggested that conditions in the cities—where as many as one-third of the population of the country are shanty-town squatters—were not so disastrous after all. They suggested that the real driving-force for progress will come from human ingenuity and enterprise, and that these new migrants should be regarded not as representing a social disaster, but as pioneers. The shanty towns have been re-christened as the 'informal sector' of the economy, and it is from such a source that it is claimed growth might come. The theory now advanced is that urban authorities should encourage and support this potential for self-help.

It is difficult to write about this 'theory' without cynicism, yet it can be linked with a cluster of doctrines which are now world-wide and of increasing political importance. The core of such proposals is a concentration on reducing large-scale social engineering projects to a human dimension. These matters are discussed in the section in intermediate technology in chapter 4. Their relevance here is that they represent a new departure in development theory which is of some interest, provided that such programmes are not advocated as a total answer to underdevelopment. Such doctrines are significant also because they may lead to change in both the rich and the poor regions of the world. Britain and elsewhere now appreciate that high-rise housing projects have been socially disastrous, and, in retrospect, it is difficult to understand how anyone could imagine that they would be an effective solution to the housing problem.

What we now have, then, is a shift from hopes for large-scale total development to an emphasis on small-scale projects which—the theory goes—when they are multiplied will begin to transform the environment. It is in a sense an admission that earlier development theory has not found an answer, and even more a suggestion that *there cannot be one answer*. Our purpose here is simply to point out that while this worldwide environmental movement can be seen to have immediate relevance in overdeveloped countries, its relevance for the Third World is less obvious, and dangerous if it means that revolutionary hopes are abandoned. The other alternative is to send the people back to the land by force, as has been done in Cambodia and is being done less brutally in Saigon where the urban population figures are going down fast. Finally, the South African policy of sending the black people to the 'homelands' is an extreme instance of compulsory 'de-urbanisation', the motives for which are not economic so much as racist and political.

Limitations of the doctrines

The topics I have just selected are representative, and certain common theoretical features can be detected in all of them. To list these characteristics should help us to appreciate why the history of 'development research' has been largely a series of absurdities.

1   *Political mystification*: Many of the earlier theories of development were not unconnected with the political requirements of the Cold War, and were geared to the global strategic consideration of the super-powers. They were also linked with the needs of an international economic system. Consciously or otherwise, the developmentalists were producing an ideology for neo-colonialsim: their theories were firmly set in a context of orthodox social science as it is understood in the USA. An outstanding instance of this world-wide endeavour was that of Indonesia. In the late 1950s Indonesia appeared to be drifting into the Communist orbit. Susan George describes how, assisted by the Ford Foundation, a strong link was built up between US universities, especially Berkeley, and Indonesia. 'The Berkeley professors turned the faculty in Djakarta into an American-style school of economics, statistics and business administration.' (9) At the same time, army officers were trained at American military bases. The ultimate result was the military take-over, the fall of Sukarno, and the massacre of at least a million 'communists'. 'Modern Indonesia now indeed has political stability; its chief ministers, and the top ranks of the army, all have PhDs from the US.'

These activities were regarded as legitimate in the world ideological struggle, and I am not suggesting that the record of the Soviet Union is free from similar methods and policies. Indeed, the same criticism can be made both of Soviet behaviour and of their theoretical analysis of

26

the development needs of the new nations. The Russians, like the Americans, have insisted that other countries, in order to progress, should pass through certain stages as set out by them and deriving from their experience and their ideology.

The political element is, as one would expect, most noticeable with regard to the literature concerning foreign aid.

There has been, of course, an 'opposition' or counter-critique, which I am not concerned with in detail here, since a criticism of development theories is implicit throughout this work. No alternative doctrines are offered, because in the different parts of the world no common realistic solution is possible for all of them. The Marxist analysis and the dependency theories mostly associated with Latin America require a revolutionary answer, but it is not yet clear where the revolution is coming from. 'The development of underdevelopment' theory mainly associated with Andre Gunther Frank has been fashionable. Frank has insisted that this continuing process is the result of several centuries of world history and is unlikely to be arrested.

All these radical interpretations are based on the concept of a global economic structure which inevitably exploits the poor countries. From these standpoints, terms like 'Third World' are inadmissible, since there is only one world. Outside the revolutionary tradition, the development researchers themselves have reduced their claims and modified their confident predictions, as in their concentration on the possibility of limited transformations in particular places. From such a standpoint even the word 'development' has become suspect.

2   *'Value-free' social science*: The attempt both in the USA and in another manner in the USSR to develop social studies as science has led to a falsification of human reality and to new forms of exploitation. Millions of words have been used to attack or defend this established doctrine and we should not add to them here except to note its relevance to development theory, and how in earlier years, particularly, there was a gap between the American and British approach.

Discussing the divergence between American and British, Colin Leys mentioned 'an abysmal gap of mutual incomprehension', (10) since the American and British movements were based on quite different methodological suppositions. The behavioural sociological theories were based on the structuralist/functionalist doctrines of Talcott Parsons, derived originally from the work of Weber. Leys notes that, in this tradition, concepts should be organised in such a way that they must be

27

derived from explicit theories about political behaviour. This use of 'ideal types' is 'a particular way of pursuing research quite alien to British traditions by looking for facts to illuminate a theory, rather than the other way round'. In consequence, facts which were not relevant to a particular hypothesis had to be set aside. In the case of development studies this usually meant that the hypotheses often contradicted the experience of those who live in the countries concerned. (It was when they clearly contradicted my own that I was moved to pursue the matter further.)

A 'scientific' model of this kind is not intended to correspond with reality, and it is this which confuses naive laymen, who tend to have an interest in a different kind of truth. As Black stated, 'The propositions asserted throughout this work . . . should be regarded as hypotheses, that is as unconfirmed propositions . . . In *scientific work it is more important to be fruitful for further work than to be right*' (11) (my italics). This is all very well in a scientific laboratory, bit it ignores the fact that human realities require social action: that, after all, is what development is about. One cannot change the world by embracing 'unconfirmed propositions'. (As has often been observed, functionalist doctrines are more appropriate for relatively static societies.) The assumption implicit in these academic knowledge factories is that it is the job of the practical politicians to get on with the action, and eventually the 'scientists' will provide them with a valid guide.

These models, then, are not so much wrong as irrelevant. This difficulty is cheerfully admitted by the behaviourists themselves—as one of them said, 'It is natural that social scientists should have such a great fixation on static models'. (12)

3 *Objectivism*: Value-free social science implies that there must be a pursuit of objectivity. Students in developing countries are particularly responsive to this ideal. They naturally want to get away from superstition and magic, mumbo-jumbo and personal bias, but in so doing they fall for the alternative myth of objectivism, which reduces science to mechanics and dehumanises the person.

The concept of objectivity is always attractive to those who wish to get away from the confusions and alarming perspective of their inner selves. Transitional man is, by definition, at war with himself internally, and if contradictory influences cannot be reconciled then it must seem better to put them aside and try to forget; that is why objectivism appeals.

But true objectivity means that you take account of personal involvement and commitment, which is indeed essential, and make allowances for it; the personal element should be explicit and declared. Whereas objectivism pretends that as a scientist you have no values and can leave yourself and your attitudes out. These are the hidden biases of the behavioural scientists.

At an academic level the objections to this approach are several. First, it is not possible to remove the personal element without dishonesty, and therefore the bias will be undeclared. Second, a split between object (the thing being studied) and subject (oneself) sets up a false perception of the world, since one is part of the other. Third, as Ziman and others have concluded, the unifying principle of science is not objectivity but the striving for a consensus. That is what many of the models in the behavioural sciences are trying to do. It is, therefore, when the personal element is left out that objectivity becomes objectivism, which, as Polyani has claimed, is a 'menace to all cultural values'. Finally, we should add that objectivism by its very nature produces invalid and lifeless interpretations which cannot be read without distress. Polyani continues: 'If the analysis is correct, history, the arts, sociology, psychoanalysis are not consensible. Similarly, law is unscientific because it has to decide without a consensus; also, law is concerned with what *ought* to be done, whereas science can only indicate what might be done.' (13)

It is this fact which causes social scientists to tie themselves up in such strange knots. One should add that similar objections can be made against scientific socialism, at least with regard to its claims to be scientific. But I am inevitably more concerned here with the Western doctrines which have affected development theories. If the sociologists are to justify their existence, they will deal not only with what might be done, but also with what should be done. Or is this asking too much, and must we return to the prophets crying in the wilderness? Perhaps. The exiled W H Auden never felt quite at home in the American atmosphere, and proceeding from an approach which was increasingly Christian, mentally reacted against the pseudo-science which is characteristic of so much sociology. His poem *Under which lyre* has two stanzas which are relevant here:

Thou shalt not do as the dean pleases
Thou shalt not write thy doctor's thesis
On Education.
Thou shalt not worship projects nor

Shalt thou or thine bow down before
Administration.

Thou shalt not answer questionnaires
Or quizzes upon world affairs
Nor with compliance
Take any test. Thou shalt not sit
With statisticians nor commit
A social science.

Social scientists, however, like sin, are necessary in this world, and these lines are no more than warning for the good of academic souls. As Wilfred Owen said, 'All a poet can do is to warn'.

Can it be said then that objectivism particularly affects development studies? The answer is that is probably influences the work of indigenous researchers, especially before they are fully established. The way the approach seems to operate is that investigators ignore or forget the evidence of their own experience because it is 'subjective'. It is in this fashion that they lose touch with their own people. They also have a corresponding tendency to over-value the literature of development theory (usually foreign). The fact that it emanates from fallible people is overlooked; it seems to exist in its own right.

4 *Reductionism*: The abuse of science which is called 'reductionism' or 'scientism' is quite general, and naturally occurs in this field. Economics has always been attacked on the ground that it leaves out human beings. Development studies have been even more suspect in this respect, since especially in the earlier decades, they treated development purely as an economic process. Economic growth as embodied in GNP came to be regarded as development, and all the other elements—cultural, historical, social, psychological and so on—were ignored; human beings were not allowed. This misuse of science became particularly dangerous when an attempt was made to transfer economic models or laws from developed to underdeveloped countries.

As Ivar Oxaal points out in the case of Trinidad, some of these countries cannot be said to have an economic system at all. How therefore can the economists make sense of it? Mostly they have not.

The knowledge industry
That academic work as organised in universities is a growth industry in its own right has received increasing critical attention. One result of this

institutionalisation is that we tend to confuse the products of this industry with 'knowledge' itself.

Librarians in particular are prone to talk about a knowledge 'explosion', whereas this vast and sudden growth is first of all in *recorded* knowledge, as set down in the laborious termite-like labours of innumerable university workers whose livelihood it is. The slogan 'publish or perish' may be sound practical advice to those whose careers it will benefit, but its connection with any kind of reality is not guaranteed. In reading the literature produced by this enterprise, one gets the impression that it has become reified or 'thingified'. This being so, it scarcely seems to matter what the theories are about, since they are painstaking additions to a structure of recorded knowledge which is already there independent of other realities. Scientific research is supposed to ensure that the accumulations of recorded knowledge correspond to something out there in the world, but this need not happen, especially in the behavioural sciences. We come back to the fact that the researchers are responsible primarily to their own careers: they are concerned with what should be done only incidentally. They are involved with each other.

Such a situation has a peculiar significance in development studies. It is that the organised production of knowledge, like other industries, is not indigenous to the developing countries themselves. In addition to the academics, the global development enterprise has spawned a motley army of international experts and advisors who have added to the general confusion. The apostles of development have become members of a jet set who tour the African continent and attend the social gatherings which are called conferences and seminars: they conduct research into problems of underdevelopment, stagnation, growth, foreign aid and above all into problems of the problems. There is therefore a development industry which overlaps with the academic one. The only impact these people have on the peasant at work in the fields is that he hears their planes overhead as they move on to the next assignment. Are we then to conclude that this industry should be dismantled on the grounds that the Africans should develop their own research capacity? Such a conclusion overlooks the fact that many of the indigenous researchers have been trained overseas and are just as far removed from the masses as the aliens whom they are supposed to replace.

As representatives of the new elite, they are also part of the international jet-set themselves. In this respect the neo-colonial pattern is the same as for any other industry, and the indigenous researchers are equivalent to the subsidiaries or local agents of a multinational corporation.

31

Another feature of knowledge factories is that there is an increasing division of labour, commonly referred to as specialisation. This has its dangers in any subject area, but in the field of development it has been disastrous. Such an approach has resulted in one of the most dangerous misunderstandings prevalent in the industrialised countries, namely that reality itself can safely be divided into a number of separate and specialised 'sectors'. I know from personal experience that when this specialisation is imported into developing countries it is intensified because of the nature of the education system and the lack of a general educational background. Unfortunately, real human problems do not fit into these academic divisions and sub-divisions. Anthropologists, economists, psychologists, sociologists and political scientists regard reality from their own particular angles, but there are not five different realities, and at the centre should be the individual person. Yet the researcher says, 'This is not my speciality', and retires to his own department in the factory. The 'problems of the problems' remain.

Conclusion

The evidence summarised here is, I suggest, conclusive. To quote two authorities at random: 'We can say with confidence, and with Gunnar Myrdal, that the problem of development in the Third World, however defined, is further away from solution than it has ever been'. (14) And 'Our knowledge about the developmental process is inadequate to provide us with either scientific theories to guide policies, or a solid perspective for predicting probably patterns of development'. (15)

Does it not seem to have been a tale told by an idiot or, rather, many of them? Certainly it does, though what we have to bear in mind is that we have simply been looking at *theories* and trying to establish how a particular field of 'knowledge' comes to be the way it is. Meanwhile the people who have been investigated and written about are still obstinately there: they have not heard of the learned doctrines and would not find them relevant. We should conclude by considering *them*, and it appears that the 'problems' can be defined in other ways.

Everything depends on the perceptions or preconceptions of the observer, some of whom may be students from the countries concerned. They are members of a new elite and are privileged persons: their hopes may not have been misplaced. Similarly, the peasants from millions of villages who will not and cannot read this book have not abandoned their hopes, because they never had any; and so on. Different groups of people should be allowed to have opinions about their own predicament. Many

32

of them, in West Africa for example, have seen enormous changes not just in their own lifetime but in less than twenty years. They know that something is happening; and if it is not what the experts predicted, so much the worse for expertise.

It seems that the assumptions which have been made were inadmissible to begin with. The other chapters of this book will try to explore the cultural implications of this state of affairs.

REFERENCES
1 Fanon, Frantz, *The wretched of the earth* Penguin, 1967, 141.
2 Nettl, J P, 'Strategies in the study of political development' *in* Leys, Colin (ed), *Politics and change in developing countries* CUP, 1969, 19.
3 Lerner, Daniel, *The passing of traditional society: modernising the Middle East* Glencoe Free Press, 1958, 46.
4 Hutton, Caroline and Cohen, Robin, 'African peasants and resistance to change: a reconsideration of sociological approaches *in* Oxall, Ivar (ed) and others, *Beyond the sociology of development* Routledge, 1975, 127.
5 Black, C E, *The dynamics of modernisation* Harper and Row, 1966, 7.
6 Weber, Alfred, *Sociology of religion* Beacon Press, 1964, 270.
7 Berger, Peter L and others, *The homeless mind* Penguin, 1974, 113.
8 Sharwood-Smith, Sir B, *But always as friends: Northern Nigeria and the Cameroons 1921-57* Government Printer, Kaduna, 1960, 192.
9 George, Susan, *How the other half dies* Penguin, 1976, 80.
10 Leys, Colin (ed), *op cit*, I.
11 Levy, Marion J, *Modernisation and the structure of societies, a setting for international affairs* Princetown University Press, 1966, 7.
12 Black, C E, *op cit*, 54.
13 Polanyi, M, *Personal knowledge* Routledge, 1958.
14 Nettl, J P, 'Strategies in the study of political development' *in* Leys, Colin (ed), *op cit*, 14.
15 Pye, Lucian, 'The international gap' *in* Weiner, Myron (ed), *Modernisation: the dynamics of growth* Basic Books, 1966, 337.

2

THE TRANSFER OF TECHNOLOGY

So far we have discussed mainly the socio-economic factors which characterise development; it remains to examine the technological component insofar as it can be usefully isolated. I shall suggest that we have difficulty in grasping the nature of technology and that this is not accidental but bound up with ideological considerations.

What is technology?
The word 'technology' cannot be fully understood by looking up the word in a dictionary. There you will find definitions such as 'science of the industrial arts' or 'the body of knowledge relating to arts and crafts' or 'the systematic study of techniques for making and doing things'. These definitions do not help much because they obscure the social element, and I have therefore followed the approach used by David Dickson in *Alternative technology*. (1) From this point of view technology, like education, is not politically neutral, although a myth has been created which would have us believe that it is. We can see all around us machines which dominate out lives and there is, in consequence, a tendency to feel that social changes are determined by technological factors. If we hold this view then it follows that when modern technology is transferred to poor countries those countries will soon become 'modernised' and will cease to be poor. But we have discovered from experience that this does not happen and one of the reasons is that technology is not an independent process.

Another interpretation is that even if technology does not determine our lives at least it makes change possible. I have not accepted this view either: it suggests that there are two stages in the process. First the machines have somehow been invented, and second the politicians or the business men come along and put them to use, for better or for worse. Using this analysis it is possible to say that there is nothing wrong with technology as such, but that what is disastrous is the way the machines

35

have been used. This has been called the Use or Abuse Theory. Thus many scientists have been able to claim that they are not responsible for the social or political application of their work. The theory has enabled them to evade the fact that they too are part of the political process which governs in the first instance what research shall be done. This doctrine, derived from positivist thinking, enabled hundreds of 'non-political' scientists in the USA to claim that the use of defoliants and other chemicals in the Vietnam War was the responsibility of politicians, not theirs. It is a view that Einstein never held. With the significant exception of those who voluntarily went into exile, the Nazis were able to use scientists in the same way. What then is the missing component in these interpretations of technology? It is simply that technical innovation springs from political and social policy decisions within society. Dickson mentions the telephone as an example: in its present form it makes long distance conversation possible between two individuals, but it excludes the possibility of group discussion without elaborate prior arrangements being made with the Post Office. Yet the system could have been geared for group communication, a process which is not dominant within an individualist society. Astronauts went to the moon because the competing Russians and Americans wanted to send them there, not solely because the technology existed. The political decisions arising from the world power structure provided the resources which led to the technological breakthrough.

In the context of development a new road may wholly change a traditional environment, but the decisions to build the road and where it shall run are social acts. Such decisions are often not dictated even by immediate economic considerations but can be political in a quite narrow sense. Many villages in poor countries have been bypassed by roads because the villages have failed to support the ruling elite. In the same fashion politicians and civil servants provide social amenities for their home towns but omit to supply them elsewhere. In areas of drought the boring of water holes is a technical, sometimes even an economic, possibility, but where they are to be drilled is a political decision; it is this which affects a thirsty citizen, not the availability of boring machines. (Bore-holes have even been discovered in politicians' back gardens.) In fact, the drought which has ravaged the Sahelian zone of Africa in recent years perfectly illustrates the nature of the problem. The various conferences which have considered this human tragedy have discussed both causes and the remedies mainly as a technical problem. Each discipline has made its contribution but they have been largely futile, first because they were independent of each other and second, because most of them dress up political and social realities in techno-logical clothes. Meanwhile food which is contributed from foreign sources does not reach its destination but is eaten by other people along the way. None of these obstacles is technical; they are socio-economic.

The industrial revolution in the West

Amongst ideological theories of the industrial revolution the same tech-nological interpretation can be found. The central doctrine is that tech-nical innovations were used to increase industrial production but other-wise they were politically neutral. The implication is that the application of technology is simply a practical process and not a political issue.

The social distress which accompanied the gathering of the workers into factories is then justified as the price that had to be paid for progress. 'Industrialisation is equated with modernisation, . . . with a better and healthier life for all . . . the same formula is held out to the underde-veloped countries.' (2) This is the same doctrine popularised by modern 'value free' sociology so that development can be regarded simply as a technical process, and societies are either backward or advanced *according to the level of technological development.*

The idea that technology develops independently of society and is subsequently imposed upon it is still the most common model used today. According to such doctrines the invention of the printing press somehow caused the Renaissance, and in the eighth century the introduction of the stirrup, by revolutionising military technology, ultimately gave birth to feudalism. History can show many examples where technical inventions were suppressed or not used because societies did not then need them. At the time of the ancient Greeks, the library at Alexandria contained a perfect working model of the steam engine. The Chinese were the first to develop paper, printing, the magnetic compass and gunpowder and that symbolic technical object the clock. But they never developed tech-nology beyond an early stage, and so it has been with other cultures. Traditional African societies did not need advanced technology and would have been destroyed by it. Societies are therefore 'primitive' only in a technological sense.

In the case of the industrial revolution, factories were set up not just to house the new machines, but also to inculcate discipline and habits which would make production possible. As one historian noted, Josiah Wedgwood, who built up the pottery industry in the Midlands in Britain, was determined to change 'dilatory drunken worthless workmen' into

37

punctual, orderly and sober persons. The conclusion must be that these revolutions were caused very largely by the rise of a merchant class which used technology to modify the attitudes of the new proletariat.

It is this same transformation which is constantly called for (mostly in vain) in the new countries and which lies behind the demands for 'scientific management'. When businessmen lament that what is lacking in underdeveloped economies is modern management skills, what they mean is that so far it has not been possible to fit the workers into an authoritarian work structure. The use of time and motion studies as developed by Taylor in the USA was designed to increase productivity by modifying the worker's attitudes. Lenin believed that this approach was a basic requisite for industrialisation in any country and declared that Taylorism should also be adopted by the new Soviet state. Thus it came about that both the capitalist and the nominally communist parts of the world developed a technology which reflected authoritarian and hierarchical control over the workforce. But in the new countries this kind of social discipline is rarely to be found; in Japan it has been present as a result of unique circumstances. It is now time to examine what form attitudes conditioned by technology are supposed to take.

Technological consciousness
We have already discussed the alleged differences between traditional and modern attitudes. I have tried to make a distinction between mere modernity and true development, but this is problematical because most technological societies at present have certain features in common. It is usually claimed that these psychological characteristics are essential in *any* technological environment. I do not believe this, but for the moment it is necessary to note what these are.

It is true that people who live in the kind of technological environment that has so far existed tend to *think* in a different way from those who do not. The modern mind has been influenced by certain attributes of industrial production which have so far been dominant and paramount. In such a world everything is measurable and reproducible, while the components in production are interdependent but separate. Technological life is rational, predictable, controllable and marked by an emphasis on linear time and accuracy. Technical ends are separate from means; for example, a worker making a cog may not know what its ultimate use will be.

Most of these features can be called 'mechanistic' and were possibly more characteristic of the late nineteenth century than they will be in the year 2000. A mind influenced by this kind of technology, in order to think, must classify. Classification has been one aspect of the scientific universe and another has been a built-in tendency to control the physical environment rather than to co-operate with it. A world which consists of many linked components has no place for what is unique. Because of this, technology has apparently been responsible for the exclusion of the arts, the downgrading of religious experience and a general dehumanisation which affects human relations. In consequence there has been a widespread and confused reaction against modern technological civilisation, a revolt which produced the counter-culture of the 1960s.

The tendency was to assume that this dehumanisation was caused by technology, and the consequent attack on industrial man concentrated on the alleged mechanisation of the whole of life including the human mind. At a popular level, deeply technical attitudes arising in the first instance from factory production have invaded human consciousness generally. 'Problem solving' attitudes, characteristic of the engineer's relationship with his machines, are carried over into human relations and become the only way that people can perceive the world. Such attitudes exhibited themselves in a sensational manner in the behaviour of President Nixon and his entourage and produced their own language to express their peculiar perceptions. At the level of theory, scientism and positivism have invaded other disciplines and the result is a kind of barbaric passivity.

Numerous analysts of American society have been prophesying Doom, and an inevitable war has been proclaimed between Eros and technology. So, for example, Rollo May' 'The lover like the poet is a menace on the assembly line . . . there comes a point when the cult of technique destroys feeling, undermines passion and blots out individual identity'. (3) Perhaps the key word here is 'cult', which implies a belief produced by the ideology of technocracy.

Sociologists have noted the same tendencies in the Soviet Union, and there is one of the reasons they have concluded that technology acquires an independent momentum of its own in any society. What I have suggested on the other hand is that both systems are authoritarian and that technological innovation is part of the political process. The institutionalisation of technology has meant that the choice of particular machines, or at least the control over this choice, remains in the hands of a dominant social class. In the case of the developing countries this class is still largely foreign and metropolitan.

39

The transfer of technology

The foregoing is intended to provide a background to the problem of transfer. We have already discussed other types of cultural transfer.

In the developed countries technological innovations have been part of their total historical experience. Economic, social, religious and political factors have combined with the accidents of geography to produce a new world. But the developing countries, still dependent on the metropolitan centres, have to import technology from the outside, and in consequence a large part of this transferring process is beyond their control, so that nobody can predict the consequences. There has always been cultural diffusion, but this is a new situation which is not yet understood. (The Russians and Chinese certainly imported technology and still do, but under different circumstances.) Within the new countries the political decisions consist of choices not about their own research but about what technologies to adopt and where they should come from. Within such a context how can political neutrality in the international power struggles be maintained?

In making these choices various economic strategies have been adopted. At an earlier stage ex-colonial countries continued to rely on the export of primary raw materials for their survival. This meant importing manufactured products and the technology stayed where it was—in the metropolitan countries. Later attempts at import substitution were made by manufacturing goods within the countries concerned, although the machines for this purpose had still to be imported. Foreign investment and international aid is part of this process. A more recent development has been the use of foreign capital, and setting up of subsidiaries by the multinational corporations to promote indigenous production. This does mean that the industrial production does take place within the developing countries for the internal market. It leads to an increased use of local capital to finance joint ventures, and governments have required that such companies should be 'indigenised' by a local majority shareholding. It is not suggested that these different strategies are necessarily stages in all cases, and in any event they usually proceed simultaneously. But whatever form this activity has taken, the difficulties have usually been more apparent than the successes. None of them has yet made much impact on rural areas. The balance sheet is something like the following:

1   *Local industry*: Industrial activity requires management and entrepreneurial as well as technical skills. These cannot be acquired from

40

academic courses and they are naturally not part of the indigenous environment. Foreign technicians can be imported (at considerable cost) and training should be one of their responsibilities, but whether this policy is effective or not, it operates only on a technical level. Meanwhile the potential managers go overseas and when they return find it difficult to apply what they have absorbed from a different environment.

The workers at the bench or on the assembly line are likely to have inappropriate attitudes. During the industrial revolution in Britain the Luddites fought a long rearguard action against the new factory system because they knew it would turn them into wage slaves and destroy their way of life which was still viable and based on small-scale production. In our context there is no parallel and the workers are not hostile to machines; they have already left the villages. But they still have a peasant outlook which has not yet been disciplined by factory procedures.

2 *Capital*: Whatever strategies have been used, there has been a drain on reserves of foreign currency due to the need to pay interest on loans, and for licences and patents which have to be transferred from the metropolitan centres; an economic dependency continues.

3 *Technical misfits*: The introduction of inappropriate technology has often failed to fit in with the environment.

The symptons of this failure are painfully apparent to anyone living amongst them. Things don't work; they remain obstinately hostile. A common predicament is that pieces of machinery break down and stay broken down; either because there is nobody to repair them or because the spare parts are not available, or because they find it difficult to survive in an alien or tropical environment—a severe case of culture shock! A common cause of immediate collapse is the fact that people do not know how to use sophisticated equipment, and in trying to learn they render it useless: the result is that bits of ironmongery litter the landscape. This high level of wastage and rapid rate of deterioration would be welcome to capitalists in developed countries, but elsewhere long delays occur while replacements are imported, or the machines are never replaced. Many are damaged on their long journeys or mysteriously lose some of their components; these mishaps occur after equipment has been ordered. But one of the reasons they may turn out to be inappropriate is that the ordering process itself is fraught with danger. One either has to accept whatever models have somehow been imported, or make orders on the basis of insufficient information, so that what eventually arrives

41

is a source of consternation. A museum of industrial technology should be set up where such abandoned items could rest in peace.

4 *Subsidiaries*: With regard to subsidiary companies, even when they are 'indigenised' much of the capital is repatriated in various forms. 'Aid' from foreign loans limits the national power for decision-making as the donors have a right to take part in formulating policy. The multi-national corporations do industrialise in the dependent countries and do cause economic growth, but they satisfy the market demands of a small middle class who maintain consumption patterns similar to their counter-parts in developed countries. An examination of newspaper and tele-vision advertising in Nigeria provides clear evidence that this is the pat-tern, since they are devoted to items which cannot be bought by the masses. The result, it has been suggested, is the 'dual economy' with local capitalist development linked to international capitalist expansion, and on the other hand a non-internationalised or marginal sector.

Agriculture

The modernisation of agriculture is rightly regarded as the key to devel-opment, but the results of research to produce grain with higher yields have produced a green revolution which has been largely negated by social and economic factors. Fertiliser cannot be afforded by poor peasants; but it is necessary if yields are to increase above subsistence-farming levels.

The mechanisation of agriculture is often regarded as the only answer to agricultural decline; but in many countries, and in most parts of Africa, the system of land tenure, quite apart from technical difficulties, makes it introduction unlikely.

The ideological reaction

Neither the form of 'technological consciousness' described above, nor the reaction against it, has developed in the Third World. This can be welcomed or deplored according to one's point of view. A common atti-tude is the wish to import technology without importing the attitudes and types of consciousness which accompany it. A variation on this policy is to attempt to exclude 'undesirable' aspects of modernisation, especially with regard to values, morals, manners and behaviour.

It seems unlikely that such an endeavour is possible, since capitalist development engenders its own value systems. Even though these de-pendent structures may differ in many respects from those in the

42

metropolitan countries, they are still capitalist. With the possible exception of Cuba, it is still too soon to assess whether non-capitalist and nominally socialist new countries have acquired an ideology which has taken root. (In this context I am excluding Eastern Europe.) The situation is extremely confused and I shall simply note certain common attitudes to industrialisation:

1 *The new élites*: One can safely say that both in their mode of life and in their attitude generally, the affluent classes in developing countries wholly welcome the transfer of technology. The remainder of the population also welcomes it, but it has not penetrated their lives. Furthermore, almost without exception, the people want the biggest, the best and the latest equipment whether it is an automobile, a television set, factory machinery or a computer. If the equipment fails to fit in with the environment, so much the worse for that.

It is an outlook which is commonly derided and labelled petit bourgeois, which it is but it cannot be ignored (there may be no true middle class in Africa, but there is a petty or lower middle class). These ambitious attitudes are regarded as unhelpful for development because they are not 'rational'. As we have already seen, theories of development have proved to be inadequate because they have been too narrowly rational in the economic sense. The fact that such perceptions are ineradicable all over the Third World, is surely a significant factor which needs to be explored and explained rather than condemned.

Characteristic of the new elites is a demand for foreign consumer products (often luxury items) even when there may be a local equivalent. This demand is condemned by governments as unpatriotic or unhelpful for the growth of local industries, but it is realistic. In the nature of things, indigenous products, at least to begin with, are likely to be of inferior quality. What is more to the point, they are often not any cheaper. The successful items are usually those like traditional garments which are not mass-produced; otherwise the only satisfactory product which springs to mind is beer, and the brewery companies are usually subsidiaries of foreign companies.

Otherwise, the products which continue to be imported are a constant source of astonishment. Toothpicks are usually mentioned in this context, but there are also more basic necessities such as mosquito repellants, footwear, tinned fruit, vegetables and foodstuffs of all kinds. Soap and detergent are manufactured in developing countries, but the foreign prototypes are usually preferred.

It is often alleged that these consumer demands are a result of a colonial mentality, whereas, on the contrary, they represent the aspirations of those who wish to be regarded as part of the new élite; they are symptomatic of a search for status. The notorious impact of imported baby food is well documented. This, together with the huge market for patent medicines, is a most suitable case study in the workings of multinational corporations. Finally, one should stress that trade secrets kept by foreign enterprise inhibit the growth of wholly indigenous endeavour.

One aspect of the 'status syndrome should be mentioned here. Objects, including technological innovations, have many other symbolic values besides their obvious economic ones. These other values are no less 'real' with regard to the satisfaction they may bring. Prestige projects such as airports, hotels, hospitals and universities are not necessarily the best things for economic progress, but they are what the people want. Should we simply say they should not want them and their attitudes must be changed? Perhaps; but in that case who is there to change them? There have always been white elephants. What are we to say about cathedrals or mosques; are they economic? They have often been surrounded by the rough dwellings of poverty-stricken people.

2   *The opposition*: Traditionalists have objected to many aspects of industrial society as it is known in existing developed countries. Many of these protests have been in the name of religion, and they have often been made by people who have already accepted the benefits of technology for themselves; they do not condemn the machines. The opposition from this quarter then, is not to technology as such—and exhibits a great deal of confusion. What they usually react against are the *symptoms* of modern capitalist industrialism such as sexual permissiveness. But meanwhile they have embraced capitalism, so the contradictions are inevitable. The objections to 'materialism' are equally inconsistent, as those who object are frequently wealthy.

What should be taken more seriously is the movement known as 'intermediate' or 'appropriate' technology. Other labels used are 'instant' or 'immediate' or 'alternative' or finally 'relevant', all of which indicate some of its characteristics. The late Dr Schumacher in his pioneering work *Small is beautiful* (4) described this type of technology as an activity coming midway between primitive manual techniques and industrial undertakings proper. In his view large-scale industrialisation has grave limitations and has resulted in the impoverishment of the rural

44

areas. It is not without significance that he was influenced by Gandhi's theory and practice in India. He was concerned not with technological transfer but with technical *innovation* from within the villages of the Third World. This work, he insisted, can only be done by the people themselves, using locally available materials and their own labour. Without such a programme young people would continue to leave for the bright lights of the cities. The main aims of relevant technology can be summarised as follows:

1 To provide essential machines for small-scale development and to identify techniques which are relevant to human needs in particular places.
2 To train school leavers to train other school leavers in simple techniques.
3 To stimulate production in the towns and villages as distinct from mass production in factories.
4 To use locally available materials.
5 To rehabilitate the disabled.
6 To provide opportunities for the employment of women in places where they live.

These headings were drawn up by myself in an unpublished pamphlet. In the same work I stressed that relevant technology should not be confused with the arts and crafts movement nor with small-scale industry. Gandhi's movement was partly a revival strategy whereas we are concerned with innovation.

This brief summary should indicate the significance and possibilities of this movement. There is an intermediate technology centre in London which publishes educational material and has conducted experimental work in several developing countries including Jamaica, Nigeria, Tanzania and Botswana. The United Nations have also publicised these ideals; the movement has therefore gained increasing support. Its attractions are obvious and I have personally been much impressed by workshops set up in Zaria and Jos and elsewhere in Nigeria. The educational role is especially significant since intermediate technology dispenses with formal educational structures. So long as it can be kept on a small scale, and preferably separate from the usual status-ridden bureaucratic processes, it can also operate with very little capital.

However, it should not be supposed that intermediate technology can be an *alternative* to large-scale industrialisation. It is not a revolutionary or even a radical movement; it must operate from within existing structures. China has used intermediate technology in her 'walking on two legs' policy (ie developing both town and countryside) with considerable success, but this is within a revolutionary framework. The conclusion must be that it represents a hopeful and valuable strategy for grass-roots development and as such could be part of a wider political strategy; otherwise 'unless the unity of technological and political practice is achieved, it is unlikely that intermediate technology, on its own, will be able to tackle the real causes of underdevelopment, nor bring about a viable solution'.

Summary and conclusion

The main intention of this chapter has been to stress the political element in development. It is a socio-economic process and it is generally agreed that economic formulae and blueprints on their own have failed to provide the answers. In fact it seems fair to say that there is still no general agreement from either the right or left of the political spectrum as to what should be done.

We have already noted however, that certain approaches have been largely abandoned. We now hear less about inevitable stages of growth, and development economists (who after all represent a new discipline) are reluctant to make generalisations about all parts of the world. Dudley Seers's statement that 'Economics is the study of economies' is often quoted. It is generally agreed that the economic doctrines which deal with the developed world are not appropriate elsewhere. What is more debatable is whether the developing countries themselves have sufficient in common for a common pattern to be discerned for proposals to be made which can be applied in different places. There is the further complication that both Marxist and dependency theories see all economic development as part of a world process. The approach used in these chapters falls roughly within these last two overlapping traditions.

With regard to technology, I have implied that economic patterns are difficult to observe, especially for the layman, but the psychological and social factors are not; they are very apparent and appear in the newspapers every day. (In 'social factors' we include class relations and conflicts.) If countries continue to adopt the 'wrong' kind of technology and the 'wrong' kind of education system, then that must have its own significance. Not for the first time one must conclude that the alternatives can only be total revolution or a continuation of the present

46

muddles. Perhaps the various armies now trampling about in the horn of Africa may eventually introduce some new perspective.

REFERENCES
1 Dickson, David, *Alternative technology and the politics of technical change* Fontana, 1974.
2 *Ibid*, 168.
3 May, Rollo, *Love and will* Fontana, 1972, 97.
4 Schumacher, E F, *Small is beautiful: a study of economies as if people mattered* Blond Briggs, 1973.

PART II

EDUCATION

3

THE EDUCATIONAL LEGACY

Education and development

The leaders of developing countries have rightly stressed the importance of education in the development process; indeed, many of them talk as if it were the key to development, which cannot be the case.

Trained and educated people are required to administer and control a new country—even more important, technological growth demands more and more skilled labour. But, as the example of India has shown, a high proportion of university-educated people does not guarantee progress. In Africa it is clear that education, for instance universal primary education (commonly referred to as UPE) may create more problems than it solves if there are no jobs for those who are leaving school. One is tempted to believe that it might be better if the children had not been to school at all. Revolutionaries welcome this condition since revolution often comes when the half-educated jobless rebel. However, in this chapter we are discussing only the aims and purposes of education as they have revealed themselves in the past, particularly before ex-colonial countries became independent.

The essence of the current problem has been well stated by Philip Coombs: 'When a society decides—as many have lately done—to transform its "elitist" educational system into one that will serve the mass of the people, and when it further decides to use that system as an instrument for national development, it is beset by many novel problems. One is that while many people want more education, they do not necessarily want the kind of education that under new circumstances is mostly likely to serve both their own future and the best interests of national development.' (1) It is this theme we shall have to explore.

Basic aims

In my book *Libraries and cultural change* (2) I simplified the matter by listing four basic aims for education which can be distinguished in any

51

society. There exist other, more sophisticated lists, but they are variations on these same themes—which are as follows:

1 The learning of skills. This is mainly vocational, and can include the acquisition of qualifications, although these are not necessarily given priority.

2 Preparation for a place in society—commonly called socialisation, or social adjustment. The norms, or *mores*, or attitudes prevalent in a society are *internalised* by this process—they become part of a personality structure. In the context of development and in post-traditional societies, this aim, insofar as it can exist at all becomes exceedingly confused and torn by contradictions. We may include value-systems as part of the socialisation. Indeed some people stress this aspect above all—to quote Schumacher, 'The essence of education is the transmission of values . . . or what to do with out lives'. (3) If this is so, how many education systems are successful? One can add character-training and moral education to this cluster of good intentions.

3 An introduction to the world of belief or ideology in the form of religious and political ethics. It is usually agreed that the socialisation aim (in 2 above) needs to take place within some framework of general belief. I suggest that much of the current talk about 'standards of behaviour' is futile if divorced from some such overall pattern or system within which the personality can develop.

4 Development of individual personality. This normally implies critical thinking and creativity. In the context of development, this 'individualism' is important because of the urgent need for innovation and new departures. Whether the values traditionally associated with 'liberal education' are equally important as they have been elsewhere is more problematical, but certainly these are civilised values based on a respect for the individual.

It will be observed that some of these aims are complementary and associated while others are in conflict. For example, an emphasis on individual growth may not be possible for societies in a hurry to develop and where collective endeavour is the first requirement. It is because of these conflicts that there is so much muddle and confusion, and why 'philosophies' of education are difficult to take seriously. In any event, they reflect whatever the social situation is. This will be discussed below, but first we should note some special features of developing societies, with particular reference to Africa.

52

Influences in Africa

Traditional education

People in traditional villages had, and to some extent still have, a comprehensive and thorough system of training from birth to the grave. Although this is neither formal nor institutional education it does embrace the aims mentioned above, with the exception of 'individualism', since in traditional society people are trained to belong, not to be different. This type of socialisation is ritualised and marked by rites of passage and ceremonial observances at all the important occasions of life. Fafunwa (writing of Nigeria) calls it 'functionalist' education, with cardinal goals as follows:

1   Physical training.
2   Development of character.
3   Respect for elders and peers.
4   Intellectual training.
5   Vocational training.
6   Community participation.
7   Promotion of cultural heritage.

Fafunwa states that 'Traditional education is not any more conservative or any less progressive than any other system'. (4) It is difficult to see why he felt it necessary to make this claim, since the merits of such systems are not that they are 'progressive' in the sense in which this word is normally used, but that they are wholly appropriate for human needs in tribal societies.

Traditional societies were probably not as static as used to be thought, but the fact remains that the system was concerned to preserve a way of life *as it was.* In such societies, respect for elders was, of course, paramount, but this and other characteristics do not fit with 'modernisation' or with 'Western' education. That such communities were mostly illiterate is not particularly relevant since they had no need for literacy; their culture was oral.

This type of education is mentioned first because its influence varies according to the nature of local cultures, but it will often conflict with more formal educational structures and even with national aims. National consciousness was not part of the former environment.

53

Islamic education

It is commonly estimated that more than 50 per cent of the population of Africa at the present time is Muslim. I am confining this section to Islam south of the Sahara with particular reference to Nigeria, not only because I am not competent to generalise about Islam elsewhere, but also because the situation varies widely in each country. Some states, such as Saudi Arabia, are obviously more traditional and orthodox, while modernising or liberal influences have had a greater impact in Egypt or Pakistan.

Here I am dealing mainly with the aims of traditional Koranic schools, which cannot be appreciated unless it is understood that (at least in the earlier stages) they are not concerned with knowledge in the Western sense, but with a religious training which culminates in the ability to join in Muslim prayers, observances, customs and ceremonies. This is the beginning of a process which is not just religious education as distinct from secular, but represents a total way of life in which the secular does not exist. Because of this, Islam, as compared with other religions, especially Christianity, which are not 'total' in the same sense, has great strength and inspires a devotion not often found in the modern world. This characteristic at the same time produces doctrinal, practical and political difficulties in relation to the secular aspects of society.

Islamic learning began as a result of the Prophet's advice to teach others without expectation of reward. It resulted in an educational movement not unlike the Christian form of education in the Middle Ages: 'This noble principle, which was successfully applied in the early stage of the development of Islamic education, reduced the status of teacher (Mallam) to that of a mere beggar . . . He had to wander from place to place . . . he had to send his pupils from door to door asking for charity. They were considered to be "Muhajiran" (emigrants) who had left their homes in search of knowledge'. (5)

Such a tradition obviously cannot survive in the same form in a modern state, but it does still exist; we are particularly concerned with its historical importance.

The education process at primary level has a significance without parallel in Christian practice at the present time, and we may find it useful to consider this separately from higher education, even if it is all part of one process. Children in Koranic schools begin by memorising a few parts or *esus* of the Koran (which has 60 parts); these are used for daily prayers. This is then followed by the learning of the Arabic-language alphabet, which enables the pupils to read over again the parts of the

Koran he has already learnt. (6) Following on from this he can then read other texts written in the Arabic script. (This is occasionally confusing to outsiders—in Northern Nigeria, what the children are learning at this stage is the Hausa language in the Arabic script.) At the end of this primary level the child can read and write in the Arabic script and he knows several of the *esus* by heart, but *he does not know the meaning of the verses* since they are intended for religious duties and for prayer, not for intellectual dissection. It is this part of Koranic learning which has puzzled non-Muslims, but such practices are not unknown in other religions—witness the use until recently of Latin in the Roman Catholic mass.

It is only at the next or 'secondary' level that the pupil begins to learn the meaning of the verses he has learned, and he is then introduced to *Hadith*. This literature is embodied in books of tradition which have established formal rites and rules of behaviour; it constitutes a chain of authorities which carry back the tradition to the prophet himself and guarantee its authenticity.

The final stages of Islamic learning, always undertaken only by a minority, carry studies into what in other systems would be called the secular sphere, and it is this level which is the heir to a centuries-old tradition that did so much to preserve classical learning during the European dark ages, and remains as an imperishable contribution to civilisation. However, the creative period lay in the distant past and, at least in the part of Africa we are discussing, it cannot be said that the higher levels of Arabic learning have much significance beyond the Muslim ethos.

This educational tradition is not a system at all in the modern sense, since there is no uniform curriculum, no prescribed qualifications and no education structure as usually understood. Leaving aside the meaning of the Islamic education-tradition at its highest levels, what needs to be stressed is that Koranic teaching has been of immense importance in the history of Africa wherever it has been established.

In effect, Koranic schools have maintained and extended the Muslim religion, especially before independence in Nigeria and also in other countries. In some regions, *eg* Yorubaland, they remained a bulwark against the advent of Christianity. That is the religion's role; the political significance, as I see it, is that this tradition is rooted in the life of the ordinary people—the masses—however poor or under-privileged they might have been. The *mallams* were not usually educated in the formal sense, but as Fafunwa points out, 'In a non-literate society, the barely literate man could be the carrier of literacy'; he was in fact an intermediary between the learned Muslims and the peasantry.

55

We should not overlook the fact that these educational methods were frequently part of a social process which supported rigidly stratified political systems and helped to prop up feudal structures, though that is not the main point here. It remains now to examine whether this tradition can be modified to suit modern needs.

Islamic education and modernisation

On a personal level, where individual Muslims have to come to terms with their environment, many adjustments are possible. Islamic truth can be separated from scientific knowledge and the two kinds of symbolic meaning can co-exist, apparently without too much stress. Any integration appears (at least to the outside observer) to be improbable because of the fundamentalist 'revealed' element in Islam. If the Koran is literally the word of God, then controversy can arise only from its interpretation. The individual is guided by authority.

On a social level, whatever form Islamic doctrines may take in the modern world, the tension between secular and religious attitudes remains. Since Islam is world-wide, there have been many schisms, many reformist movements and *Jihads*, or holy wars, to convert the infidel, and attempts to get back to the true message of the Prophet when it has become corrupted by the usages of the world.

As in the case of Christianity, some of these movements attempted to recover the egalitarian elements within the faith. Many practices which are often thought of as Islamic were the consequence of semi-feudal social systems. Repressive regimes have always used religion for their own purposes, and religious faith produces theocratic movements which become powerful vested interests in themselves. Marxists have classified religious belief as the opiate of the people, but this is so only in the sense that religion has been appropriated and misused to drug the masses by rulers who control them for wholly irreligious purposes.

Alongside and often in conflict with these attempts to preserve Islam there has been the rapid growth of modernisation and secular ideas. In countries such as Egypt, Syria, Iraq and (possibly) Pakistan, the anti-colonial struggle produced *two* elites, not one. On the one had were the new Western-style schools and colleges; on the other were the ancient Muslim academic and religious institutions. The first elite was rich and materialist, while the traditionally-orientated Muslim one was less rich but honoured and respected. Their common ideology was nationalism, a struggle against the Imperialists.

Initially, the modernising elites formed 'revolutionary' governments which were firmly linked to Western capitalism. While the emphasis was on anti-imperialism, the traditional Muslim element could go along with it, but in recent times there has been globally a fundamentalist backlash against Westernisation and materialism, whether it be Marxist or capitalist. At the centre of this world-wide resurgence of Islamic traditionalism is a movement to return to *Sharia* (the Islamic legal code) and a corresponding rejection of Western law. In the Gulf States, the *Sharia* has always been in force so that, in theory at least, adulterers are stoned, thieves have their hands chopped off, and those who break the Ramadan fast are publicly flogged. These punishments are not always carried out but they are official state policy. During 1977, in Egypt and the Sudan special committees were set up to draft new legal codes to adapt the *Sharia* to the realities of modern states. Both committees proposed the death penalty for adulterers, and communists and Muslims who renounced the faith. At the same time, a conference in Cairo demanded the prohibition of the drinking of alcohol, of gambling and the charging of interest by banks. There have also been attempts to reintroduce the segregation of men and women in public places. These movements are of course mostly pressure-groups, not governments. For example, according to newspaper reports, the orthodox *dakharahs* (missionaries) in Malaysia have urged the poeple to throw away their radios and televisions and to burn their furniture. Naturally, the government tries to restrain such people, but the pressures have been growing.

This political swing to the right in the Islamic world is beyond dispute. The reasons for the trend are less easy to establish. It has been suggested that the growth of a superifical and imported modernism has left a cultural vacuum which traditional forces are rushing in to fill. This has happened even in Turkey, where the founder of the modern state separated religion from the secular power, a division which is contrary to Islamic doctrine. Kemal Ataturk was determined to reduce Islamic cultural influences, which he saw as an obstacle to modernisation. He proclaimed that 'There is only one civilisation' (by which he meant the West) and introduced the Latin alphabet and European headgear, marriage and family law. A typical symbolic act was the banning of the call to prayer from the minarets.

Turkey was a special case in that independence was fought for and won much earlier than elsewhere, but the point is that the political reaction (as represented by the political parties' capture of rural votes) is visible also. The modernisation was skin deep and it did *not re*ach the rural areas.

We have suggested that the 'silent' peasantry might one day rebel and produce a real revolution. Obviously, the movement based on the revival

57

of religious institituions is not that at all, but an instinctive reaction against modernisation. When one considers what form the new way of life has taken, and how it has benefited not the peasants but only the new élites, when one reflects that the new Western values have not been able to penetrate their lives, such a response is understandable. The peasantry never appreciated the new ways; for one thing, after their brief schooling (if any) they had little or nothing to read. They have remained outside the modernising process.

Meanwhile, the rulers of the oil states in the Persian Gulf, with their tiny populations and vast wealth, constitute an important political influence. In those countries public cinemas are forbidden, and women are not allowed to drive cars. The current religious reaction in many countries is fueled by the riches of Saudi Arabia, in a form of religious imperialism under which client states must take account of Saudi views. Yet the world is well aware that religious taboos, though rigidly enforced among the masses, are not for their rulers. These contradictions are so extreme in Saudi Arabia that the survival of the regime for very long in its present form must be open to doubt.

These political trends naturally affect schools and, especially, universities where the students reflect the cultural climate. In practice, political regimes are more liberal than many critics suggest. However, if the word of the Koran is to be taken literally, the message is quite clear and it is not compatible with modernisation as defined in the West, where the concept was invented. This is most evident in the position of women within the societies. 'Men are the managers of the affairs of women for that God has preferred in bounty one of them over another . . . Righteous women are therefore obedient . . . And those you fear may be rebellious —admonish, banish them to their couches and beat them.' Elsewhere in the Koran there is a reference to the 'tillage' of women. It is a doctrine which men of other faiths have also preferred not to abandon. Yet the doctrines based upon the *Hadith*, and to a lesser extent the *Sharia*, are somewhat different, since they are systems which have grown up over the centuries and do not have quite the same undisputed authority as the verses of the Koran, nor the emotional force.

Since this book is largely concerned with Africa south of the Sahara, we should add that Islam in that vast region, not being a state religion, does not have the same *national* significance, although among the faithful strict orthodoxy may prevail. That it does not do so everywhere is exemplified in Yorubaland in Nigeria where, for example, the practice of *purdah* is not customary. As one authority has noted, 'In its Yoruba form Islam is largely a matter of ritual observances'. (7)

So we see that, at least on a social level, there is a conflict between Islamic and Western education. What compromises may be possible cannot be suggested in detail by outsiders. One must conclude that non-Muslims are not really in a position fully to understand the essence of this type of education, nor to appreciate all the issues involved.

Christian missions
The historical role of the Christian missionaries in establishing their own kind of education in the colonised parts of Africa is probably so well known to readers of this book that it scarcely needs repeating here. As with Islam, the primary aim was conversion, but the results were the acquisition of literacy and access to Western education. The consequences of education systems do not necessarily correspond with the aims of the educators.

The missionary schools provided the foundations for modern education both before and after the colonial period, and their influence is still not negligible, though varying according to the different histories of each country. The debit side of all this activity is also well documented. Most of the missions were not tolerant, and in their early stages violently attacked both the traditional and Islamic systems. (Not infrequently they also attacked each other.) They claimed to be suppressing barbarous and vicious practices—which they sometimes were; as one Methodist statement had it, 'The substitution of a civilised authority for the accursed despotism of Pagan and Mohammedan powers is divine and gracious interposition'.

The religious consequences were ambiguous and, as one African authority notes, 'For anyone who can notice such things, there is abundant evidence to show the prevalence of native customs and beliefs under a thin veneer of Christianity'. (8) Or again, 'The new deity is added to the totality of supernatural forces on which they can call for aid. Generally speaking this is the present state of affairs'.

But we are concerned with purposes, and in relation to the four educational aims mentioned at the start of this chapter, it is apparent that although the missionaries contributed to socialisation in the new (colonised) societies, and set up some vocational instruction, and inculcated certain beliefs and values (whilst attempting to destroy traditional ones), they cannot be said to have stressed the fourth aim, which is individualistic or liberal or scientific. This is important, because none of the three historical influences described here, (traditional, Islamic and Christian) was 'modern', in the sense that for different reasons and in different ways they have remained authoritarian.

59

The fact that the missionary schools were boarding schools (they usually still are) is also significant, since their influence, as opposed to traditional culture, was thereby strengthened. Up to quite recent times, life in some of these schools resembled with remarkable fidelity the kind of world depicted in *Tom Brown's schooldays*. Such a milieu as a foundation for a new country had severe limitations and was naturally imbued with a colonialist ambiance.

These are broad generalisations, and no doubt there were exceptions. Also, variations occurred in different parts of Africa or within particular countries, according to the kind of missions they were. Such differences can still be seen, and some schools were more liberal than others in their interpretation of Christinaity and in their attitudes to indigenous cultures.

In view of the tendency to equate missionaries with colonialism, it should also be observed that they were often in conflict with the colonial authorities and an embarrassment to District Commission Officers. In Nigeria it was only after 1920 that the colonial government really began to bother about an official policy for education.

Concerning Northern Nigeria, there has been much debate whether the known resistance of Islamic leaders to 'Western' education was due to their own 'reactionary' views or to the attitudes of the Christian missionaries. In fact, the colonial government favoured Islamic education. But because of the Christian activity, Muslims identified Western education with Christianity and were inevitably suspicious—a suspicion which remains, even though Western education ceased to be Christian in any precise sense at the beginning of this century—at least in the mother countries. The real danger, of course, was not a waning official Christianity, but a secular type of education which had no special or privileged place for either Islam or Christianity. The ancient conflict between the two great 'religions of the book' was no longer relevant. In consequence, the educational emphasis was totally shifted.

Western secular education

Many Third World citizens who were later to become prominent in their own countries were exposed to 'modern' forms of education in the USA, Britain, France or elsewhere in Europe. I have distinguished this type of education from the religion-based systems of Islam or Christianity because its aims have been different. If we take these overseas systems we must note that the four aims can apply to foreigners from the Third World only in a partial way. Western secular systems are not designed to prepare them for a place in *their* society nor to introduce them to their own values (whatever these might be). They do, however, provide them with necessary skills and qualifications, and they equip them (it is to be hoped) with the type of enquiring mind which modern education at a higher level is supposed to produce. The modern systems, at least in the liberal capitalist West, do make some attempt to foster individual thought, even if it is not always clear what people should think about.

So much for the impact of education in advanced countries on visitors from abroad. It should not be supposed that the systems are considered appropriate, nor the aims satisfactory, even by the domestic inhabitants themselves. There is always a 'crisis' in education, since it holds the balance between opposing social forces. From the political right comes the criticism that education has failed to maintain traditional values or academic standards. The development of comprehensive education in Britain has been met with increasingly virulent attacks on these grounds. These conservative protests are first cousins to the similar complaints about falling standards which arise in developing countries when education expands or begins to provide for a higher proportion of the population.

Much of the alarm arises because members of the more affluent groups or classes in society grow anxious that the quality of their children's education is being eroded and that their life changes will suffer. There are some grounds for this reaction, and a tension between liberty and equality always exists. 'Middle-class' freedom to ensure the best possible education for their children may clash with a comprehensive system which provides for everybody. Yet it is ironic that parents now expect schools to uphold values which they no longer believe in themselves; this is a kind of moral insurance policy. Thus in part the English public schools are gaining a new lease of life since they are thought to provide stability for children whose parents have divorced.

From the left, on the other hand, has come pressure for a truly democratic system with the same opportunities for all, including education in the most complete sense, and not just vocational training which fits people for their place in a hierarchical society. (There is a parallel here also with demands made in developing countries.) There is also a similar insistence that education-content should be relevant to a changing world, but since these changes are now so rapid, education always seems to be lagging behind. Thus one writer in *New left review* offered the unequivocal assertion that 'British education is from a rational point of view grotesque, from a moral one intolerable, and from a human one tragic'.

One of the most positive contributions from within this democratic socialist tradition has been made by Raymond Williams. (9) He suggests a minimum standard for every educationally normal child. This should include:

1   Extensive practice in English and mathematics.
2   'General knowledge of ourselves and our environment' to be taught at the secondary level, not as separate disciplines.
3   History and criticism of literature, the visual arts, music, drama, landscape and architecture.
4   'Extensive practice in democratic procedures' and in 'the use of libraries, newspapers and magazines, radio and television pro-grammes, and other sources of information and influences.'
5   Introduction to at least one foreign culture, including its language, history, geography, institutions and arts, 'to be given in part by visiting and exchange'.

This common education would stop at 16. It will be seen that this programme provides for all the aims we have recognised. It does not, however, allow for the present social set-up in Britain and is to that extent Utopian. For example, teachers in some of the 'blackboard jungles' may well boggle at 'democratic' procedures. Also, most teachers in British schools at present show little sign that they are capable of implementing such a programme. Many are afraid of deal-ing with controversial issues with religious or political implications; it is safer to be neutral, non-committal and, in the last resort, not an educationist at all.

If such proposals seem remote from reality in Britain, it is evident that they are even less relevant for the countries under review. I have quoted them in order to indicate that this educational tradition needs radically to be modified to meet rapidly changing circumstances. Mean-while, education structures in developing countries have been modelled on patterns which are obsolescent in the countries which produced them.

Conclusion
The foregoing refers to the impact of four wholly disparate traditions which are in conflict with each other. In consequence there is a con-fusion which, whilst it may be fascinating to the detached observer, does not indicate the way forward that apostles of development require; indeed the signposts point in contradictory directions or none. On the

political level there is an ideological vacuum which ultimately may be filled by absolutist doctrines such as those which prevail in China. In Africa this process has officially begun in Somalia, Ethiopia, Angola and Mozambique—the outcome remains to be seen. Meanwhile in other developing countries individuals are increasingly conditioned by influences emanating mostly from the capitalist West.

It is now time to look at this educational legacy and the Western secular system which has been transferred to the new nations. The Western model, it has been hoped, can be adapted to indigenous aims, and it is this enterprise which must be considered in the next chapter.

REFERENCES
1 Coombs, Philip H, *The world educational crisis: a systems analysis* OUP, 1968, 7.
2 Benge, R C, *Libraries and cultural change* 1970, 123
3 Schumacher, E F, *Small is beautiful: a study of economics as if people mattered* Blond Briggs, 1973, 73.
4 Fafunwa, A B, *History of education in Nigeria* Allen and Unwin, 1974, 48.
5 *Ibid*, 55.
6 Arberry, Arthur J, *The Koran interpreted* OUP, 1964, 77.
7 Fadipe, N A, *The sociology of the Yoruba* Ibadan University Press, 1970, 318.
8 Nduka, Otonti, *Western education and the Nigerian cultural background* OUP (Ibadan), 1964, 17, 19.
9 Williams, Raymond, *The long revolution* Chatto, 1960, 142-144.

4

EDUCATION NOW

It is now appropriate to examine the aims of education in the new countries—always bearing in mind that official policies may not relate to what takes place in the classroom.

The structure and policies of education are determined by historical, social and economic forces such as those we have already discussed. One should distinguish, then, between the 'real' aims and official pronouncements. This may seem obvious, but in fact much education literature and even official reports ignore it. For example, it is frequently stated that the new education systems are unsatisfactory because they are likely to produce educated or half-educated people *for whom there are no jobs*.

This certainly happens and is already becoming a social problem in many countries. But the fault is not the education system, but the fact that societies are still not organised for production. If one assumes a social *status quo*, then it follows that education should not be expanded; but it is the assumption which is wrong. Those who are alarmed by expansion should remember the statistics. As a rough average it is usual in most under-developed countries that only about 5 per cent of the people or less receive university education; 20 per cent may have primary education, 30 per cent about four years in school, and 45 per cent no education at all. That is why the Universal Primary Education planned for Nigeria is such a tremendous undertaking.

Most Third World countries inherited a system set up before they became independent. It is a notorious fact that some countries reached independence with only a trivial number of university graduates among the population. This was especially the case in Zaire, Mozambique, Angola and Guinea Bissau, not least because it was not originally intended that these countries should eventually govern themselves. It was not an auspicious beginning. Most of the universities followed a British pattern, often with an admixture of American policies and methods, and this, together with a somewhat confused local reaction against such models,

65

resulted in systems which satisfied few. The British prototypes were humanistic in the European tradition, while the American influences were more 'practical' and technological, resembling in this respect the educational policies in the USSR.

Vocationalism

Education structures are partly determined by what people want for their children. In most parts of the underdeveloped world, people at all social levels have been remarkably consistent in seeing education as the key to advancement in this world. This view is realistic, but the kind of education they have instinctively wanted does not necessarily relate to national development as seen by planners of long-term growth. This has always been so, even in colonial times.

It has often been claimed that the neglect of practical and technical education which was apparent in Africa was deliberate colonial policy. It is probably more accurate to say that the kind of societies which were brought into being required certain skills, notably those of clerks and junior administrators, and this is where advancement lay. The colonial educators themselves were constantly lamenting that not enough was being done to relate schooling to life as it was lived in the villages, but parents did not want this type of education for their offspring. In this view they were correct, and they understood very well the nature of their society—which in many respects is the same now as it was then.

Technological skills were not required since, after all, these were not industrial countries. At an intermediate level there was (and is) a need for artisans of every kind—mechanics, plumbers, electricians and so on. They were required to service the machines which were imported from abroad. Yet their status was low and technical training was neglected in all the colonial territories.

Some attempts were made to set up higher education with a vocational bias. For example in Nigeria, the colonial government set up a 'Higher College' at Yaba as early as 1934. This institution was not a success, and Nduka describes it as a 'pathetic waste' and the product of half a century of imperialist blinkers. (1) Within the colonial context, it was rightly regarded with suspicion, and popular resistance to vocational education at the lower levels remains very strong; the acquisition of practical skills is not seen as desirable. My own students have always insisted that 'hoe-power' is not for them, and that the purpose of their education is to get them away from the land, not to provide for their return to it. It should be obvious to everyone by now that unless and

66

until basic necessities such as roads, electricity, water and modern cultural amenities (cinema, television, schools for adults, and the rest) are provided in the villages, the young people will not wish to return in any capacity. What does happen is that people retire back to their villages when their life's work is done.

In some respects this imbalance in educational demands is worse now than formerly, since international trade and mass-production of even the smallest items tends to kill indigenous art and craft. It is scarcely credible, but commonplace objects like pins have to be imported from Birmingham, or Tokyo, or Hong Kong.

In view of the resistance to vocational training, we may conclude that society does not provide for future development as much as the planners hope, and in spite of serious current efforts to expand technical and vocational education. From a development point of view this neglect has been unfortunate, but popular doubts are healthy, since they may reflect an instinctive understanding that vocational training is only one part of education and represents only one of the aims we are discussing. In hierarchical societies citizens are trained to take their place within rigid structures, and that is not democratic education. Nobody supposes that parents are concerned with visions of ideal education for their children; they are, however, interested in vocation and life-chances, but not at the bottom of the heap or on the lower rungs of an exclusive social ladder. They are aware also that too many are pushed off the ladder altogether—those commonly (and unfairly) called 'dropouts' or, more appropriately, 'kickouts'. Vocational education is fine if it leads to a place at the top.

But the social reality remains that agriculture, not education, must provide the key for development, and that somehow the education system must provide for agricultural training. But how and when? The view that this should be done at a primary level is now largely discredited. Yet many official pronouncements have recommended, or seemed to recommend, that the primary curriculum should include practical farming. As recently as 1960 the Ashby Report emphasised that 'since for a long time to come large numbers of primary school leavers will be unable to attend secondary schools, it seems imperative that sound and effective agricultural education be imparted to those who will be returning to the land'. (2) Another typical statement was made in the Report of the Banjo Commission in 1961: 'It was hoped that the literate primary school-leavers would go back to be better farmers, carpenters, bricklayers etc, but all the pupils themselves want to be are junior clerks in offices'. (3)

There are many other complaints of this kind, but the reports have not been realistic. The task of primary education is not to provide instruction in practical farming, but to offer foundations which will reconcile children to their rural environment. Also, pupils are sometimes exploited when they are put to work in the headmaster's garden.

Nevertheless, valuable experiments towards an education more suited to the villages have been made in many parts of the world by missionary bodies, by intermediate technology units and by individual pioneers. One of the best known of these projects is that of Patrick Von Rensberg at a school in Botswana. There, the children were required to build their own school, to produce their own food, and generally to provide their own means of livelihood. This experiment attracted much support and attention, but it ultimately ran aground for the usual reasons, that it was an isolated endeavour. These were secondary-school children, and they compared themselves unfavourably with children from other schools who did not have the same programme of manual labour. Inevitably, although their cooperate efforts did produce results, their values in the last resort came from the society around them. At a national level the system of Basic Education initiated by Gandhi for rural India is also well-known. There the anti-modern bias was more pronounced, and not everybody could agree that spinning with the hand-wheel should be the foundation of vocational training, even in villages which had not known the spinning wheel before.

But considerable efforts are now being made to increase and improve technical colleges. It seems that the type of informal and unstructured training provided by intermediate technology could be an attractive and much less expensive supplement. These schemes can be entirely free from foreign support or importation, since they train young people in the village to make useful and appropriate machines using local materials. They can be multiplied indefinitely, because trainees can start up similar projects in other villages and no elaborate or stultifying bureaucracy is needed. They have been advocated as one answer to the urgent problem of unemployment amongst young people. This kind of development is at the grass roots and could do much to revitalise stagnant villages; technical training is done on the job and linked to production, yet such schemes are not prestigious and 'small is beautiful' is not a slogan that usually appeals to the planners of new countries.

For technical and agricultural education, there are other possibilities. Many have advocated an increase in adult education outside formal schooling structures, since it is the school-leavers and 'dropouts' who are most in need. The popular colleges of the USA have been urged as models and colleges of rural technology recommended. The aim would be to emphasise tertiary non-university institutions. Meanwhile the problem remains and vocational training, except for white-collar and professional workers, is an unrealised aim. There are academics with PhDs in electronics, but not enough electricians.

One should mention that there have been since time immorial many traditional apprenticeship schemes in trades like tailoring or carpentry. Most of these are in the towns; they are not unlike the systems of the Middle Ages in Europe, and trainees are not free from exploitation.

Socialisation

It will be recalled that another essential purpose of education is to introduce the student directly or indirectly, consciously or by subliminal processes, to his own culture—by which we mean way of life. The first thing to take account of is that this socialisation process is rarely straightforward and always ambivalent, facing both the past and the future.

A necessary part of culture is the preservation of the past, which is one reason why libraries which preserve records of all kinds are important cultural agencies. However, some post-traditional societies are rejecting the past, which makes it doubly important that education should prepare people for their roles in a new and unfamiliar society. The school, the university and the adult-education class develop new knowledge and perceptions. In this way formal education is both a conservative and a progressive force (which is why both the staff and students of universities so often come into conflict with governments).

One of the most obvious and typical characteristics of traditional society is a respect for the elders. They are honoured not only because they are shortly to join the exalted company of the ancestral dead, but also because, over the long years, they have absorbed the complex forms of customary wisdom which have sufficed for human needs for centuries. In such a world proverbs, riddles and moral fables play an important part— the rich paraphernalia of a non-literate culture. Since nothing is written down, all this can only be passed on by the old men and women of the community.

It is at once apparent that modern education undermines this symbolic world, and since so much of knowledge and knowhow is new, the experience of the old people becomes irrelevant, so they are bewildered by and often hostile to the muddled manifestations of transition. In the more remote village their ancient authorities may still survive, which is yet another reason why young people emigrate to the towns.

The question which will not go away concerns the erosion or collapse of the old certainties. Since society is in transition, what framework of reference can be passed on to the young? In another form the problem is familiar enough in the adolescent absurdities of the West. It is significant that both childhood and puberty are modern concepts; traditional society has rites of passage and initiation ceremonies, but they do not last for twenty years and a child or a teenager is not a separate human species.

I stress this point because it lies behind so many of the lamentations about decaying standards of behaviour. In the old days children did not smash up the headmaster's car or burn down the school because there was neither a school nor a car. What then is to be done about this lack of discipline? One method which the military are advocating in Nigeria is to send soldiers (corporals seem to be most favoured) into the schools. On a less preposterous level there are calls for religious revival and re-generation—any religion, it seems will do so long as it makes young people behave.

One is reminded of the angry exhortations of the Old Testament, and it is difficult to take such appeals seriously; official religions have never provided solutions in matters of conduct at times of social disorder, if only because the same remorseless processes which undermine old modes of behaviour also weaken religious observances and beliefs. Young people cannot but observe that eminent persons whose political or business behaviour is dubious in the extreme are often practising Christians or Muslims. As Nduka observes: 'All authorities appear agreed on the fact that one of the effects of the contact between the indigenous cultures and the dominant Western culture is the lowering of moral standards of both the indigenous and the foreign culture'. (4)

Another hope is the resort to patriotism and high ideals. For example, in Nigeria the National Universities Commission (in the section of its 1977 report on the new universities) stated *inter alia* that the universities should produce 'Patriotic and fair-minded men and women of intelligence, of good character and with some understanding of the purpose of human life and observance of the rules of conduct which should be followed for achieving this purpose'. (5) The dilemma is indicated by those five words *the purpose of human life*. Who will pronounce on such a theme—one which has occupied religious and political thinkers since thought began?

Ideology

Behind all these formulations lies an awareness that the socialising process must rest, if it is to be successful, on some coherent frame of reference, on some sort of political or religious foundation. Here one encounters the irreducible fact that pluralistic societies cannot produce an all-embracing official structure of belief.

Monolithic countries such as the Soviet Union or the Islamic theocratic states need only lay down that a primary aim for education is to produce good communists or Muslims. For in such societies free criticism is tolerated only so long as it does not question the fundamental tenets of belief as expressed by the leaders of political or religious institutions. There is no dilemma until dissidents refuse to keep silent. In the Soviet Union, dissenters are confined in mental homes; in South Africa those who believe in human equality are imprisoned and tortured.

Meanwhile, in less totalitarian countries (and this includes many African states), the calls for an official ideology persist. They are the concomitants of social movements and conflicts which have arisen in societies which need goals and purposes, for development by itself is only a process and requires a goal to make it work. It is for this reason that 'African humanism' (Kaunda in Zambia) and Nyerere's 'African socialism' have been developed. The official ideology of Tanzania is in fact *an attempt to link traditional African values with development.* (6)

For us this enterprise is significant because Nyerere rejects 'modernisation' as it has been defined in chapter 2. Claiming that African traditional life is communal, he is hostile both to the competitive and materialist element in capitalist models, and to a Marxist socialism based on doctrines of class-conflict. All temptations of personal gain must be resisted since 'true socialism is an attitude of mind'; he also notes that there is no word for 'class' in indigenous African languages. Furthermore, 'The foundation and the objective of African socialism is the extended family'. Finally Nyerere emphasises that in Africa (until the colonialists came with their notions of property) there was always *the right to use the land*, not to own it. There is also the usual stress on the need for hard work. 'Women who live in the villages work harder than anybody else in Tanzania, but the men who live in villages . . . are on leave for half of their life . . . their energies are wasted in gossip, dancing and drinking.'

This last indicates what the Tanzanian revolution is up against, and it is true that in a country with few resources the obstacles have seemed

71

almost insuperable. But it must be admitted that this type of African socialism is open to many objections. One is that the problem is not just to create or recreate Ujamaa villages, but to develop a *national* community. Extended families tend to be exclusive: communality is restricted. With regard to the elimination of self-interest and avarice, the Utopian element is strong—Tanzanians are probably just as greedy as everybody else. But at least a genuine attempt is being made, which is in marked contrast to other developing countries.

Elitism

It is necessary to look at the difficulties encountered in those countries where there is no official ideology. Obviously, various value-systems are transmitted from within societies, or transferred from other parts of the world. Many, perhaps the majority, of teachers, both in schools and universities, still retain coherent religious and/or political beliefs, and these naturally have an influence on the next generation. It is remarkable how many young people are deeply affected by dedicated individual teachers, especially at primary and secondary level. One cannot generalise about these processes except to note that many teachers were themselves the products of an education such as that of the mission schools, which were firmly rooted in a system of religious belief. African society is still not secularised in the manner of large parts of the developed world. Indeed, it is that hostility or indifference to institutional religion which is typical of advanced societies that surprises and shocks any African student who goes abroad for the first time. In Africa the churches have not yet emptied, and many devout Christians, when they attend colleges or universities in Britain or elsewhere, join Christian evangelical unions and become missionaries in reverse, as it were.

This is one aspect of the transmission of value-systems; the other is a quite different, indeed a contary, influence. The new countries generate materialist values which derive from a relatively unbridled pursuit of wealth; these attitudes are a reflection of transitional societies where the old loyalties have gone and where a get-rich-quick morality prevails. Such an atmosphere inevitably affects everybody, including the young— even though these attitudes are constantly deplored by all, including those whose behaviour illustrates the new processes most conspicuously. The hapless individual feels trapped in a system where he must concentrate almost exclusively on material success in order to survive. Such values are of course not transmitted as part of a social or educational philosophy—on the contrary, a chorus of exhortations from politicians

72

from press and pulpit and from military men rails against evils 'in our midst'. But the evils persist, and produce a cynicism which affects education.

The new societies are characterised by a new social élite. When the term is applied to education it has several meanings. Firstly it refers to those societies (the majority at all times) which do not give equal opportunity to all, irrespective of the social position or status of the parents. Historically, the children of the poor received no education, or only a minimal amount. When privilege begins to be eroded, opportunities are created for children from unprivileged homes who show exceptional intellectual ability. This is a second form of élitism, which is based not on social position but on academic merit, and usually justified on the grounds that talented people should be given opportunities for secondary or higher education, but society still does not require than everybody should be educated in this manner. Furthermore, there are differences between people which require not only different levels, but different kinds of education. At present, most countries have systems which exhibit both these two types of elitism, and it could hardly be otherwise.

But the twentieth century has also witnessed the growth of the ideal that everybody has a right to both basic education and its higher forms. Accordingly, many underdeveloped countries are currently using as much as a third of their limited resources to increase educational opportunities. But schooling for all is beyond their means, so that the schools have proved to be an improvised, expensive and narrow bridge designed to carry all the children across a widening social gap. It is in this context that we must consider the concept of elitism as it applies in most new countries now.

President Nyerere has insisted that elitism exists because the nature and quality of primary and secondary education is geared to and distorted by university requirements, a level which the majority of students will never reach. Neither primary nor secondary schooling is 'terminal', so that for the majority it does not relate to their later lives or to national development. The existing systems therefore have come into being in order to meet the needs of a new administrative, professional and commercial class. Opportunities and success and social rewards are available only to university graduates, so that a degree becomes a passport of 'meal ticket' by which one enters a privileged caste. In such circumstances the purpose of suffering education is simply to pass a series of examinations, and any other goals education might have recede into the background. The new governments are well aware that the system is unsatisfactory

73

and wasteful, but within the present social structures remedies are likely to elude them.

It is from this standpoint that we must regard official demands that education should quit its 'ivory tower' and relate more to the environment. The appeals are largely doomed to failure, firstly because élitism is a dominant value in society, and, secondly, because these same value-systems are strongly entrenched within the universities themselves. Regularly one reads statements about the appropriate functions of a university which list three activities—teaching, research and 'service to the community'. One is obliged to ask: what community?

Many praiseworthy efforts are made to bring about more vital links with 'the masses'—for example, in health, agriculture and education—but they come up against obstacles which are characteristic of élitist societies. In the nature of things university services tend to be indirect. It is rarely possible for efforts to improve agriculture or community medicine to pass straight from the university to the people (although this *is* done with radio programmes). If only in the interests of economy, the thrust has to be in training civil service extension-officers, who are then intended to go out into the field (commonly called 'the bush'). For reasons we have already noted the officers tend not to do this, and end up in bureaucratic posts instead, and in view of the nature of the rural environment one can sympathise!

Relevance
Educationists with experience in the new countries have been known to pronounce that there is a conflict in education between standards which are presumed to be international and those of indigenous relevance. This varies according to subject-fields and educational levels. It was always obvious that the available textbooks for primary and secondary schools would have to be rewritten to get rid of a Eurocentric bias, and this has largely been done now, and the more glaring absurdities have been removed. But it is only a beginning, and it will be a long time before people in Third World countries become the *centre* of their own symbolic world.

The knowledge industry has grown up slowly in a few metropolitan cities, and has helped to make it possible to invent a myth of 'internationalism' and a doctrine than 'knowledge' is universal and can be transferred—whereas the trees of culture are rooted in particular places, and a view of the world which calls itself international simply represents a pervasive cultural imperialism; we do not have to condemn or deplore this historically determined situation, nor should cultures be rejected because they are 'alien'. I do not recommend chauvinistic nationalism, only that we should be aware of cultural influences and able to create our own perceptions. That is the meaning of cultural freedom. As Onibonoge has said: 'The indigenous is the insistent voice demanding that we be ourselves, that we . . . perceive the reality of our particular world and that we be faithful to it. Reality is not just what we see, hear and feel; it is also our perception of these things'. (7)

Liberal education

The notion of relevance is central to any form of liberal education—a concept which students in underdeveloped countries find difficult to understand, since it is rarely part of their background. It is therefore necessary to ask: what is liberal education and can it be transferred?

The emphasis on 'liberalisation' derives from the classical western world and a humanist tradition which includes the scientific enterprise. At the level of teaching it is a matter of *making connections*, just as they are made in an electrical circuit. With such an approach the 'subjects' of the curriculum are related to each other, because it is understood that the world does not really divide into separate subjects—they have been invented by the knowledge factories. But 'breadth' is not necessarily achieved by teaching a wide variety of different subjects, since the result of doing so may still be illiberal if the subjects do not add up. Nor is liberal education, as some have thought, a matter of avoiding intensive specialisation; there is nothing wrong with specialisation at the right time and in the right place. We are all specialists, but we should try to be human as well.

Liberal education embodies an approach to the world which illuminates facts or provides a meaning to what is otherwise an inert or lifeless collection of bits. The assemblage of facts is, of course, essential at the first level of the education process. Once they are gathered up, what shall be done with them? At the more primitive levels of education—the illiberal, let us call it—nothing is done with them except that they are *memorised*. (The Hammonds, in their book on nineteenth century British economic history, record how a class of children had been taught to repeat in unison that the cow is a ruminant quadruped. Whatever other significance a cow might have was not pursued.)

Illiberal concentration on facts for their own sake is an attempt to empty out or suppress the human values which a true education system requires. Philanthropists in early industrial Britain tried to ensure that

75

artisans who studied in the mechanics institutes stayed in a narrowly technical area of study lest they should absorb dangerous or subversive doctrines. Somewhat later, in faraway colonial regions, the administrators similarly restricted education to a limited vocational training.

When education is not liberal, facts are collected like pebbles from the shore; then, to add to his collection, the industrious educator goes further and *turns values or ideas into facts as well.* Then it is alleged that this potted 'knowledge' is better than none at all—it is certainly popular with students who can memorise the concepts as if they were facts in order to pass their examinations. A stage is reached when the teacher becomes superfluous: there is nothing for him to interpret to his students because 'knowledge' has been pre-packaged. This is another reason why illiberal education is popular—the teacher need not teach.

The need for radical change
In the light of the above I believe a case has been made for the transmitting of liberal or humanistic values (I am not suggesting that they can be transferred in any direct way from one country to another).

Wherever such values are strongly held they will lead to a radical or a revolutionary ideology. As Basil Davidson has urged, 'Most authorities agree that nothing can avert disater in Africa except an accelerating rise in African productivity. But no such rise is possible without a great change in rural attitudes and any such change must call in turn for radical shifts in socio-economic structures'. (8) One must add that these transformations must be accompanied, even preceded by radical shifts in educational strategy and methods.

Yet it is still possible to use education for quite different purposes—to transmit wholly opposite value. In many parts of the world education is a key element in repressive policies consciously designed to keep the majority of the people down under savage tyrannies. The committed teacher, faced with these realities, can only do foundation work to prepare people's minds for the wrath to come.

Individuality
I have used this dangerous word in order to focus on the last of the aims of education as set out in chapter 3. One Nigerian academic has observed: 'The growth of individualism is probably the most important of the social changes that have been brought about by contact with Western culture. But individualism is most apparent in the economic field. Its connection with the other cardinal value of the West, i.e. the individual personality, is rather remote.' (9)

Traditional education reinforced social norms and a customary way of life; the individual found himself within the community and not in opposition to it. From a psychological point of view it was probably a more healthy and stable condition than the 'modern' one where the private and public spheres have become separate. This produces mental tension, and what has been called 'the homeless mind'. Traditional education was primarily devoted to security both material and spiritual, and in it, anxiety (so it has been claimed) was reduced to manageable proportions. The individual was not alone in traditional society, but integrated in a community which shared the same values, beliefs, traditions and codes of behaviour. To what extent actual security was achieved is a matter for dispute. What is not in doubt is that an individualist approach to the world does not provide security.

The kind of education which endeavours to provoke people to think for themselves is not a comfortable or comforting process. Similarly, the pursuit of truth, goodness and beauty may lead the lonely mind into cold and inhospitable realms. Often condemned as bourgeois preoccupations, these precepts remain foundations of liberal education; and the alternatives are either vague or sinister. One of them is Stalinism, which would have us believe that existing communist countries are free from all unhealthy manifestations and have recreated community and human solidarity on a national level. The evidence does not quite support this view.

Individualism has been associated with liberal capitalism and, indeed, many anti-socialists insist that without capitalism liberty is impossible. President Truman, in his usual forthright manner, once declared: 'All freedom is dependent on freedom of enterprise . . . the whole world should adopt the American system . . . the American system can survive in America only if it becomes a world system'.

It is true that freedom for businessmen is one form of freedom, but it does not follow that intellectual freedom or academic freedom can only be realised in a capitalist state. Because of this association of liberalism with capitalism, many have pointed out that individuality is not the same thing as individualism. The former can be realised only in co-operation with other people and as part of social activity, whereas it is possible for the individualist to function, just as the businessman may do, entirely for his own benefit and without reference to the needs of other people.

What, then, does this emphasis on the individual mean in relation to education? It involves a critical approach to the world which must include an examination of the self. It means that structures must be created which are not authoritarian and which allow the child or the adult to grow or develop in his own way. The historical origins of this approach are to be found in classical Greece and its rebirth in the Renaissance; in the New Testament and its many interpretations since the Reformation and finally in the growth of modern science and technology. It has been present in most religions including Islam—whenever the dead weight of fundamentalist traditions and priestly vested interests have not stifled it. In this sense an insistence on critical thinking which is student-based is a necessary attribute of modern education although not of course the only one. In the education systems of the West, this stress on the individual has been most successful at the primary level, whereas secondary and tertiary structures have been much more geared to social needs in the narrow vocational sense, or to the preservation of a class-structure in society. Of all the educational aspirations we have mentioned, it is the most difficult to achieve. It is easier to reinforce the under-development of the mind than to unfreeze its rigid structures.

We are dealing with developing post-traditional societies, but any country which is committed to rapid change must foster creativity and the personal initiative of at least some individuals in order to promote innovation. If the education system fails in this respect, and attempts to impose only conformity, then it cannot meet the needs of the modern world. But, to thwart this endeavour, there are formidable obstacles notably present in the underdeveloped countries. They can be summarised as follows:

1   When governments plan a rapid expansion of education at all levels, they require a large number of new teachers to be produced in a crash programme. The teachers, so produced cannot be expected at whatever level, to reach a high standard, or to be concerned with the difficult problem of free enquiry; indeed, they may consider that too liberal an atmosphere would undermine their authority.

2   In these same countries teachers are not usually dedicated or committed persons who regard teaching as a terminal career. They are mostly engaged in obtaining further qualifications to proceed elsewhere. In consequence their contribution to an improvement in the quality of education will be minimal. One ex-teacher referring to his experience of school in the 1960s in Northern Nigeria wrote that at school 'I was taught some morals—to be respectful to my parents and any other elderly somebody I may come across anywhere.' Later when he became a teacher, 'My teaching life was very dull. I never consulted or read books apart from what I had to do with my children. This was to conform with our plan of "giving our brains a rest".' (They needed the rest of course from their private studies.)

78

3   The teaching profession anywhere tends to be conservative. One authority (Beeby) notes that teachers are a product of the system to a degree that is true of no other profession. In developing countries this is especially the case.

4   In many peasant societies there is a resistance by parents against sending their children to school, for the sensible reason that schooling will take their children away from the land either temporarily or permanently. In parts of Nigeria these attitudes are reinforced by religious suspicions about Western education. This resistance is weakening as a result of official pressure but it is still there. I quote another extract from a student's written work: 'School in those days in my village was meant for outcasts and slaves and not for a fathered child. School to my father was a remand home, a place for orphans and bastards. School children were thought to be thieves and their masters cruel ones'.

5   A fundamental difference between advanced societies and the countries under review is that in the former there are a great many educational influences outside the formal schooling system. These societies are usually pluralistic in the sense that the individual at an early age encounters pressures and influences which pull or push him in different directions and this is just as much part of his education as school. In the poorer countries on the other hand the students or the teachers as noted above are wholly dependent on the system. 'There may be no library within reach, no newspaper of a standard to enlarge their horizons and no one in the village to provide intellectual stimulation'. (10) In consequence 'beyond the pasteboard covers of the one official textbook lies the dark void where unknown questions lurk.'

6   One of the requisites to make modern methods of teaching possible is exposure to a good library. Thus on the eve of independence in Nigeria Nduka wrote: 'Because schools often lack adequate equipment, in particular a reference library, teachers and pupils have falled back on the readily available books and pamphlets giving model answers'. (11) He notes further that if students are fed with facts and dogma they cannot find things out for themselves. This state of affairs has changed very little in many schools.

These, then, are some of the obstacles to progressive education as it has developed in the West. It is apparent from this list that the *quality of the teachers* is the key element. In this context I consider that the four stages in the development of education as worked out by Beeby (12) are illuminating and useful: they can be observed almost anywhere and are as follows:

1 The 'dame school' stage: This terminology refers back to early education procedures in Britain. At this level teachers are not trained at all and schooling consists of the three R's and the memorising of words whose meaning is not understood. It is paradoxical that this kind of education is abstract and is not *applied to the practical world*. (In education when content is 'unreal' the formal element has to be increased.)

2 Formalism: At this level teachers are 'ill-educated' but trained; they cling to the official syllabus and what the children learn may still bear no relation to the world outside the classroom. The facts which are absorbed do not mesh either with one another or with the personal life of the child. This brings to mind the instance of the medieval monks who used to copy inaccurate pictures of herbs from books even when these same plants were outside growing in their garden. Beeby gives a modern example where a teacher and the children drew a picture of a fish with the scales pointing the wrong way; yet they were all members of a fishing community. Within living memory British soldiers were trained in this way and were expected to memorise manuals which did not relate their circumstances.

The emphasis in formalism is not on understanding but on memorising facts. I have stressed this formalistic bias in education because this is the stage which many, perhaps most, primary schools have reached in developing countries. In Nigeria I witnessed on television a teacher (non-Nigerian) getting the children to memorise three *tenses*:past, present and future. It was apparent that their connection with the meaning of time was not revealed. In such a context, how can a school library help?

3 Transition: The teachers are trained and are better educated, usually having completed a secondary course. There is a greater gap between them and the pupils so that they feel more secure. It is at this stage that 'supplementary readers' are likely to be used and there may be a library of sorts. Emotional or aesthetic values are still not dealt with but there is a chance for the more adventurous teachers to make their own contribution.

4 The stage of meaning: At this fourth level the teachers are both well-trained and well-educated. They will find it impossible to ignore the emotional and aesthetic life of the pupil and an attempt is made to deepen understanding. This is the stage where the gap between real life and the classroom is reduced and individuality can be developed. As Beeby notes, not all societies regard this stage as desirable since it may conflict with the other aim of socialisation: that there should be 'a subtle and pervading resistance to change'. Once again we are brought back to the political kingdom and to the presence or absence of ideology. Teachers who are committed to nothing except the security of their own careers are not likely to reach this stage, particularly if they live in societies where the pursuit of meaning or understanding is regarded as heretical.

Beeby did not claim and I do not wish to suggest that these are chronological phases which must follow one another. He was referring mainly to primary education, but examples of the 'lower' stages can be found in both secondary and university education in any kind of country. The stages are perhaps better understood as *levels* in the teaching process rather than as a pattern of historical development, for which there is very little evidence.

Changes in quality as distinct from quantity emerge in an unpredictable manner in unexpected places. There have always been a few inspired teachers within any system; we have to legislate for the majority who are not. Illich has insisted that modern systems of education are so constructed that the desired level of true education as envisaged in the fourth stage above is impossible. In consequence society must be 'deschooled'.

It is pertinent to add a warning note. It has been suggested here that concentration on the individual should not and cannot be considered in isolation. Creativity is certainly desirable, but if by some means everybody became endowed with creative powers, society would probably disintegrate. The prisons and mental institutions of the world are crowded with creative people.

In the construction of new societies other values and other qualities are required, notably the willingness to work together for the common good. These national endeavours are wholly social and necessarily communal, so that individual development must be part of the public weal. As collective entities such societies can achieve something; they cannot do so if individuals set themselves up as a law unto themselves. 'Do what you will' may be a possible slogan for a society in an advanced state of over-development or dissolution, but it is inadmissable elsewhere.

One can conclude therefore that it may be too much to expect that this type of learning can be developed fully at the present time. Learning by rote will probably continue to figure prominently and facts will be given an importance they do not deserve. However, it is an aim which will be realised in the future. Development as a matter of faith requires that there must be a future.

Conclusion
The aims of education as considered here do not add up to a full blown 'philosophy'. the history of education is littered with philosophies which nobody ever cared about. I have been concerned to make an analysis of present fantasies, realities and future needs. Precisely what has to be done to transform these unsuitable structures, policies and methods, is something which must vary for each country. The first requirement is fully to appreciate that such a transformation is required.

REFERENCES
 1 Nduka, Otonti, *Western education and the Nigerian cultural background* OUP Ibadan, 1964, 55.
 2 *Investment in education: the report of the commission on post school certificate and higher education in Nigeria* (Chairman Sir Eric Ashby) Federal Ministry of Education, 1969, 103.
 3 *Report of the Commission on the educational system in Western Nigeria* (Chairman: S A Banjo) Government Printer, Ibadan 1961, 4.
 4 Nduka, Otonti, *op cit*, 93.
 5 *National Universities Commission report on new universities in Nigeria* (Federal Government unpublished report 1977)
 6 Nyerere, Julius N, *Essays on socialism* OUP, 1970.
 7 Onibonoge, G O, 'Wanted! a cultural revolution, not a dialogue' in Oluwasanmi, E, and others (ed) *Publishing in Africa in the seventies* University of Ife Press, 1975, 271.
 8 Davidson, Basil, *The Africans, an entry to cultural history* Penguin, 1973, 324.
 9 Nduka, Otonti, *op cit*, 95.
10 Beeby, C E, *The quality of education in developing countries* Harvard University Press, 1966, 43.
11 Nduka, Otonti, *op cit*, 142.
12 Beeby, C E, *op cit*, 48.

5

ADULT EDUCATION AND LITERACY

To the popular mind in Africa any reference to adult education suggests
classes in literacy. This belief stubbornly persists and, like most views
held by the masses, is substantially correct, at least at the present time.
It has been pointed out, however, that there need be no connection. In
advanced countries adult education and literacy are linked only in reference to new immigrants and the underprivileged, since adult illiteracy
is not a problem for the majority of the people. (Although we should not
underestimate the size or importance of the minority and it is a fact in
Britain, for example, that some children are substantially illiterate when
they leave school.) Here we are dealing with countries where 70 per
cent or more of the population is illiterate and amongst such people adult
education cannot be divorced from literacy programmes.

These statistical percentages are of course not evenly spread and in
some backward areas within individual countries illiteracy may be almost
total. For instance, in Egypt the national figure for illiteracy is 75 per
cent, but for the *fellahin* on whom Egypt depends as much as it does on
the Nile, and who make up over half of the population, the figure is 90
per cent. As one reporter has pointed out, 'The *fellahin* . . . spend their
lives being swindled by bureaucrats who force bribes out of them for
services that should normally be either free or very inexpensive'. (1) He
concludes: 'The strength of the fellahin is their silence', and I shall refer
to this 'silence' below.

It is of course possible, especially with the use of film, radio and television, to spread 'public enlightenment' about health or farming to illiterate people, but except under revolutionary circumstances the impact of
such campaigns is limited. We are concentrating therefore in the first
instance on the illiteracy problem.

There is no suggestion that adult education in the complete sense is
unimportant; in any society we can now take it for granted that education should be life-long. This applies not only to professional and

83

vocational retraining in fields where people now soon get out of date but also to liberal education designed to overcome the uncivilised effects of specialisation. But for the countries under discussion that type of liberal education unrelated to career structures must remain a luxury for some long time to come.

The persistence and significance of illiteracy
It is now a commonplace that although the percentage of people in the world who are illiterate may be slowly declining the total number is constantly increasing because of the population explosion. There are now about 800 million illiterates, and of these 143 million are in Africa. By the end of the century the figure is likely to be well over 900 million. For the world as a whole about one third of the population is thought to be illiterate and for Africa one recent figure (1970) was 73.7 per cent (for women 83.7 per cent). These figures are of course approximate

Even amongst experts in Unesco the gravity of this situation was originally underestimated and its significance not fully understood. At one time it was thought that if universal primary education (UPE) could be introduced the problem would be solved in one generation. If any authorities ever seriously held this view they do not hold it now. We have already quoted figures for Egypt where free compulsory education has existed for some time.

This particular illusion has subsided but another is still present. Some enthusiasts even now seem to believe that adult education, or indeed any form of education, can generate development, whereas there is overwhelming evidence to show that illiteracy is not a cause of underdevelopment but a symptom of it. This means that so long as other social transformations do not occur it cannot be eradicated. Educationists must be aware that poverty causes illiteracy but they frequently write as if it were the other way round.

There are three main reasons why illiteracy cannot be eradicated in underdeveloped countries and a host of minor ones. First, school leavers after primary school lapse into illiteracy (this has been called 'illiteracy by atrophy'). Second, if there are no tangible economic reasons—such as job opportunities—for learning to read, then the people have no motivation. Third, they may positively resist literacy campaigns for sound social and political reasons. For example, traditional farmers did not need to learn to read; for them literacy was irrelevant. In modernising circumstances, on the other hand, it is apparent in may countries that governments do not really want to educate the people although they

84

usually pay lip service to adult education; or they use literacy campaigns for oppressive political purposes, in order to manipulate the masses more easily. As was noted in the Final Report on the Iran literacy symposium of 1975 some participants 'even went so far as to state that, especially insofar as it reinforces the . . . reactionary role of the petty bourgeoisie, education today constitutes an obstacle to development in a good many Third World countries'. (2)

In such circumstances a certain lack of mass enthusiasm may be expected. Everything depends on what social purpose their literacy is going to serve—whether it will satisfy their needs or simply make them more useful or more amenable to their rulers. In some places learning to read may not benefit anybody at all.

The foregoing sounds negative so I should make it clear that I am not questioning the value of universal literacy as such, merely emphasising that any form of education can be abused or misconceived. Once people are caught up in the process of development if that process is to succeed and to be a reality rather than a sham then literacy campaigns become essential.

A Unesco statement claims that for illiterate people the twentieth century does not exist: 'They naturally cannot read notices . . . they cannot find their way about; they cannot tell the time or know what day it is, or how old they are, or what lies beyond the frontiers of their village. They are at the mercy of swindlers, bureaucrats and tricksters of every kind. It is even difficult or impossible to buy tinned or bottled or packaged goods in a shop.' (3) This list of trials could be lengthened and perhaps it omits the most serious handicap of all—the feelings of inferiority or inadequacy which, in modern circumstances, illiteracy may bring.

Obviously in the traditional village there was no need for clocks, nor did it matter precisely when anybody was born or what was happening in the world outside. All that, if the people are to escape poverty and oppression, must be left behind. What Freire calls the 'Culture of Silence' which still blankets a large proportion of the earth must be lifted; where I am writing this at the moment that 'silence' extends in every direction for thousands of miles and across frontiers. Meanwhile administrators and academics and journalists are pontificating about the needs of the masses.

As Chesterton once said about another place 'they have not spoken yet'. Once they are involved in their own destiny they will become literate soon enough and what they have to say may not please their rulers. This, then is the deeper significance of literacy in our time: it can be the key to open the door into the future. It can also be a means of changing people's perceptions.

Definitions
It is not possible to offer a definition of literacy which will allow us to say where illiteracy ends and literacy begins; there are different kinds as well as degrees of illiteracy. It is not a precise concept and can easily be manipulated for political purposes. Some western observers have considered that people can only be classified as literate if they can read and write in the Roman script. Alternatively if an Irish or Welsh man cannot read his own language are we to call him illiterate? It would be an unpopular view.

In the case of African languages which have been deliberately revived for national reasons there is a discrepancy between common speech and literacy. Many African can read and write in English or French but not in their own spoken language; they are not usually classified as non-literate. On the other hand, many people who are officially classified as literate are unable to read or write in any language. This includes many who have certificates after attending literacy classes.

One education handbook states that adults are literate 'when they can show that they know how to write a letter and can read and understand anything printed in their language including numbers 1-1000 and symbols of money, weights and measures that are in common use in their areas'. This definition will not bear close examination—what kind of letter will they be able to write and who will understand it? Nobody is likely to understand '*anything* printed in their language', and some definitions would leave us all illiterate. In short these concepts are relative. For a particular individual the term is not constant, since he will always be in the process of becoming more, or less, literate according to his circumstances.

The question of numeracy is important. People who cannot read or write at all usually cannot add up, subtract, divide or multiply figures. Simple trading becomes a lengthy and laborious process. (In traditional circumstances, before time became so insistent, this did not matter; such transactions were a pleasant part of social life.)

The above definition refers to 'symbols of money' and it is significant that in Nigeria and Ghana, where currency reform has been undertaken and an indigenous decimal system introduced, the traders continue to think in terms of pounds, shillings and pence for years after they have ceased to operate. The same manifestations have of course been apparent in developed countries.

Traditional literacy

Earlier efforts to combat illiteracy consisted of campaigns to enable people to read and write particularly *in the vernacular*; that is to say in their own first language. Both the emphasis on vernacular languages and the methods used came under attack. With regard to indigenous languages we have already noted that they often have the disadvantage first, of not being national but local and second, that so long as English (or French or whatever the colonial language was) remains the official language they do not constitute a passport to material advancement.

At one time, indeed, vernacular literacy programmes were condemned by nationalists as a colonial manifestation and some still regard them as a colonial legacy. Possibly for this reason, amongst others, there is less activity of this kind in Nigeria and elsewhere than before independence. However, the majority of the campaigns undertaken at present in the nineteen states of Nigeria take this form; they are 'traditional' both in their use of the vernacular and the method employed. This consists of using primers, often story books, which are not necessarily related directly to the everyday life of the people, although some attempt is made to connect them with the environment. Their history in West Africa and elsewhere is one of partial failure.

Economic functional literacy

As a result of earlier dissatisfaction with the traditional literacy programme, Unesco developed (at the World Congress on Illiteracy in 1965) the concept of 'functional literacy'. In its simplest or crudest form this can be defined as work-orientated literacy related to the problems, needs and interests of given groups.

Just as a child learns to speak his or her language by reference to his immediate needs, so it would seem to be commonsense that people who are being taught to read for the first time should be interested in reading and writing words which will help them deal with their environment. I have described this form of functional literacy as 'economic' because it can be restricted to an education which is ideologically 'neutral' (that is to say in support of an existing regime), in which case little attention is paid to values and more to work problems. (Many of the early Unesco experiments such as those in Nigeria and Tanzania were organised through farmer co-operatives.) When this is done well it is of course worth doing.

To be effective the instructors and the people who write the primers must be able to identify with the people. (It has often happened in literacy campaigns that instructors are openly contemptuous of their students.) At their best such campaigns may enable them to write their names and read simple instructions, or it may help them to get a job, but it does not transform their lives. This, from the point of view of some enthusiasts for functional literacy, has been most disappointing, because they were concerned with the potential role of literacy in generating development.

A notable example of this kind of literacy campaign is provided by Brazil, which undertook in 1970 a most ambitious programme which has shown impressive results. The planners of this movement, called MOBRAL, claimed that is 'functionality' was different from that of the Unesco programme. No less than 130,000 literacy units were set up throughout the country and considerable successes were registered. However, criticism has been made that there has been no noticeable improvement in the socio-economic life of the participants.

The programme set up in Tanzania with the co-operation of Unesco has the advantage of being run by a government which is genuinely concerned with true development (as distinct from mere modernisation) but even there success has been only partial. (Tanzania as is well known has run into severe difficulties with its development policies.) Elsewhere results have been even less satisfactory and we must now turn to the possible reasons.

Functional literacy: Paulo Freire and cultural revolution
A radical critique of literacy programmes has been developed by the Brazilian Catholic priest Paulo Freire and others in Latin America, many of whom are also Catholic priests. Their ideas have become widely influential as can be seen from the proceedings of international conferences on literacy programmes. Their starting point has been that the outstanding successes in mass literacy activity have been almost entirely in communist countries, particularly the USSR, China and Cuba.

In these countries illiteracy has been drastically reduced or abolished in a relatively short time. All these movements have included an element of coercion. Absentees from classes in the USSR were at one time fined and I have seen it stated that at one time the Chinese taxed illiterates. This coercive element is bearable if the people know that their lives are being transformed and that they will benefit by it. At other times, for instance in the Turkey of Kemal Ataturk and in parts of India, the people have responded usually for nationalist reasons.

A common element in all the successful campaigns has been that the people have become *actively involved in their own development*; it has not been simply imposed from above although that is where the initiative had to come from. I call this type of functionalism 'cultural' to distinguish it from the kind which is merely economic ('modernisation'). The additional factor is of course political. As Illich says, 'Freire . . . discovered that any adult can begin to read in a matter of 40 hours if the first words he deciphers are charged with political meaning. Freire trains his teachers to move into a village and to discover the words which designate current important issues, such as the access to a well, or the compound interest on the debts owed to the patron. In the evening the villagers meet for the discussion of these key words. They begin to realise that each word stays on the blackboard even after its sound has faded . . . discussants grow in social awareness and . . . they are impelled to take political action as fast as they learn to read. They seem to take reality into their hands as they write it down.' (4)

The central approach in cultural functionalism is that literacy training, like any other education process, is not politically neutral and can be a basic instrument for social changes; it is not a simple matter of learning to read and write but a movement of liberation. As the preface to *Cultural action for freedom* states, 'the situation which engendered the Freire approach . . . is the emergence of the popular masses into the national political scene in the so called underdeveloped countries, more precisely in Latin America. The decolonisation of the Third World opens the way to the true liberalisation of all mankind or to its more efficient domestication. It is a situation, therefore which calls for a reappraisal of the meaning and methods of education'. (5)

There are Utopian elements in these proposals, an important one being that what is implied is a revolution from below. Conservative governments are not likely to tolerate such behaviour, which is no doubt why Freire has left his own country. However, the influence remains and his experience and that of others in different parts of the world support both the conclusions reached and the methods used. It should be added that the African political situation is very different from that in Latin America. The programme implies a revolutionary situation which is not present everywhere—instead of claiming that literacy can engender development these pioneers are insisting that literacy is a necessary part of a cultural revolution without which economic development cannot take place.

Reasons for partial failure

I have accepted the Freire critique to some extent and consider that the evidence supports it. Some of this evidence is summarised below and these factors can be found in most underdeveloped countries outside the communist bloc.

There are certain basic ideological reasons why all forms of adult education including literacy have not flourished. The fundamental problems have not always been understood and were therefore underestimated; some authorities have referred to illiteracy as a 'disease' which has only to be cured, whereas the disease is underdevelopment and illiteracy is its symptom. Similarly others have described illiterates as 'marginal people' —marginal to what?

They are obviously oppressed persons caught in an existing social structure, and the elimination of illiteracy can only be part of other strategies for changing the structure of society. If governments are not wholly committed to development than naturally they cannot be committed to adult education.

Similar conclusions were reached by the 1975 Iran symposium, which was jointly sponsored by the Iran government and Unesco. The symposium subsequently published a manifesto called *The declaration of Persepolis*. (6) Having noted the outstanding results achieved in China, Cuba, North Korea, Somalia and Brazil (which as I have noted above is in a different category) the declaration concluded that 'the most favourable structures' for the successful accomplishment of literacy projects would be:

1   Those that, from the political point of view, tend to bring about the effective participation of every citizen in decision-making at all levels of social life: in economics, politics and culture.

2   Those that, from the political point of view, aim at an endogenous and harmonious development of society, and not at blind and dependent growth.

3   Those that, from the social point of view, do not result in making education a class privilege and a means of reproducing established hierarchies and orders.

4   Those that, from the professional point of view, provide communities with genuine control over the technologies they wish to use.

5   Those that, from the institutional point of view, favour a concerted approach and permanent co-operation among the authorities responsible for basic services (agriculture, welfare, health, family planning etc.)

There are many societies, including a number in Africa, where such favourable 'structures' do not exist. In such cases the illiterate majority represent in a sense a separate culture (but not a sub-culture) within the nation.

The other fundamental weakness has been that adult education has been separated both administratively and ideologically from formal education for young people. When this happened in developed countries at an earlier period it did not matter so much, because adult education had been a movement with its own momentum and social origins. The form which illiteracy now takes in the Third World has no exact parallel in the history of Western industrialised countries although an analogous historical situation might perhaps be found in the Soviet Union.

The difference in the old countries was that long before the state became fully responsible for education there were various bodies inspired by religious or political ideals who concentrated on the education of adults as well as children according to their own ideas of the purpose of life. These movements coincided with or preceded universal state education for young people and were partly a consequence of the industrial revolution which also produced an extraordinary increase in population and in Britain particularly, the appalling conditions in the new factory towns. Both the organisers of these movements and the teachers were committed people, so they were able to make an impact on society. This dedication, mixed naturally with other motives less pure, derived from their wider beliefs—an important point since no sane person is devoted to education for itself: education for what? and for whose benefit?

With regard to the Christian religion this same movement spread overseas as missionary endeavour and became part of the colonial enterprise, but the political secular stream (necessarily radical) did not and in the nature of things could not. This is one of the reasons for the absence of radical thought in ex-colonial countries. The ideology of the people who actually governed the colonies could not include such dangerous notions as adult education for human freedom, and they were never quite happy even about the missionaries, some of whom showed signs of taking the New Testament seriously. It is of some significance that serious attempts to formulate mass literacy programmes in the British colonial territories dated from World War II and reflected radical socialist attitudes then dominant in Britain. But it was not an indigenous growth and the new nationalists were mostly concerned simply with taking over the seats of the colonial 'masters' whose values they shared.

Since we are here discussing the transfer of ideologies we should add that the liberalising tendencies in modern Islam, such as have occurred in national movements in Turkey (under Ataturk) and Egypt, have likewise not been transferred to Africa south of the Sahara, where Islam has remained firmly traditional. This religious conservatism has reinforced the ideology, and in some places the social structure, of a semi-feudal past.

Ths historical factor is stressed because it helps to account for the fact that adult education was and is an activity artificially separated from the education process in general and secondly that for the reasons I have suggested little development occurred. The need to close this gap has been recognised in many new countries especially those with some kind of socialist orientation. In Tanzania for instance primary schools have become 'community schools responsible for adults also. Such programmes require entirely new methods of training for teachers.

These ideological factors above conditioned the growth of adult education in new countries. They have led to various deficiencies which I summarise below. Most of the examples are taken from Nigeria but doubtless similar circumstances exist elsewhere.

1   As a general rule attendance at adult education classes, including literacy classes, has been voluntary, so that where motivation has been weak there has been a high drop out rate. The effect of coercion in communist countries has already been discussed.

2   Insufficient resources, human, financial and technical have been devoted to this purpose. In this area as in other similar 'non-productive' services like library provision there seems to be some law that the more inadequate the services the more extravagant are the claims made for its value.

3   The administrative structures, mostly inherited from colonial times, have been and are inappropriate. There is often a division of responsibility between adult education officers employed by the state and local government staff including organisers and instructors. These instructors, on whom the burden of teaching falls, are frequently half-trained, poorly paid and harassed by a top-heavy organisation which is part of a different setup; in consequence they are not committed.

4   Difficulties are encountered in producing 'follow-up' literature without which people become illiterate again. The need for this is

recognised, but in many places such literature is not produced nor are there libraries or bookshops to distribute it. The possibilities, including mobile library or mobile bookshop services, are discussed elsewhere. A common obstacle has been that adult education and libraries are provided by two different agencies who may find it difficult to co-ordinate their activities. Ideally of course the organisers involved with the adult education programmes should also produce the literature tailored to the needs of their own people.

5   The various agencies involved, for instance those dealing with health and agriculture as well as education and libraries, pursue their activities independently of each other.

6   One reason that statistics are unreliable is that in some programmes instructors have been paid according to the number of certificates issued.

7   Functional literacy even now may be regarded as a new departure to be treated as experimental. It is obviously more difficult to set up and requires a dose relationship with the people to be taught. Furthermore the principles are not easily understood by those unfamiliar with them and have in any case been interpreted by the use of different methods. For instance, in 1972 a scheme was introduced in Northern Nigeria introducing functional literacy teaching in farmers' co-operative societies as a pilot project. After an initial success the scheme collapsed because firstly, a Unesco expert left and secondly, the Adult Education Department had insufficient control over instructors. This may be one of the reasons for the present emphasis on traditional literacy in Nigeria. The other may be that as a result of the Universal Primary Education policy there is renewed emphasis on the cultural importance of vernacular languages.

8   We come now to the education of women, without which all these programmes must be regarded as a failure. Efforts have been made everywhere by state and local government agencies, with some success, to provide literacy and homecraft classes for women. But the motivation of women tends to be even weaker than with the men. Modern hygiene may conflict with traditional practices. Some modern practices are difficult to carry out for environmental reasons and opposition (for example with regard to education in family planning) may come from the men.

Many women do express the need for literacy; as one woman is reported to have said: 'How can we prepare our children for a world we do not understand?' But the obstacles are often too great. For instance, in one Muslim area in the former Benue Plateau State only one woman out of thirty attended classes. In some regions, because of *purdah*, special classes open only to married women are held at night. Otherwise in several states in Nigeria those who participate in literacy classes, at least in the towns, are mainly 'free' or unattached women. (The word 'prostitute' is used but it gives the wrong impression to those unfamiliar with this type of society since all ladies who are unmarried for whatever reason may come into this category. I have been told in the old Zaria city that men who frequent the company of 'free' women do so mainly because they are good company and can discuss current happenings.) It is recorded that in Kano State *blind* instructors used to go from house to house to educate women in *purdah*.

I am not suggesting that this is typical or particularly significant but it is quoted to indicate the nature of the problem. Because some women have become professionals at the top of the tree there is a common belief amongst men in Africa that women are already on the way to becoming liberated. This is far from the case, and I should add that the resistance to education for women and girls is not confined to Muslim regions. Assuming that there is a genuine intention on the part of official leaders to introduce adult classes for women there is still a long way to go.

9   Finally, in the light of the foregoing, it is not surprising that the people's demand for adult education is not always very loud or persistent; it tends therefore to be imposed from above. In the case of Kabba, a town now in Kwara State in Nigeria, one research student discovered that 'adult literacy is no longer the thing that adults in the 1950s wholeheartedly accepted with enthusiasm'. (7) In attempting to discover the reason he could elicit no explanation from the Ministry of Education, but some of the people reported the following problems:

(i) The adult students had to pay for their work books and other materials. Many of them claimed to be poor.

(ii) There was the feeling that there was no material gain. This feeling was rampant with the traditional literacy adult classes.

(iii) State subventions to the local government authorities had stopped, so their enthusiasm in organising the courses had been diminished.

(iv) The state library had not been able to help.

These reactions are predictable and corroborate the points we have made. It is of some significance that the enthusiasm of the 1950s which is mentioned was before independence. It is a curious fact that the colonialists at that time were able to involve the people to a greater extent than has happened since at least in the region mentioned. Doubtless one of the reasons for a decline in interest is the disillusionment born of experience.

To conclude this catalogue of partial failure or partial success we should bear in mind that the task is daunting and formidable. We are dealing mainly with societies where there is no revolutionary dynamic and in such an environment it would be wrong to denigrate the devoted efforts of many dedicated individuals, both expatriate and national. For example the Principal Adult Education Officer in Kano State, Alhaji Wali, stated in 1975 in a lecture to students 'It is regrettable to note that developing countries have not recognised adult education as a key factor in development . . . The Government has not yet declared any dynamic policy in respect of literacy campaigns and adult education in general'. Meanwhile certain people, like the speaker, do what they can.

Hidden literacy
The general belief that Africans were formerly totally illiterate is not correct. There were and are several forms of marginal or hidden literacy. 'Traditional societies in Africa . . . were decisively influenced by key individuals who could read and write.'

In Africa, and in other parts of the world, in pre-industrial societies, writing was not a means of communication in the modern sense but a magical and religious activity. As Goody has pointed out, 'In the shadow of the fixed and established Books of God that form the core of world religions, another category of text has circulated, one that deals in magic formulae and magical squares in providing specific solutions to particular problems'. (8) Even at the present time some of the older men in Ibo-land have a form of 'writing' which they use for those magical purposes by making marks in the sand. These signs are incomprehensible to younger people; Professor Kotei of the University of Ghana has described the early system of writing, the Vai script which existed in Liberia, (9) and there are also other traces of early forms of writings in West Africa. In all cases they were part of a secret activity designed to preserve tribal or religious identity against outside pressures.

Attention has been drawn to another form of hidden literacy, the widespread use of Arabic script by people in West Africa. These people have been officially regarded as illiterate since 'from the onset of colon-ialism the European attitude towards literacy was to define it *strictly with reference to European languages*' (my italics). (10) By the late nineteenth century Arabic script was used not only for devotional reasons, but was also widely employed in the making of religious charms. The language was also used for documentation of political and trade matters.

There can be no doubt even now that many 'illiterates' such as cook stewards and night watchmen have some knowledge of both reading and writing in their own languages in the Arabic script; this has usually been the result of Koranic education. The fact that the Tuaregs, the veiled people of the Sahara desert have always had their own language (Tamashegh) still written in their own script (Tifinagh) has been seriously neglected. This unique script links them to the societies of the ancient world and a considerable literature survives, including poetry and imaginative writing. With regard to the use of Arabic much work remains to be done in this area of study.

Other forms of adult education
In spite of the limitations mentioned, a great deal of activity goes on in all developing countries, and it should be appreciated that in stressing deficiencies I have been using a particular yardstick: I have been considering these programmes with regard to their revolutionary potential for transforming the lives of the people, and have suggested that unless they can be used in this way they will continue to be very limited in scope. Not everybody regards the role of adult education in this fashion and those who hold other and more conservative views about the nature of development are likely to be more impressed by the results achieved so far—they do not expect very much. It remains briefly to summarise some of these programmes.

Traditional education
In the chapters on education we have noted that traditional education in illiterate societies was life-long in the best sense, and made no distinction between childhood, youth and age except as represented by the rites of passage which everybody had to undergo.

In a somewhat different sense Islamic or Koranic education can also be called traditional because it is not new. Throughout the literature on education in the Third World there is a tendency to neglect this contribution, as already described.

Koranic literacy has only been 'hidden because there has been an ethnocentric or religious bias which has caused people to play down Arabic literacy south of the Sahara whether it manifests itself in the use with vernacular languages or with Arabic proper. However in the context of Western education it is understandable that this type of literacy has been misunderstood, partly because outsiders have thought wholly in terms of learning the Koran by heart. Whatever its religious significance may be, this is not 'functional' in the sense which Unesco has used, nor is it even literacy as commonly understood in Western definitions. There is always the extra religious dimension which to the devout Muslim may be paramount—a passport to Paradise is more important than one to a university. There are learned Islamic scholars in parts of Africa who cannot read an Egyptian newspaper printed in modern Arabic.

Throughout this chapter we have been dealing implicitly or explicitly with motivation, which in the case of Koranic education is clear, but has little to do with national development except in a moral and psychological sense (training good citizens). It is this moral education which Muslims stress as important in combating the evils of transitional societies. This form of adult education is therefore largely a different kind of activity from what we have been discussing, but this is not sufficient reason for its dismissal. For those trained in Koranic studies from their earliest years the modern forms of secular adult training may seem secondary or irrelevant. In view of our comments about individuals voluntarily undertaking instruction, it should be noted that in the earlier years of Koranic instruction a coercive element is present. We should not forget that literal doctrines of free will are not relevant to subsistence societies; if Rousseau had lived inside such a society, would he have been so convinced that people are born 'free'?

Practical and vocational training
As part of development projects all the new countries have recognised the need for instructing adults to take part in the modern world. It is possible to distinguish between programmes directly concerned with training people to do technical jobs and activities which arise out of a working environment.

Formerly vocational training was taken care of by the apprenticeship system, which was often restricted on a hereditary principle. Whatever form the system took, young people learnt 'on the job'. This type of training continues officially and unofficially. For example, the famous roadside mechanics found all over Africa usually first learn their expertise from working for a large firm; after that they set up on their own. However, a modernising economy requires more official types of training and various courses are run. Programmes of this kind, whether vocational or not, are run by university extension services, by state agencies and by some industrial organisations. New communications media are used and radio programmes mostly run by universities meet with some response from farmers. But the problem of unemployed youth remains. Many of the difficulties and limitations already discussed affect these campaigns. It should be noted also that in some countries missionary and foreign aid activity still makes a contribution, mostly with regard to particular projects.

Continuing formal education

In our various comments on education we have noted four main sectors: (i) the formal education structure, primary, secondary and tertiary for young people, (ii) adult education, particularly for those who have had no formal education at all, (iii) vocational training, and (iv) continuing education for academic qualifications. It is the last of these which remains to be considered and which in some respects constitutes a problem which is most characteristic of many countries at their present stage of development I have called it a 'problem' because there is some doubt as to whether these extensive, expensive and often wasteful programmes should be undertaken at all.

In this sector demand is the key factor as within present education systems only a minority can get to secondary school and a very tiny percentage to the universities. We are brought back to questions concerning the fundamental nature of development. What is supposed to happen to everybody else? In developed countries until quite recently there were job opportunities at reasonable levels of remuneration for young people who left school at primary and at secondary level. Partly because of class structures their status was not in question and many were able to take pride in belonging to the 'working class', a term which, in Africa is not used in this sense. All this was partly a consequence of industrialisation and the creation of a proletariat (peasants are not so much proud of their social position as resigned to it). Since, in most developing countries there is no settled class system of this kind and job opportunities and rewards at the lower levels are few it is difficult for individuals to step off the education ladder without disaster. On the other hand even if the state should provide for them to continue their formal education to higher levels ultimately there will obviously be no room at the top.

The answers to these dilemmas lie outside the sphere of education. But meanwhile *the demand is there*; a tragic sympton of underdevelopment. I use the word 'tragic' with reason because it is a most depressing spectacle to watch thousands of young people desperately spending years of their lives struggling to obtain O and A levels in a GCE system which came originally from a foreign country and which will shortly be dismantled even there. One should add that it must be equally depressing for themselves, especially for those who are regarded as 'dropouts'—a term which implies that everybody must join the elite or perish. The waste in terms of human energy is obvious.

However, as long as society makes this kind of demand for higher education it seems that provision should be made to provide at least for the more persistent students. Accordingly in most English-speaking ex-colonial countries, particularly in recent years, state agencies and some university extension services run courses for O and A level qualifications. Ultimately these students hope to pass into university or, failing that, a higher technical college. There will naturally be a high failure rate, and at this point we should mention briefly the numerous profit-making institutions, mostly based in Britain, which offer correspondence courses not only for school certificate but for many clerical and professional qualifications. Some of these are respectable, with high standards, but many are not; once again the human waste is obvious.

Finally we should look at the possibilities of distance-teaching, with or without the use of radio or television. Benefiting from the British Open University experience, some countries, for example Iran, are experimenting with similar projects. The fact that the Open University can provide courses for 50,000 students at once at a cost which would pay for only about 5000 'normal' students naturally commends itself to poor countries. There is also a post-secondary distance-learning scheme which operates in Eastern France, the main difference from the British system being that the Centre de Tele-Enseignement Universitaire (CTU) uses existing university lectures modified for radio broadcasting.

The best-known project operating in developing countries is that in Kenya, the Correspondence Course Unit (CGU). The special feature in this case has been the presence of large-scale technical assistance from the United States so that the experience is not very relevant for those countries without foreign aid for this purpose. The Unit is a full-time organisation not burdened with other teaching responsibilities and it operates mainly within an urban setting. It has been suggested that the French model might be applied to other countries and plans are now being implemented in Nigeria to set up schemes based on existing universities, including the new ones. The British model is not suitable for African countries and even a modified form of distance-teaching would encounter many severe obstacles, the most serious being poor postal facilities and the lack of available reading material in bookshops or libraries. Nevertheless, as with all other forms of continuing education, the demand is there and attempts are likely to be made to meet it, particularly as it can be said to bring the existing universities closer to the people outside.

Conclusion

In the foregoing survey the stress throughout has been on the political context. In communist countries and in the revolutionary regimes of Cuba, Mozambique and Angola, much greater emphasis is naturally put on political education both for children and adults. Inevitably this will take a crude or blatant form and by hostile critics is labelled 'indoctrination' rather than education in the liberal sense. Tanzania, which is non-communist, occupies a middle position but the ruling party's whole programme based on the Ujaama villages depends on adult education programmes for its success; the effort is consciously being made there also to produce people with new values and new perceptions. Whether this is meeting with success is not the point here. It is the policy which is relevant and those who object to this politicisation should be prepared to admit that they are in effect advocating the preservation of existing and indefensible social arrangements. In the non-radical countries many adult education classes have ended with perhaps five minutes devoted to 'civics'. Whatever 'civics' turns out to be in such a context makes little difference, since neither the individual nor the society will be affected; the education is divorced from social and political action.

REFERENCES

1　Peroncel-Hugoz, J P, 'Report on Egypt' *Guardian weekly* 19 September 1976, 12.
2　Final report of international symposium for literacy. Persepolis, Iran, Unesco, 1975.
3　Benge, R C, *Libraries and cultural change* Bingley, 1970, 104.
4　Illich, Ivan D, *Deschooling society* Calder and Boyars, 1971, 18.
5　Coutinho, J da Veiga, Preface to Freire, Paulo, *Cultural action for freedom* Penguin, 1972, 8.
6　*The declaration of Persepolis* Unesco, 1975.
7　Fashagba, Steven O, *Library possibility in traditional areas: case study, Kabba* (unpublished MLS thesis) Ahmadu Bello University, 1978, 43.
8　Goody, Jack (ed), *Literacy in traditional societies* CUP, 1968, Introduction.
9　Kotei, S J A, 'The West African autochthonous alphabets: an exercise in comparative palaeography' in *Ghana social science journal* Vol 2, I, 1
10　Harrell-Bond, B E and Skinner, David, 'Hidden literacy' in *West Africa* 5 September 1977, 1812 (and in subsequent issues.

PART III

COMMUNICATIONS

6

THE USE OF READING

In writing about reading one need not fear that it has all been done before.
The few scattered references (including my own) to reading habits in
underdeveloped countries have concentrated on some fairly obvious points
and there the matter rests. The time has come, it seems to me, to follow
up these observations with some attempt at further analysis, even if the
results are partly speculative. Inevitably I am influenced mainly by my
experience in West Africa and especially Nigeria.

Africans as non-readers
First we should review some of the conclusions reached so far. Two
quotations will illustrate the typical approach. First, Achebe notes that,
'The overwhelming majority of the adult population only reads newspapers, journals and magazines, as has been observed even among intellectuals'. (1) Or again, Adegbonmire notes that the reading habit among
the literate has never been there and the bookseller 'must realise and
accept that he does not have the type of reading public which his counter-
part in Europe and America has'. (2) Quite so; most observers then go on
to note that necessarily almost all reading is utilitarian, in the sense that
it is carried out for some immediate practical purpose and mostly as part
of formal education. As a broad generalisation this is true, but this does
not take us very far.

The psychology of reading
There are certain commonly accepted notions of types of reading using
such categories as achievement, devotional, cultural, recreational, compensatory. These categories are commonly understood and are vaguely
useful, but they obscure the fact that reading matter cannot accurately
be classified in this way. It is reading as an *activity* which counts, so
that a worthwhile analysis has to be psychological. It is the *psychology*
of reading which should concern us and we are dealing with the psychology
of people in transitional societies.

103

There are two objections to the use of categories of reading; the first is that reading processes, like any others, are culturally determined. This means that the use of loaded terms like 'achievement' or 'compensatory' or even 'devotional' merely cause confusion if they are transferred from one culture to another. The second objection is that the reading activity involves an interaction between the reader and the reading material and how the reader reacts is wholly personal.

We cannot therefore apply value judgements to literature without reference to human responses. People respond to the same piece of writing in different ways and what is inspiring to one is boring to many; what is pornography to some is not at all to others. If a reader uses a great novel solely to improve his English, or to find out about a foreign culture, or simply to say that he has read it, are we to claim that these uses are inadmissible? I hasten to add that this approach is not intended to remove the need for value judgements whether aesthetic or moral. Such matters are important but they involve answers to another kind of question which we have not asked. What concerns us here is what kind of reading activity people need in a particular social situation.

It is at this point that we can return to the concept of practical utility. It need not be disputed that developing societies require readers to read for socially useful purposes rather than to develop their mental or spiritual potential as individuals. A distinction between the individual and society is always dangerous and often unreal, but it is one which in this context we have to make. Reading is primarily an individual pursuit, even though it may have social consequences. Reading for examination purposes is personal in the sense that it leads to material advancement, but it is also social since it is required for collective vocational needs.

In societies where for development or ideological reasons a heavy emphasis is placed on collective activities this practical use of reading is paramount. Books are regarded as tools for social engineering rather than as guides for the exploration of the soul. These are the uses of reading in the USSR and in China. There even the imaginative literature known as 'socialist realism' is pressed into the same mould, and it must be geared to social purposes—it must be optimistic and healthy, and it should help with economic production.

We can say that this type of reading is 'short-term' in the sense that it is meant to benefit society immediately, whereas what has been un-wisely termed 'culture reading' involves an act of exploration into emotional, aesthetic, spiritual or intellectual worlds which seem to be purely personal and to have no direct value to society. In fact such reading may well lead to anti-social or subversive attitudes or an indifference to the accepted goals of the nation. Just as in traditional villages those who read have sometimes been greeted by alarm and hostility, so on another level students in transitional societies who read 'outside curriculum' maybe pose a threat to existing social arrangements.

The conclusion can only be that in a just or dynamic society *both* types of reading are necessary, since the 'subversive' readers of today may be the architects of tomorrow. It may well be that the dissident writers of the USSR will ultimately contribute more to the development of their country than the latest literary hack who produces a novel to encourage 'correct' attitudes amongst the workers.

There is nothing original in what I have just written but I have emphasised it since there is a danger that we might suppose that developing societies only need the more immediately useful sort of reading. Indeed, in a previous work, I have stated that at the present stage of development in many countries we should not expect or even hope that reading should be anything but practical—Dostoevsky can come later. I no longer hold this view and I shall try to suggest that unless individuals read the literature which they need to revolutionise themselves then the revolution will never come. But first it should be useful to summarise the factors which have limited the range of reading in Africa so far.

Limiting factors

1   African culture has been communal and individual reading is regarded as an anti-social activity. One cannot expect traditional villagers to appreciate behaviour so foreign to their customs. Cases have been reported where students who were reading were declared to be possessed by demons. But we are not dealing with demons or life in the villages, so too much should not be made of such extreme reactions. However, even with the 'new breed' of young people, leisure time is still largely spent in communal social activities.

2   Much has been made of physical and social impediments such as overcrowding (with its attendant noise), lack of electricity and other factors. Such circumstances help to explain why people at one social level read very little but they do not account for the reading habits of those who are free from such problems.

3   Africa is still largely illiterate and this inevitably affects the minority who can read. The valuable traditions of an oral culture are still around even if they are passing away. Furthermore there is a fair proportion of neo-literates who have never read with ease. This type of semi-

literacy exists even in developed countries; after all reading as a customary activity is a minority thing *in any culture* and it should not be supposed that Africa is peculiar in this respect. It has frequently been observed that reading habits vary a great deal amongst the countries with a high rate of literacy. It is well known that a higher proportion of the population in Northern Europe spend their spare time in reading than in the Catholic Latin South. And it is held that in France there is an intellectual élite which reads a great deal while the mass of the population do not read widely. There are many other examples.

4   In Europe and elsewhere, the use of reading, especially for recreational purposes, preceded radio, film and television. In Africa they have been introduced at the same time and for many people the mass media have preceded literacy. In spite of the claims by McCluhan and others that this must have a profound effect it is difficult to establish what the consequences might be. There have been suggestions that reading may not be necessary at all. Two points can be made: first, that illiterate people, for several reasons, may not be able to respond fully either to television or radio. There are difficulties in perception and understanding partly caused by their basic ignorance of the wider world; this is discussed further in the section on mass communication. Second, it does not need research to prove that if people, especially children, spend many hours each week in front of the television they will read less. Elsewhere this has largely affected recreational reading more than other forms. (It should be remembered that in West Africa over half the population is less than 15 years old.)

5   A significant factor is that neither children nor adults in Africa have been exposed to the written word as a constant feature because of the lack of libraries, bookshops and indigenous publishers. The usual vicious circle occurs: the materials are not there because there is no demand, and there is little demand because the reading is not available. Also those printed works which do exist are often unsuitable or in the wrong languages.

6   Control of free expression limits the value of publications such as newspapers and periodicals so that people may prefer to obtain their information through oral sources.

7   We have already noted that an authoritarian tradition in education has stifled free enquiry and the critical spirit. If this is absent there is no incentive to read and students will instead rely on the word of their teachers.

8   Developed countries, because of their production systems, have increased the amount of leisure time which is available to almost

everybody. This is not the case in underdeveloped countries except for the unemployed or the underemployed, who are not likely to read anyway.

9   Climatic factors have often been stressed, especially heat and humidity, which are ennervating.

10   The hardships involved in reading or learning to read English as a second or even third or fourth language must interfere with reading for pleasure and affect the rate of any reading exercise.

These ten negative factors have been dealt with summarily because I wish to explore them further in relation to each other. The real problem is not the undeniable existence of such circumstances but which of them are of primary importance; which of them are temporary and whether they add up to a set of influences which will remain indefinitly. Finally, one needs to ask if it really matters whether or what people read.

The available literature
If we look at a typical environment (I am obliged to take anglophone West Africa as an example) numerous qualifications have to be made to the interpretations we have accepted so far. It is here that we can begin to present a more balanced picture.

Many of the alleged barriers, for instance the high rate of illiteracy, will not remain forever, at least not in their present form. The book production problem will also eventually be solved, but meanwhile it is my view that the absence of suitable reading materials has been under-estimated as a decisive factor, particularly with regard to the reading habits of those who are not students. The fact that the indigenous book trade has barely survived a protracted infancy is one more symptom of underdevelopment. This has meant that in some areas there have been gaps which have not been satisfactorily filled and cannot be filled by overseas publishers.

Imaginative literature, particularly the novel, can be regarded as a part of 'culture reading' although novels may also be read for various practical purposes. The popularity of such British writers as Marie Corelli (once taken seriously in Britain before World War I) and Bertha Clay (a more recent and most unserious novelist) is well known. At the moment in the University where I work female students tend to read Denise Robins and the men James Hadley Chase. What is remarkable is that the same authors, once introduced, continue in demand decade after decade. Ten years ago I noticed the popularity in Ghana of an unpleasant German novel called *The basket of flowers*; this eighteenth-century work is still advertised in the Nigerian press at present. Why should these particular novelists and not others still survive?

An examination of the sugary confections of Denise Robins does not reveal any basic difference from any other of the numerous British producers of light romance. James Hadley Chase (an Englishman writing in an American idiom) might seem slightly more relevant to African society. In his stories the police are just as wicked as the criminals. This is a modern convention which people in African countries will readily understand. However, neither of these novelists is unique, and the evidence suggests that the popularity of such works is a consequence of publishers' plugging of particular authors.

Once a demand is established the popularity persists over a very long period; indeed, there is no evidence that it will come to an end. Some of these novels were imported as much as 50 years ago by the missionaries (as must have been the case with the *Basket of flowers*.) Needless to say such concoctions do not relate to *any* environment and certainly not to development. (The mere fact that they appear to be set in some other country makes them more attractive as escapist literature. If the term 'compensatory reading' applies to anything at all then this must be it.) It must be admitted that in most cases the standard of English is high enough to be of use to students, although some do absorb characteristic American slang expressions from James Hadley Chase and use them in their writing. The term 'compensatory' could be applied to this type of reading.

If we examine bookshops in the large hotels or in multiple stores we shall find, in addition to this light fiction, a fair number of British and American works which can best be described as 'soft porn', together with some indigenous attampts at this genre. They are probably read more by business and professional men (including expatriates) than by students, and are certainly too advanced for the masses. They are significant only in the sense that they indicate the growth of one kind of sophistication. Some of the popular African periodicals also contain sexually explicit stories and features; they have the merit that whatever fantasy might be present is recognisably African.

In or outside many stores one also finds from time to time, large consignments of comics published in Britain and done in the American manner. Some students read them and they are popular with neo-literates; one recalls the prevalence of such material for adults in the USA. There is no African element in these comics, but habitual addicts rapidly get to understand the conventions. It is this literature, if it were indigenous and exhibited more appropriate values, which could be used by those who have just learned to read.

At the same popular level we encounter the famous Onitsha pamphlets about which so much has been written. Here we are concerned only with readership of these pamphlets. I wish to emphasise its significance in view of the statements which have been made that Africans do not read. As E N Obiechina has pointed out, this literature appeals mainly to the new literate class of elementary and grammar school boys and girls, low-level white-collar workers, primary-school teachers, literate and semi-literate traders, mechanics, taxi drivers and, above all, to the numerous products of adult education classes and evening schools who find more sophisticated literature, such as the novel proper, too cumbersome and difficult. (3)

The sales figures of the pamphlets prove that there is a constant demand for light and simple reading matter. One of them entitled *Veronica my daughter*, by Agali A Ogali, has sold 60,000 copies in the twenty years since its publication in 1957. Obiechina gives a useful analysis of the literary influences behind this movement, which are summarised as follows:

1 The African oral folktale (with an explicit moral);
2 the study of English literature;
3 newspapers;
4 the cinema:
5 Christian education.

With such a combination of influences the cultural significance of this and similar literature can readily be appreciated. They include pamphlets which give practical advice on all important matters, especially love and money.

Their importance is of course now partly historical as the original movement was destroyed in the civil war. However, a similar literature in various forms still exists. It is rooted in the environment and is written only for local readers. The key characteristics of the pamphlets are, first, that they are relevant and topical (typical titles *No longer a minister*, *Lagos is a wicked place*), second that they are easily available when other literature is not, and third that they are cheap. This type of popular literature is the only genuine local article; such material suitably modified would be relevant for national development.

It might be thought that 'serious' African literature like the 150-odd titles in Heinemann's African Writers Series could have a similar appeal

109

to a national readership; they compare favourably with much American and British fiction. But the appeal is limited by several factors: they are read mainly by students (often as set books in universities and secondary schools) and it is doubtful whether they are much read for recreation; also they are not easily available. Another unexpected obstacle is ethnic incomprehension. In Nigeria the novels of Chinua Achebe may be just as alien to a Hausa man as those of Harold Robbins, perhaps even more so. As many of the other novels in this series consist of dressed up social anthropology they lack universal appeal.

Finally there is another difficulty. It has been generally admitted that in view of a limited local readership, African writers have to write with British and American readers in mind—in any case their works are published in these countries. This is not a criticism but a recognition of fact; one which must limit local appeal to a small minority.

We have dealt with foreign light fiction, which is much in demand. What remains is serious non-African imaginative literature, especially the novel. In considering its possible readership we have to remember that, even in the non-traditional sectors, African society is not fully individualised in the Western bourgeois sense. In consequence novels which concentrate on explorations of the isolated self, the soul or the 'solitary mister' have not great appeal and are not understood. Our experience of students is that they more easily respond to Shakespeare where the plays are firmly set in their social context (one which is not vastly different from many present-day African societies) and where they can identify with certain characters. This cannot easily be said about so many modern British novels, with their internal, psychological handling of individual characters and intensely subjective news of the world.

There are of course other cultural differences which limit response to European or even American literature. Most, if not all, African societies are still close to oral literature with its tradition of explicit morals. But many modern foreign novels are 'immoral' or amoral. The hero" is not often heroic; indeed, he may well be an anti-hero. Again, the modern trend towards unisexuality and playing down of the difference between the sexes finds no echo amongst African readers, who are still largely used to male chauvinism. The approach to sex and the appeal of the erotic is bound to be different, but we must not pursue these matters too far; they are mentioned to indicate first, that the modern novel lacks appeal, and second, that a more truly indigenous literature is required.

I have concentrated on imaginative literature as one branch of non-utilitarian reading; many outsiders have lamented its neglect. What has emerged is that the serious novel, along with other non-utilitarian work, is not much read, while certain types of popular literature are.

One cannot leave the theme of literature for the masses without reference to the religious (mainly Christian) publishers. Their importance is that even if their literature was disseminated in the first place by foreigners, it was intended for an indigenous flock. Insofar as the Christian pamphlets or books were biblical they were not mainly Eurocentric, and the world of both the Old and New Testament was strikingly similar to much of Africa today. This same relevance is present in the pages of the Koran. Christianity (like Islam) came from the Middle East, not Europe, and it was never originally thought that God was a white man. Tracts and translations were of course written by white missionaries but they were based on the Bible and in many respects suited to African needs. The message of the Koran is less directly connected with the mass literature in English which we are discussing.

The two great 'religions of the book' have the universal appeal which is necessary to cross boundaries—that has been the significance of their literature. The Christians have built up a distribution network which has no parallel in secular publishing. They printed and are still printing in the vernacular languages, and they were *committed* at the popular level. That the Christian gospels have been published in 560 African languages must surely mean something. One must assume that much of this literature has been widely read; indeed, the evidence is available in the speeches and literary style of many African political leaders. What would be valuable is something at the secular level with the same appeal. A last discouraging word must be added, which is that such publishing is heavily subsidised.

Children

We have implied that the African environment, and particularly formal education, stifles the imagination and limits curiosity. (In many traditional societies curiosity was regarded as a moral failing, to which women in particular were prone.) It is for this reason amongst others that children's literature is so important. At this early stage they do want to read.

Here we encounter the odd fact that in countries which have a rich indigenous oral culture, much of which is suitable for children, the majority of published works available are still written by expatriates and imported. (I am not referring to school textbooks here.) These are of course not always appropriate. Stories with foreign settings are often ridiculed on cultural grounds, but such criticism may be ill-founded, since children do not always prefer the familiar. The goblins and *ghommids* of Yoruba folk tales, like fairies everywhere, exist perhaps only in the mind, but for the child that is his privileged kingdom. (One British equivalent is the world-of-the-public-school story, popular in a country where such schools are not public at all and to which most children will never go; that also is a kind of fairyland.)

However, the need remains for stories and other works relating to the child's own environment. Much imaginative literature deals with animals and birds and it is absurd that these should often be foreign when indigenous oral culture teems with the local fauna. Must they all be locked up in zoos? If African children sing *London bridge is falling down* or *Ring a ring of roses* or *Baa baa black sheep* is that cultural imperialism? Or is it possible that the world of the very small child is a universal one?

In spite of these advisable qualifications it is obvious that more indigenous children's literature could be produced because the demand is there. The people of the new transitional societies now recognise that their children can be granted the luxury of childhood and need not work —at least not all the time.

There has been speculation about the relative absence of African writers for children. It has been suggested that Africans are reluctant to write for children lest it be thought that they are still children themselves. When one considers how many of the classic British writers for children never 'grew up' there is something to be said for such a fear. On a more serious level, however, we should appreciate that all creative artists, even when they do grow up, have to preserve the direct vision of the child. It is this kind of imaginative creativity which the developing formal African education systems may do much to suppress. The main difficulties are that first, modern structures cause a break with the non-literate past; and second, these same structures cannot allow new imaginative faculties to develop. No doubt the black equivalent of William Blake is wandering abroad somewhere near Sokoto classified as the village idiot. Meanwhile, as we shall see, most people are too preoccupied with everyday chores to spend much time 'living like children'. Writing for children cannot be 'serious'.

After this brief look at popular reading, the conclusion I wish to submit is that in most developing societies there is an enormous untapped demand. Others with experience of the book trade have noticed this potential. (Librarians are less likely to observe it as they do not normally provide for such readers.) Thus Omotosho says: 'It is not that people do not read. It is what they read, what is available for them to read; this is the problem'. (4)

112

I have observed many people who are just literate—workers such as
messengers, technicians, domestic servants, and drivers—spending a great
deal of time struggling with some unsuitable literature, often children's
stories or the popular local periodicals such as Drum, Trust and *Woman's
World*. They are concerned not only with learning to read properly for
the usual advancement reasons but to find out about the world; there is
a genuine curiosity which is often killed quite early amongst the educated
classes. The reference to illustrated magazines indicates that there would
be an immediate response to comic strips of *the right kind* if they could
be produced by local people. These could really be used as a literature
of national development. I am not speaking of crude propaganda although
even that might be more healthy than the comics imported from abroad
with values which are not just irrelevant but anti-social. It is ironic that
one country where popular indigenous comics have been launched is
South Africa, but they are not quite what I have in mind.

Vernacular literature
We now arrive at the intractable problems of language. Of all the negative factors listed above the language confusion should be given priority,
since the use of English as a second but official language in the greater
part of Africa is a problem attended by many ramifications.

For many countries there is no solution in sight. One might easily
think that the answer could be found in a changeover to a vernacular
language for all purposes as soon as possible, as is happening to some extent with Swahili in East Africa. The playwright and poet Wole Soyinka,
on behalf of the African Union of Writers, has even advocated the use of
Swahili in Nigeria where Swahili is not an indigenous language. He has
been driven to advocating such desperate remedies because the existence
of ethnic language divisions in Nigeria makes a common vernacular
language politically improbable.

The British colonialists in Nigeria, at different times and in various
places, made efforts to introduce vernacular publishing, although necessarily the languages used were not national but what were then called
'tribal'. At that time, before independence, most nationalist leaders opposed this policy on the grounds that it was helping to keep their people
out of the mainstream of history and therefore perpetuating their inferior
status. Similarly, popular demand then and now has been for the English
language which will lead to advancement and rewards. One can say that
if none of the local languages is the official national language, then these
objections are partially valid. Vernacular publishing needs to be encouraged
113

most obviously at an elementary and primary level, but it cannot be a sole answer to the reading problems we have discussed so long as English remains the official language.

Mass literacy campaigns have been mostly in the vernacular and these have encountered the same objections—that they represent a colonial-type policy. In Nigeria there are between three and four hundred languages—the figure differing according to how you distinguish a language from a dialect. Even if we restrict ourselves to major languages there are still too many to make a mass publication programme practical. The situation is similar elsewhere in Africa.

From a national point of view a concentration on several languages would be ethnically divisive. There are also technical difficulties in printing some vernacular languages, for example, in printing transliterated Yoruba it is necessary to use a number of special signs as the language is tonal and a written word may stand for several things. The word *Owo* has four different meanings, depending on the position of the stress and inflections. These have to be transcribed into marks above letters on the printed page, which becomes a problem for publisher, printer and reader alike.

In view of all these factors it is clear that the dilemma is acute; It is difficult, if not impossible, to preserve an indigenous culture without the language which is central to it—yet to concentrate on vernacular publishing would be a waste of resources, for English is still essential. The solutions will naturally vary from country to country and region to region.

Reading difficulty
Meanwhile with regard to the use of English we should note difficulties which cannot be easily eradicated. Those who have read books in their own language from an early age will not easily understand what it is like to read from the beginning in a language which they do not speak at home or even at school. It is often said that there was once a similar situation with refard to the use of Latin in Europe, but the parallel is not sufficient, as Latin was used only by a small, educated élite, and, furthermore, right from the start of printing there were publications in the separate national languages.

What happens is that it takes a long time before anyone can read with easy or rapidly enough to make it an efficient process. There are also limits to comprehension. For all university students, lecturers are needed to *interpret* set readings. Students in African universities obviously will need this assistance to a greater extent. In addition to an inevitably slow rate of reading they may not be able to understand certain texts at all. In such a context it is pointless to complain that students rely too much on lecturers. If they do not understand the lecturers either—what then? As everybody knows one does not get a full understanding of a foreign language for a long time—add to this the fact that the standards of English teaching will probably continue to decline and then one can begin to appreciate the problem.

We must conclude, with particular reference to formal education, that the language blockages will not easily be removed. One does not need to go further to find the reasons for a lack of interest in reading which is common amongst the educated classes. To struggle for an education and a qualification, an effort is required which may seem to be out of all proportion to the intellectual rewards, even if it pays off in a material sense. The statement by students that after graduation they will never open a book again is often heard, and one student is reported to have said that he would ensure that his wife read the newspaper to him!

The prevalence of stress
There is still another circumstance so far not discussed. We have noted the hostile social material conditions which weigh particularly upon the less affluent groups in the community, whether in village or town.

The educated elites are not so much troubled in this way—their living conditions compare favourably with those elsewhere. What does bother them is the *stress* which is endemic in the new circumstances of post-traditional society. Situations of stress exist everywhere but their incidence varies in intensity; they apply equally to expatriates living in under-developed countries. I refer to the time spent in everyday life in visiting the bank (a lengthy process), in obtaining petrol (often a lengthier one), on taking children to and from school, in getting the last tin of something from the shops, in haggling in markets, in looking after innumerable relatives who expect the 'big man' to help them, and not least, in many of the cities, struggling about in the new jungles of traffic (possibly the most time consuming of all). Furthermore human relations may consist of protracted negotiations with every sort of person, none of which can be summarily dismissed.

This is not all: the above refers to the world outside work; at work in offices, shops, schools and institutions of every kind the number of capable and responsible people is still such that quite small transactions are difficult. Decisions can be made but how, in such circumstances are

115

they to be carried out? They are of course eventually followed through, but the effort is disproportionate. The average conscientious Nigerian in a key position probably has about ten years or less of productive life; one can watch the grey hairs appear almost daily. How could such a one settle down at the end of the day with Kant's *Critique of pure reason* or even *Gone with the wind*?

It is not just a matter of the time-consuming distractions but of stress in the clinical sense. From a development point of view it may not matter very much if businessmen drop down dead in airport queues, but if everybody is under too much strain we have to note the consequence that a bottle is more likely to help than a book. It is against such a background that we should consider the habit of not reading.

The plight of women
To this catalogue of struggles one should add that the women of the new elites have an extra burden. In countries with a developed bourgeoisie career women often have a tough time but not necessarily any worse than the men, who may share responsibility for bringing up the family. But in many developing countries the women have always done most of the work, manual or otherwise; the men who used to go hunting or into battle no longer do so but have an office job instead. This is, for them, has to be the sum of all their labours, so that if a woman also goes to work she is expected to look after the home as well. How in such circumstances could reading habits develop? The question seems almost frivolous.

It is of course true that there are always exceptional men or women who can transcend such distractions. Our responsibility, however, is to deal with the typical, and how long conditions remain typical is a matter for conjecture.

Interlude: false interpretations
I have dwelt upon what I consider are the most decisive influences. Other alarming notions have been introduced such as those quoted (apparently with approval) by Professor Kotei. (5) I have to mention these in case we might be led astray. He quotes G Jahoda, to the effect that Africans find the abstract thought of Europeans difficult because they have 'different cognitive structures and different cognitive skills'. Kotei also quotes Sapir, to the effect that the languages of underdeveloped societies do not have abstract words. Finally, in his own words, he claims that, 'For the majority of our people, it would seem that alien abstract notions

116

have first to be translated into concrete terms before they are understood. When we read books that cannot be related to our direct experience the book will either bore, confuse or totally confound us.'

Passages such as this are themselves confusing and confounding and could be used (similar doctrines have been used) to draw racist conclusions.

Underdeveloped countries are a short step away both in time and place from traditional societies, which were pre-industrial, pre-scientific; most of them were oral cultures. One would not expect the languages of traditional societies to have had 'abstract' words concerning realities which they have not experienced and did not need to know. The people of Wales have a language which lacks many modern words—so also does Arabic; but nobody has ever suggested that such peoples find reading difficult.

In earlier cultures there was an oral literature and a theology often of a very complex kind—all of which was part of a unified perception of the world. When 'development' breaks these up, new perceptions have to be received and it is these which can be difficult or 'abstract'. The symbolic universe of the European working classes has or had the same non-abstract characteristics as traditional African cultures and, as Bernstein has shown in the case of English, their language was and is inevitably more 'concrete' than that of other classes. They have preferred the old Anglo-Saxon to Latin constructions because they relate most to their experience.

It is for these reasons that abstract notions are alien, not because they are European. Such ideas on an intellectual level are simply the conscious and developed forms of attitudes which everybody has, although not everybody needs or wants to work them out in such a way. For the majority of people in every society the world of ideas as it is developed in books is not necessary—that is why they do not read them.

However, the ideas themselves are still essential and how they are transmitted is a complex social process. At times of social convulsion and upheaval the ideas become paramount and (to simplify very much) one would expect more people to read in order to sort out what they should do or whom they should follow. In more stable or static times such explorations are not necessary, and there are times of defeat and desperation when all that is left for the individual is to survive. In order to survive he will not read but simply watch and pray. One can agree with Professor Kotei if this is what he means, but not if there is any suggestion that Africans have some inherent difficulty in reading. That is how their societies have been; that is all. Nevertheless, the official languages are alien and modern industrial cultures have first been developed in another place, so reading represents an introduction into a world which is not yet an African one. That is why the upheavals will continue and why a variety of reading is essential.

Conclusion

We started with our list of ten largely adverse factors and have tried to show that many of these may be only temporary since all are symptoms of underdevelopment. I have not tried to suggest that reading in itself is a 'good thing'. It is a neutral activity without any absolute value unless you are learning to read for the first time. This neutral process acquires a meaning, when the reader has certain psychological drives, according to the literature he uses to meet them.

I have argued that in the circumstances prevailing wide reading beyond utility is necessary for personal development even if it should lead one to wild and lonely places. On the social level, national development implies urbanisation to some degree and the use of literature and libraries has always been associated with towns. Also implied is not simply an exodus from but the transformation of the villages; this may be the heart of the matter. It is beyond dispute that for the people who work on the land there has been hitherto neither the wish to learn, nor to read, nor much use to which reading could be put. If physical labour, whether in factories or in fields, is sufficiently intense and prolonged, then reading is irrelevant. While such conditions remain (as they do for most people in the world) it scarcely matters whether people can read or not.

But if and when radical social transformations take place they will be accompanied and stimulated by the use of the printed word. Reading can then become a basis for social and personal liberation. It will help to provide alternatives to the old authorities who are passing away and a defence against the new ones which will appear.

REFERENCES
1 Achebe, Chinua, 'What do African intellectuals read?' *in* the *Times literary supplement* 2 May 1972.
2 Adegbonmire, Wanmi, 'The hazards of bookselling in Africa' *in* Oluwasanmi, E and others (ed), *Publishing in Africa in the seventies* University of Ife Press, 1975, 48.
3 Obiechina, E N, *Onitsha market literature* Heinemann, 1972, 10.
4 Omotoso, Kole, 'The missing apex, a search for the audience' *in* Oluwasanmi, E and others (ed), *op cit*, 259.

5 Kotei, S I A, 'Some cultural and social factors of book reading and publishing in Africa' *in* Oluwasanmi, E and others (ed), *op cit*, 182-3.

7

THE CULTURAL PREDICAMENT

Scope
We are not here concerned with the numerous possible meanings of the word 'culture'. Our purpose is best served by regarding 'culture' as a 'way of life' which can then be divided into its various categories, such as political, economic, social, ideological, spiritual, historical, and so on. These components are often conveniently grouped into those concerned with material things (technology, for example) and those which exist largely in the human mind (value, beliefs, art forms, doctrines and symbols).

The connection between the two areas of activity, ie the material and the ideal, is one of the most basic of all human problems. In this chapter the emphasis is put on 'ideal' culture—what someone has called 'the world of symbolic meanings', and I am more particularly concerned with the way that people regard changes in their own culture than with interpretations from outside. If revolutionary material transformations occur, what changes in human consciousness must take place to accompany them? The other chapters in this book, such as those on development and technology, deal with material culture, and all of them including this one are intended to be limited to developing countries.

The ideal content of culture
It is not possible wholly to isolate the ideal elements in culture without grave falsifications or distortions. For example those who try to understand imaginative literature or art without reference to its social context are guilty of an intellectual triviality which is usually rooted in political prejudice and ignorance. The connections must be made, and part of the problem is not just what the connections are but how they should be established; this is the arid and daunting sphere of *methodology* which produces so much unreadable literature.

What we are attempting to elucidate includes some of the following cultural manifestations. People may discontinue magical practices or come to believe in a different kind of God apparently because electricity has been installed or father has gone away to work in the mines. But this is not apparent to *them*. Lenin said that he had come 'to abolish the village idiot'—by this he presumably meant not the idiot in person but a *concept* by means of which it is possible to idealise him.

The culture of other people as it variously appears to the anthropologist, the sociologist, the missionary, the tourist—even the administrator—is not seen in this light by the people themselves. In consequence there must always be an element of condescension or arrogance in the presumptions of outsiders. The people who are studied, converted, administered or organised do not formulate such problems in a conscious fashion. They have *attitudes*; that is all.

Every reformer or revolutionary (in the underdeveloped world the man of good will must be one or the other) comes up against the stubborn fact that those whom he wishes to change may not be aware that they are miserable. The 'wretched of the earth' have to be told that they are wretched—in other words, they are not politically conscious. (It is of some significance that the title of Fanon's seminal book in the original French is *Les condamnés de la terre*, a phrase which more accurately expresses the human predicament.) We are often damned or doomed because we are not conscious of, and therefore cannot understand, what is happening to us. Before taking up this point again it is worth noting the various possible attitudes towards cultural change in developing countries.

The traditionalists

Those who wish (whether inside or outside a community) to preserve the past at all costs we may call traditionalist ('conservative' has too many loaded implications). They are concerned that a stable way of life which has been sanctified by the passing of centuries should not be allowed to fall apart.

The idealisation of tribal life by outsiders from developed countries has been a constant element in cultural history for centuries, and the concept of the noble savage is only one form of this myth. In the twentieth century such attitudes have persisted, often because Western observers are reacting against the deficiencies of their own technological environment. There is the phenomenon known as 'Masai-itis', which has consisted of the idealisation of the Masai herdsmen of East Africa, who

122

have resisted modernisation and assimilation. They are easy to romanticise because they are doomed. The elegaic tone characteristic of those who lament the passing away of ancient nomadic traditions is unmistakable. For example, a passage by Colin Turnbull on the death of a Masai man: 'When he dies he is not buried in a hole in the ground, a thought that is horrifying to these herders, but he is laid out in the open with a clump of grass in one hand, a pair of sandals and a cattle stick in the other, ready for whatever onward journey there might be. The useless body is disposed of by vultures and jackals, spending its last moments under the stars that, for the Masai, represent celestial herders driving celestial cattle across the sky. If there is a heaven, for the herder this is surely how it must be'. (1) Colin Turnbull has done sensitive and moving studies of two other 'lost' peoples, the Pygmies and the Ik, the last being a terrifying account of a Ugandan tribe who have ceased to be human in the sense usually understood.

Such studies of doomed communities, who cannot be reconciled to or assimilated into the modern world, tend to irritate the new educated Africans. Faced with the almost insuperable social problems of the exploited masses, is it these small dying minorities that we should concentrate upon? Those who have taken up the cause of aboriginal or 'stone age' peoples elsewhere, such as those along the Amazon or in Papua-New Guinea, have met with similar criticism. These studies, it might be said, represent traditionalism in an extreme form, and Turnbull is consistent when he deplores Western education on the grounds that it is wholly destructive: 'What may prove to be Zaire's greatest blessing has been held to be the greatest defect of the Belgian colonial system, the lack of any substantial body of educated elite. There were little over a dozen university graduates for a country almost the size of India when the former Belgian Congo won its independence. That means, however, that there were only little over a dozen colonialised minds'. (2) It is significant that those who take this view identify Western-type education with colonialism. I would prefer to believe that there are other Western traditions which can provide hope even if they have not yet been absorbed;

I do not wish to leave the impression that this type of traditionalism from the outside should be wholly deplored as foolish or sentimental. Traditionalist observers have noted that 'modernisation' as it has existed so far is largely a mess of pottage. Their reactions are significant also because the peoples who are doomed in this fashion are either nomadic herdsmen or hunters. Such groups have been rejected by settled cultivators since the tilling of the soil began. In the fourth chapter of Genesis,

'Abel was a keeper of sheep but Cain was a tiller of the ground . . . and it came to pass that Cain rose up against his brother and slew him'. The prophetic accuracy of the Old Testament is further indicated when the Lord cursed the peasant Cain: 'When thou tillest the ground it shall not henceforth yield unto thee her strength; a fugitive and a vagabond shalt thou be in the earth'. Such are the people today who are leaving the villages in thousands and flocking to the towns. The hunters and the nomads have fared even worse, as can be seen in the age-old oppression which has been the lot of the bushmen of the Kalahari desert; a persecution from the black and white races alike.

It is not too fanciful to suppose that these conflicts represent forces within the human mind and soul, and it is for this reason that the psychology of the Masai or the Pygmies or the Kalahari bushmen have been regarded as symbols of a lost purity and innocence. We deplore the peasant mentality because he is obsessed with property and is not his brother's keeper; we do not like to feel that this is how we are. Meanwhile the gypsies are still in the symbolic wood.

It is time to turn to the traditionalists proper. These include the old people who belong to the old ways and the traditional rulers whose responsibility it is to preserve them. Formerly these were mainly illiterate and therefore not liable to defend their cultural heritage in academic terms, but increasingly the educated 'natural' leaders of their people are conscious of the dilemma discussed here. They co-operate willingly or reluctantly with the modernising administrators and are regarded as valuable links of communication between national leaders and the still largely illiterate masses. It is possible, but not certain, that as Western-type education affects more people their importance will be reduced. A gulf already exists between them and young people whether fully educated or not; but meanwhile, in varying degrees and according to different circumstances, they are accepted.

Finally, there are those indigenous persons who are traditionalist for religious or ideological reasons and whose personal position is threatened by change. Paramount amongst these are the Islamic defenders of the faith, who are discussed in the chapter on education. They are probably right in holding that their beliefs (in this case consciously worked out) cannot be reconciled with a 'modern' viewpoint. Their responses, like Turnbull's but for different reasons, are logical and consistent. I have chosen a quotation to illustrate them, taken from the press record of the debates on the proposed Nigerian constitution which included a reference to Human Rights: 'Take the law of inheritance for instance.

When my father died seven years ago, the little he left was shared between his wives and children *according to a formula*; [my italics] when my mother died later, the same formula was used ... According to this formula, in the case of the children of the deceased, each male child shall have twice as much as each female child'. (3) The speaker then notes that for the Muslim this procedure derives from the Koran, and if it conflicts with what have, in modern times, been called 'Fundamental Human Rights', so much the worse for them. 'This is the way such things have been with us Muslims for ages and this is the way they should continue up to the end of time.'

No better example could be found of the essence of strict traditionalism. It is a view which has to be respected even when deplored. I should repeat that what I am discussing here is not the threatened traditions themselves but how they are regarded. (The moderniser refers to such religious traditions, whether Muslim or Christian, as 'fundamentalist'—as distinct from 'liberal' or 'progressive'. It is interesting that the above speaker turned the tables and referred to those who stress human rights as fundamentalist; it is of course a clash between totally different assumptions. Either human rights are fundamental or they are not; similarly what is regarded as the literal word of God in the Bible or the Koran is fundamental or it is not. That there are other forms of religious faith and that these total contradictions need not exist is not our concern here.

Lest it be thought that this last example is simply a religious manifestation, I must add what should be obvious, that much of the resistance to change comes from those whose privileges are in hazard. Frequently what is threatened is a centuries-old domination of society by men in their own interests in order to keep women in their subject role. The modern answer to this is not a women's liberation movement, although this might help, but a struggle to liberate everybody.

Modernisers

The modernists can also be divided into the indigenous and the outsiders, the latter mainly experts on development whose economic doctrines we noted in chapter 1. Here I note some of their usual approaches. They are no longer guilty of the more blatant forms of neglect or ignorance of the indigenous way of life, particularly when involved in transferring technology. The Russians sent snow ploughs to Guinea only once, and possibly there are fewer tractors now rusting unused on the plains of Accra.

Typical of all modernisation is the emphasis on scientific control. They are right in asserting that conscious control of new societies is inevitable, because the old ways have been undermined or shattered first by imperial conquest, then by technology and trade. Traditionalists note with nostalgia that tribal societies were self-regulatory—that is to say, they had inbuilt and unconscious controlling mechanisms. These regulatory mechanisms are no longer there and social machinery of a new kind has to be invented. It is at this point that the masses have to be involved, otherwise the new national mechanisms do not work. But such involvement might turn them into revolutionaries, so it is not carried out. However, the point here is that 'modernism' implies rational organisation in Weber's sense; something which is foreign to traditional society and which helps to destroy it.

The other strong suit in the moderniser's hand is his wish to eliminate barbarous practices. Partly in reaction against the former myths about darkest Africa, traditionalists and some liberal expatriates have minimised the significance of customs which offend what are supposed to be modern concepts of behaviour. Violence and cruelty have their own characteristic modern forms including torture for political ends. In our century these crimes have been committed on such a scale that we can scarcely comprehend them.

However, this should not blind us to the fact that modernisation in underdeveloped societies may help to eliminate inhuman practices of a more old-fashioned kind. Sometimes these customs have been culturally central, and it is these especially which constitute a problem for the moderniser. Female circumcision (clitoridectomy), still widely practised in many parts of Africa, is one such custom. President Kenyatta (in *Facing Mount Kenya*), and the Kenyan novelist Ngugi (in *The river between*) have defended this system as it exists amongst the Kikiyu on the grounds that the old culture should be preserved and also that the women freely accept it as a basic element in their way of life. Yet there can be no doubt that clitoridectomy is repugnant to a modern sensibility which embraces human rights (in this case those of women). It is also claimed with some justification that women in total Purdah or seclusion are perfectly content, at least if they are not exposed to Western education. All that need be said here is that the outsider should be wary of hasty condemnations, since the answers must eventually be found from within these societies and that other modernising influences will produce change.

These transformations are likely to occur because indigenous modernisers tend to share the attitudes which we have identified in Chapter 1. They will also have their links with the old traditions so that they are sometimes more realistically aware of the difficulties of development.

126

Similarly they never minimise the disorders and corruptions of the new transitional societies. They also, in historical terms, had to struggle against the colonialists, so it was necessary to stress the value of their own culture. It is only in such a way that we can appreciate the doctrines of 'negritude', which elevated into assets the characteristics alleged to be African which the white racists had scorned or condemned. Such traits included the ability to live in harmony with natural forces instead of trying to control them. The 'noble savage', originally a white and alien concept, returned to its homeland and was adopted by Leopold Senghor, the poet President of Senegal. Both the West Indians and Africans who had been colonised by the French had become 'Westernised' and were in search of their roots. Black people in the two Americas naturally share the same predicament; such persons are partly outside the scope of this enquiry.

Transition and its interpreters
In noting reactions to the passing of traditional society we do not mention 'transitionalism'. There can be no such doctrine, but only various types of practical persons who struggle with the way things are. Inevitably this is Everyman who is likely to criticise severely the disorders of contemporary life, but since he is aware that a breakdown of old communality has led to rampant individualism, his main concern is to get as much money and property and position as he can for himself and his family.

In this struggle the fittest may survive, but much also depends on luck and the ups and downs of political fortune which changes with bewildering rapidity. In order to climb up within such a social system one has to pull other people down. There is an unstable social mobility which depresses the sensitive and exhilarates the aggressive. Because of this, almost everybody is forced to become a businessman in addition to his other occupations. These conditions exist in an extreme form in Nigeria but they are noticeable in all new countries. For most people therefore 'development' means development for themselves and for their brothers and sisters however these may be defined.

All this has to be stressed, as otherwise we may leave the impression that hordes of theoreticians go about armed with sociological abstractions. People have to live; if they were to express a point of view at all it would be that they must salvage what is useful from the past at the same time as they welcome anything new that will benefit them.

It need hardly be said that transitional man is usually not hampered by a 'bleeding heart'. A social conscience is a luxury which only the truly privileged man can afford, and even he can only indulge it when his own achievements and gains are secure. (Tolstoy could try to give away his lands because he was a member of the landed aristocracy.) These privileges are spiritual as well as material, and one of the more foolish aspects of the counter-culture of the 1960s was that its adherents rejected an intellectual tradition which had been built up at such cost for two thousand years.

The Surrealists and the Dada movement idealised the primitive. Transitional man does not make that mistake; he knows how fragile civilised tradition is, and that the barbarians are always at the gate. The predicament then is not just theoretical but primarily practical; the new elites are caught up in a world-wide process which they do not expect to control or understand. The remainder of this chapter examines some of their dilemmas.

The sources of change

Auden's words, 'The winds must come from somewhere when they blow', express the poet's intuitive appreciation of the problem of the 'prime mover'. What causes change? If agreement were to be reached on such a matter we should not be arguing how development can come about.

There is no need to repeat the classic formulations here: some are monistic in the sense that one principle is identified, such as 'the Will of God', or 'the mode of production', or simply 'technology'. Other interpretations profess to see the fortuitous interplay of various forces. Whatever application such doctrines may have had for industrial societies, it is more difficult to use them for the societies we are discussing.

With regard to religious determinism, if there exists some purpose for us all in the mind of God, how can we find out what has been ordained for us? Political leaders who claim to have a direct communication line to heaven have always been suspect. With regard to technological influences, it seems that technology may be a decisive agent only in the first instance. The building of a railway or an electric light system is in each case sufficient to modify profoundly or even to destroy an old culture, but it cannot create a new one. Tractors may replace donkeys and telephones take over from smoke signals or the beating of drums, but when they have taken over, what then? Suppose we have nothing to say. As far as economic determinism is concerned the difficulty has been that even in their more refined forms which give due recognition to human activity, Marxist theories are notoriously clumsy when applied to underdeveloped countries, partly because class systems are embryonic and partly because modes of production are not mainly indigenous, but are controlled from other parts of the world. Finally, there are still some old-fashioned interpretations which are based on Weber's concept of the march of 'rationality' in the world. This bleak doctrine is also difficult to apply to transitional societies, which are often irrational in the extreme, and many have preferred this human absurdity to the life-less, more 'rational', bureaucracies of the West.

During the last twenty years various new attempts have been made to chart the movements of late capitalist society. Daniel Bell's *The coming of post-industrial society* is an example. Like Marcuse, he tries to account for the decline of emphasis on a work ethic and the prevalence of new consumption values involving hedonism and play. (Why do so many intellectuals in Europe or USA try to reject a bourgeois society from which they benefit?) In a less noisy manner the 'adversary' or 'counter-' culture of the 1960s still survives. Bell claims in fact that at least in the USA bourgeois culture vanished long ago.

Dependency

However, we are not concerned primarily with these post-industrial societies, but with countries where capitalism is still embryonic and parasitic. For the people of the Third World the attitudes of counter-culture are irrelevant. A developing bourgeoisie is not likely to embrace anti-bourgeois values.

What is most relevant here is the manner in which the people of poor countries regard their own societies. It is a striking fact that most African peoples are not much interested in ideologies and give their allegiance to people and to individuals rather than to causes. This in itself is probably a symptom of transition. Most intellectuals are aware that new tools of analysis are required in order to interpret their societies and as a guide to action, but they are also aware that they have not found them yet. A key factor is the religious one, since, unlike the people of the industrial-ised world, most Africans still adhere to some organised religion. It cannot be said, however, that it is the kind of faith which expresses itself in political action except at the level of individual charity. The radical priests who have taken up the cause of the masses in Latin America have no parallel in Africa, perhaps because the people are oppressed in a different way.

Survivals

As cultures pass away they leave some behind. This happens to individuals when they migrate either within their own country or to another one; it happened to the ethnic groups who went to America, and above all to millions of African who were forcibly taken to the Caribbean and to North and South America.

Persistent residues of old cultures can be found without difficulty, even after a people has spent several hundred years among different social customs; there remain oral traditions, music and dance, festivals, folklore and religion. They have survived in spite of, perhaps even because of, persecution and policies designed to exterminate them. In Latin America and the Caribbean they are more noticeable because many of the slave communities were allowed to remain in tribal groups, whereas in the Southern States of the USA they were deliberately dispersed. The traces of Yoruba culture in Brazil are considerable, an impact which became two-way when some of the ex-slaves returned to Nigeria bringing with them, amongst other things, the Brazilian style of architecture. In Trinidad and elsewhere in the West Indies there is a commercial saving system called *susu*, which is a direct survival of an identical Yoruba custom still called *ususu*. In Trinidad, as in most parts of Latin America, the carnival is a Latin festival. It is now African also; the carnival drums later became dustbin lids and eventually the steel bands which are now a part of world culture. These too were formerly banned by the colonial government.

Religious remainders in the same area include the *Voodoo* practices of Haiti, and the *Shango* cult in Trinidad and other Caribbean islands to which the Yorubas were taken. In this context most people think of the various kinds of soul music which have persisted in the USA and now affect the whole national culture. Music, although it always arises in one place out of special circumstances (like Reggae in Jamaica, spreads and become international. Reggae is particularly significant because the Rastafarians of Kingston believe in their strange mystical fashion in a return to Africa. The Reggae sub-culture, consisting of modes of speech, dress and hair-style, is now being transferred to deprived West Indians in Britain.

The above examples constitute green shoots from roots of the transplanted tree of culture, which in its original form could not survive. A similar process occurs within any society, since in one sense culture is a preservation of the past. In most cases where total transformations like the industrial revolution have taken place, the culture of the pre-industrial folk survives only as something which blows in the wind. In all European countries, in addition to age-old irrational superstitutions, there are pagan religious survivals somehow now incorporated into Christianity; examples are the Roman Catholic festivals in the Mediterranean lands. The Christian customs of Christmas include ancient pagan elements like the presence of Santa Claus and the ritual burning of Christmas puddings.

In Africa the traditions are of course still there, especially with the older people, but the educated youth have lost them. Young people from the villages are flocking to the cities, but their powerful ancestors and traditional gods are left behind and no longer have to be propitiated.

Life in the old days was based on respect for elders, a respect which still remains, but in a diminished form, as a contemporary Nigerian poet, succinctly put it in his poem *The dead culture*:

In days gone
To salute seniors
We remove our shoes
And go prone
Today juniors
Salute seniors
In high tone
Wearing high shoes (4)

African art was also part of a total way of life. If the religious beliefs are taken away, old art forms lose their meaning so contemporary Africans no longer appreciate them. They are then considered 'primitive', and one is more likely to find on middle-class walls a flight of china ducks. (When artists themselves lose this same sense of totality what they produce, of course, is 'airport' art for toursts, economically important but otherwise without much value.) Likewise religious ideologies may survive; but only in disguise and often underground; they remain potent and alive but only as preserved mythologies like those of ancient Greece. Such are the Yoruba deities whom we encounter in the plays of Wole Soyinka. (They have also become, as it were, an alternative insurance policy if the new gods fail, as they often do.) Again, African dances used to mean something, being associated with the cycle of the seasons and the planting, tending and harvesting of crops, with birth, fertility and death. Now Africans will dance for quite other reasons in disco halls, and the village dances become a show of spectacle to be preserved as part of a museum or tourist culture. They have become strangers in their own land; spectators of the folk.

Oral traditions, once so totally part of culture, are disappearing fast even in largely illiterate societies. The elaborate structures of riddles and proverbs which young people were once taught by their elders, must pass away if only because we now do not have the time. The complex

rituals of greeting in Hausaland will have to be modified since they too
are leisurely; if civil servants spend half their mornings greeting each
other or saying farewell how can they do any work? (It seems appropriate to greet a labourer in the fields with, 'How is your tiredness?'—but
much less so a fat man at his desk.)

Finally, one should mention hair styles and costume, a sphere which
registers cultural influences like a seismograph. In Egypt the late President Nasser once made his belly dancers wear body sleeves; now his suc-
cessor has taken them off. President Nyerere frowned on the mini-skirt,
which President Banda banned, and Lee Kuan Yew has forbidden long
hair in males. Elsewhere girls were made to cover their breasts, but now
at cultural shows they are commanded to uncover them again. Such are
the cultural dilemmas of presidents.

Revivals

Some survivals are deliberately preserved or revived, in which case they
may change their form and much of their meaning. The English still
put up phallic Maypoles to dance around on village greens, even if they
do not know why, but May Day is now an international Labour Day.
Some revivals are notably artificial and faintly ridiculous, such as Morris
dancing in England, but the Scottish kilt is a natural survival because the
Scots are not yet independent; no doubt when they become so they will
remove it just as the Irish stopped talking Gaelic after freedom came.
The white-robed priestly caste known as the Druids (once the leaders of
a resistance movement against the Romans) now move in procession
through the Welsh valleys each year at the Eisteddfod, the national
festival of Wales and in the USA the United Ancient Order of Druids—a
kind of Rotarian body with harmless secret rites—performs good works.
The bloody conflicts of the past are turned into pageantry, which is nevertheless a genuine cultural event involving the people. Can one say the
same for Ben Hur or the Ten Commandments on the screen?

It is apparent from these few selected instances that survivals and revivals are both political and religious. They are also essentially artistic
activities. As John Cowper Powys so powerfully demonstrated in his
monumental novels, the defeated Celtic gods still haunt the British
countryside in many areas for those who are attuned to their presence.

Nationalism

The fact that I have unconsciously returned to my own culture is an
indication of the tenacity of national cultural roots. That is how it has

132

been for a long time in Europe, and the USA has been able to American-
ise so many different ethnic groups, including the Africans, because they
were gathered from separate places all over the earth.

In the modern world conscious attempts to create or preserve cultures
are fueled by nationalism, which takes the form of liberation movements
or national consolidation when independence comes. Nkrumah's 'African
personality' myth makes no more sense than a European personality. It
is sometimes said that the obstacles to African unity are political, not
economic, whereas they are both, since the economic links are still not
between African countries but between these countries, Europe and USA.
This is why, in francophone Niger, one of the poorest countries in the
world, you can buy caviar, croissants, bottled Vichy water and holly and
mistletoe at Christmas time.

This is why culture must *first* be national, as Fanon insisted, and must
be fought for if necessary on the battlefield. That so many African
countries did not have to fight, is one reason for the frailty of their
nationalism. What the newspapers always refer to as the 'rich culture' of
the African peoples is still largely traditional and ethnic, so that the
leaders of the new nations have to play down or modify tribal customs
in the name of national unity. Central to many Nigerian and other African ethnic cultures was the existence of secret societies, whose annual
masked festivals figure prominently, for instance, in Yoruba and Ibo culture. But now in the cause of national development, the Nigerian government has found it necessary to attempt to curb their activities by insisting
that persons holding public office should cease to belong to them. The
result is that something which was at the heart of traditional tribal culture has somehow to become marginal and less vital. Yet the persons
who are responsible for carrying out the decrees, themselves belong to
both worlds, the local and the national one, and if they are secret how
are we to tell who the members are? In spite of these complications the
political process has to continue and there is no other way.

Conclusion

The answers to some of the predicaments we have noted are implicit in
the questions. Transition is inevitably a time of confusion. Parts of older
cultures fuse with parts of new ones, as is most evident in the sphere of
religious belief (where indigenous Christian churches more suited to
African needs have multiplied).

Otherwise the story is mainly one of the co-existence of diverse, even
contradictory elements. These are apparent everywhere within material

133

culture, symbolised by the simultaneous presence of ultra-modern air-conditioned buildings and mud huts; of donkeys and cows and camels mixed up with the city traffic. Similarly with regard to ideal culture, contrasting concepts, values and beliefs co-exist inside individual heads. People are not consistent even in relatively static and stable societies; we should not be surprised therefore if 'transitional man' has a transitional mind.

It follows that if the denizens of the Third World are to embrace other peoples' technology they are unlikely to abandon all their yesterdays. Indeed, the fact that it was not their own technology to begin with makes it less likely. An extreme example of one kind of cultural co-existence is provided by some Middle East cultures, especially Saudi Arabia, where the same man who attended a technological university in the USA can apparently inhabit what modernists would regard as a medieval mental world. In other countries the solution (if it is one) is less simple, since the countries with no oil money have to develop themselves, whereas the oil-rich countries are importing not only technology but technicians and teachers. For religious reasons they are therefore able to keep the two spheres, the material and the mental, wholly distinct. This is less possible elsewhere, but precisely because of this the old cultures are largely doomed.

Traditional leaders talk of preservation and revival, but their own lives may not correspond. They also talk of bridges between the old and the new; the imported Western customs and indigenous behaviour. What I have set out above is intended to show that this is a dangerous fallacy. It is particularly dangerous when foreigners talk of building bridges between advanced countries and those which are not. It is not 'bridges' which are needed but a recognition that, in historical terms, the affluent part of the world is rich because the rest is poor, and vice versa. Disraeli, with reference to the nineteenth-century British proletariat, talked of 'two nations' when it should have been one; at that time those middle-class persons who thought in terms of bridging the gap went in for charity and good works. In the modern global economy the parallel is exact; we have foreign 'aid'. But the two economic spheres are not separate. There is only one world.

REFERENCES
1 Turnbull, C, *Man in Africa* David and Charles, 1976, 79.
2 *Ibid*, 268.
3 *New Nigerian* 16 November 1977.
4 Vatsa, *Col* M F,

8

FREEDOM OF EXPRESSION

Any discussion of intellectual freedom is in danger of getting stuck in
the deep bogs which are the traditional controversies on the nature of
human freedom, a conflict which is likely to continue until doomsday.
The positions we take up on this usse rest on political and religious assumptions and on the kind of society we live in. All that we can provide
is a rough map of the battlefields and a guide to the forces which are engaged.

The mood of idealism generated by the death of millions of people in
World Way II caused democratic political leaders to formulate slogans for
the better world which it was hoped that victory would bring. As early as
1941, President Roosevelt, in his State of the Union message, propounded
the four freedoms which should constitute human rights everywhere.
These were: freedom of expression, freedom from fear, freedom from
want and freedom of religious faith. Later, after the war, in 1948, the
United Nations issued a Declaration of Human Rights which the Soviet
Union did not sign.

It has long been appreciated that there are several kinds of 'freedom'
and that religious and political freedom is conditioned by economic
freedom and vice versa. When the United Nations became disunited, one
of the issues which divided the two power blocs was that concerning human liberty. The liberal capitalist camp insisted that individual freedom
to say or think what one likes had to be based on an absence of political
control and coercion. The opposing communist camp declared that these
intellectual freedoms were meaningless to ignorant people who had nothing to eat. When the necessities of life are absent, the opportunity to say
or write without interference is an irrelevant luxury. They declared that
the right to unfettered expression could not make the people free if the
only liberty they have is a freedom to starve. These controversies were not
new, and were based on the fact that there are no absolute freedoms but
only different kinds and degrees of liberty which often clash—the freedoms of the few have depended on the slavery of the many. In the harsh

135

world of Great Power confrontation it became increasingly clear that in most places these freedoms remained remote abstractions. Both sides claimed that their kinds of freedom alone were real and that their opponents were hypocrites or monsters. The arguments have been intensified since President Carter launched his campaign on human rights.

Meanwhile, the countries of the Third World proclaimed that they were non-aligned and neutral. This has never really been the case; some were more neutral than others, according to their strategic situation. In one respect the Third World is closer to the communist bloc because they are poor and freedom from want should receive priority—these countries are demanding the right to share in the wealth of the industrialised world. As an African delegate at the United Nations has remarked, 'Human rights begin with breakfast'. China can provide a model for them to follow, but even the most well-disposed observer cannot claim that absolute freedom prevails in that country. Are we to conclude, then, that one kind of freedom precludes another? Must we accept as a dreadful necessity that social, economic and cultural development require coercive direction and an absence of individual choice? Hegel defined freedom as 'the recognition of necessity', and Marx insisted that the necessity was economic. It is these questions we must now examine.

Types of impediment

Our main concern in this chapter is with official attempts, by positive intervention, to control free expression. However, we should not overlook the fact that underdevelopment by its very nature sets up almost irreducible barriers to the unfettered transmission of ideas, information, news and communication generally. It is difficult to apply these freedoms in a society where people cannot read, or where they are too poor to care whether they are theoretically 'free' or not.

In various contexts we have already discussed the undeveloped structure of the communication industries and the limitations imposed by the lack of an efficient economic infrastructure (roads, railways and so on); also the deficiencies noted in publishing, printing and bookselling, which cause information materials not to be available. Communications do not have to be controlled if they do not exist. Any discussion of these matters, therefore, must examine problems which differ both in kind and degree from those in developed countries. The following are the main categories of material which may cause offence.

136

Obscenity

The considerable literature on censorship in liberal or pluralistic societies has concentrated in recent times on the alleged evils of obscene materials and the social dangers of the commercial exploitation of sex.

This concern mainly dates from the time when the masses in Western societies became literate and when mass-produced literature became cheap. Before the nineteenth century there had always been a market for pornography (politely called erotica), but it was not available for the common people, mainly because it was expensive. This has been called censorship by the purse. At the present time the publication of such materials has become big business, but it has not yet been transferred to developing countries, even where there is no official attempt to prevent their importation. If there is a small market for literature generally (apart from textbooks) the demand for 'dubious' literature will be equally small.

Such materials are symptomatic of affluence and characteristic of 'permissive' societies. People who live in subsistence economies find life too basic to bother with such frivolities. Even those who are part of the more transitional sectors of society are in any case restrained and conditioned by religious sanctions which have largely dissolved in the industrialised West. It is possible that governments may be faced with a flood of pornographic literature at a later date when their peoples become more sophisticated. Meanwhile, there is merely a trickle and it is not a social problem; so much so that many university students do not know what pornography is.

It therefore seems necessary to explain what we are discussing at a popular level. Books exploiting sexual interests are certainly on the bookstalls, particularly in hotels and airports, but these are mostly the 'soft' porn to be found all over the world. Almost any kind of literature can arouse sexual feelings, but this literature is written solely or mainly for that purpose. Although from a literary point of view these paperback novels are rubbish, it is not these which come under attack. It cannot be said that they contribute to development or the elevation of the human spirit, but they are relatively harmless. More significant are the illustrated magazines, mostly imported, whose prototypes are *Penthouse* and *Playboy* and their British equivalents. There is certainly a greater demand for these for the obvious reason that they have visual appeal. Again, they are expensive and do not constitute a serious cultural threat. There is undoubtedly a considerable demand for pictures of nude ladies, which decorate many domestic walls, even in Muslim areas where pictorial representation is supposed to be taboo. It has sometimes been claimed that pre-literate people cannot recognise pictures, but there is evidently no difficulty here. In some countries periodicals of this type are banned, but not in West Africa.

It needs to be emphasised that a large part of true or 'hard' pornography, as distinct from that dealt with above, consists not just in pictures of the nude, but depicts human sexual activity in all its variations. It is this type of material that is unlikely to be found in developing countries, first because it is too expensive, and second, because it would be seized by the authorities as offensive to public opinion, particularly to religious susceptibilities (a small underground market exists, of course, as it does everywhere, mainly consisting of little men selling postcards unfit for posting). Those who advocate total freedom of publication sometimes forget these 'action pictures', which would probably strike them as being alarmingly unsuitable for their daughters' education. (Most of the argument on this subject revolves around the possible harm which might be done to children and unbalanced persons.)

One of the difficulties which arises in attempting to control indecent material (including films as well as books), has always been that many serious works of art contain matters which puritan critics have considered to be obscene and which, therefore, in some countries have been banned under censorship laws. This is a loss to literature and an unjustifiable interference with cultural freedom. Once laws about obscenity are on the statute books, it is likely that serious literature, especially fiction, will be affected. In European countries and in the USA, where formerly repressive legislation existed to control expression on these grounds, the laws have now been liberalised.

Similarly, there are few objections now raised against medical work and literature on sex education and family planning. There were once pressure groups which tried to ban this type of educational activity but now, except in some countries where the laws of state and religion are combined, that particular battle has been won. In the same way books investigating or depicting sexual habits and practical manuals of sex techniques are usually not considered offensive. That kind of repression has mostly been swept away, but more recently there has been a backlash against the alleged permissiveness of modern society. In Britain a 'gay' periodical has been successfully repressed because it published a serious poem implying that Jesus Christ must have been familiar with sexual love. Legions of light have been recruited; alarming ladies and eccentric peers have appeared on public platforms with Malcolm Muggeridge.

Meanwhile, in the new countries, critics of cultural imperialism have deplored the importation of Western decadence in literary as well as other forms (such as the wearing of platform shoes). Wickedness, it is asserted, is an alien invention to be fought against and stamped upon. In Africa there has also been a tendency to insist that all sexual perversions and variations, including unorthodox positions, have been imported from Europe or America. They represent, it is alleged, a form of sexual imperialism designed to undermine indigenous institutions. Transfer of technology may have failed but the transmissions of wickedness succeed. Concerning these notions, a certain healthy scepticism is appropriate; sexual exploitation, as part of the history of colonialism, was a reality, but it manifested itself mainly in the relations between rulers and ruled.

Violence

There is evidence to show that in many countries crime and anti-social behaviour have been prompted or triggered off by gangster values portrayed in literature, especially comics, or in films. Young people have been influenced by exposure to these things. Allowing for such tendencies in human nature, the social sources of criminal behaviour are to be sought in the conditions which exist in the countries of the Third World.

With regard to the extent of the influence of the cinema, a warning note should be sounded. In Nigeria, with a population of perhaps seventy million, the country has only about a hundred cinemas as against at least two thousand in Britain. With this qualification, we can certainly point to probably undesirable influences from violence on the screen, but more significant is the fact that there is no suitable alternative to such entertainment. In Nigeria one can see small boys playing as fighting, imitating the techniques popularised by the actor Bruce Lee in films from Hong Kong. Does this matter? No doubt it does, but the films are symptomatic of a general social situation rather than the cause of it. Children have always played soldiers.

With regard to the comics which feature violence and spread fascist values (including racism) there is a case for banning their importation. It is an example of a control of freedom which can be justified, but again the only positive solution is to provide healthy alternatives.

Blasphemy and heresy

In earlier centuries heretical literature and often the writers themselves were burnt. The denial of religious freedom was also fundamentally political; it is a ban which still exists in some countries. With regard to

139

African ex-colonial countries, all that can be noted is that religious freedom does usually exist and state governments are secular: that is to say,
the state is separated from religion. This is one method of preventing religious tyranny and was one of the reforms carried out by Kemal Ataturk,
the founder of modern Turkey.

In these secular societies, literature in favour of various possible religious faiths is tolerated, but there is a general tendency (perhaps supported by public opinion) to reject atheism. For example, in Nigeria in
1977, the Head of State declared that newspaper articles attacking organised religion would not be allowed. However, there is no censorship law
to that effect; the similar attitude which existed in Europe for so long
no doubt persisted because atheism was often associated with disrespect
towards the state as well as a rejection of the deity. It was symptomatic
of a subversive attitude, since rulers like to pretend that God is on their
side, especially in war time; He legitimises their authority and their behaviour.

Political control
In the widest sense, control of free expression for any of the above reasons
is a political act. Obscenity, heresy, and the advocacy of violence may
undermine the authority of the state, or to be more precise, the stability
of a particular government. We now come to the various controls which
are directly political in the sense that they deny the right of citizens to
criticise the form of the state or the behaviour of its leaders.

Some kind of censorship has existed since government came into being,
and in certain areas (for example, national security), still prevails in all
societies. (The difficulty is that national security can be interpreted in
such a fashion that tyrannies are established.) Liberal capitalist democ-
racies, including those which have mixed economies and democratic
socialist governments, aim at reducing all forms of control over the expression of opinion to the minimum consistent with the safety of the
nation. Marxists have denied that this freedom is real, since it exists within class structures where capitalist exploitation still prevails. Whether it
is negated or not, the fact remains that with some minor area of restric-
tion, people in the West are relatively free to read, publish or broadcast
what they like. The main characteristic of the countries which call themselves socialist, such as the Soviet Union and China, is that they reject
such lack of control on ideological grounds.

The reaction against Stalinism amongst socialists has produced Euro-
communism and an insistence that communism can have a human face

and a liberal content; this remains to be seen. Meanwhile, socialists claim that the lack of freedom in existing radical societies is a perversion of Marxism, while their antagonists insist that it is inherent in the ideology. I am writing from within a liberal tradition (however tattered that may be) and cannot accept the arguments for censorship in the name of building a just society; such arguments have been constant since Plato's Republic, and they are not consistent with individual freedom.

With regard to the non-communist world, the situation ranges from the savage total kind of censorship which now exists in South Africa, through the various, scarcely less vicious, methods used in Latin America, to the relatively benign state of affairs in African countries such as Nigeria. It is difficult to generalise, if only because a lack of freedom may suddenly be relaxed by a change of government (as recently in India) or the reverse process may happen—a repressive government will clamp down further controls. In Argentina in 1977 at least a dozen journalists were arrested or 'disappeared', and the country's leading journalist and publisher, Jacobo Timerman, was imprisoned and tortured; another, Hector Ferreiros, was riddled with bullets. Some of these abductions and murders are carried out by extremist political groups, but the security forces are usually directly or indirectly involved. All this happens in a country where the President, Jorge Rafael Videla, is on record as being in favour of a free press. In Nicaragua in January 1978 a journalist was murdered under similar circumstances.

Compared with these brutalities and with their own former policies, the current Soviet habit of incarcerating dissident writers in mental homes seems relatively mild. An alternative practice adopted in the Soviet Union and in East Germany and other countries in Eastern Europe, is to 'allow' dissidents to leave the country. Likewise in South Africa, the white editor Donald Woods made his dramatic escape in January 1978.

In those countries where human rights have been systematically violated, it is obviously not safe for people to express themselves freely. However, there are many countries in Africa where writers can feel reasonably safe most of the time. In new countries political stability is not to be expected, and governments consider that some kind of guidance is necessary. They are not usually democratic societies, and if other forms of individual freedom are curtailed then one would expect some restraint to be put on expression. It is claimed that standards of journalism are not high and the press may lack responsibility. Governments often state that they welcome constructive criticism, by which they usually mean comment which is not unfavourable. In the countries under discussion press, radio and television are usually owned or controlled by the government. The most likely alternative (not usually possible in new countries) is ownership and control by private enterprise. This is equally open to objection as business interests are socially irresponsible and may finance and support political parties. It is, of course, usual for advertisers both in the press and on radio and television to provide income for the mass media, but this does not represent control or even influence in any direct form. Purists object to commercial advertising which is, of course, notably absent in communist countries, but in most countries there are worse evils to contend with.

With regard to radio and television, the British model of public corporations, which are to a large extent free from Government interference, can be quoted as a satisfactory solution to a most difficult social problem. But in countries with a shorter history and less stable circumstances, such a desirable state of affairs is not possible. Even where public boards exist, they have not sufficient autonomy to be free from the interference of governments which provide their money. With radio and television the censorship position is very sensitive. The argument is used that a largely illiterate population can easily be misled or misinformed and is peculiarly vulnerable to alarmist rumours. There can easily be inflammable situations involving, for example, ethnic antagonisms which can get out of control; accordingly the need for guidance does seem to be there.

In the same way it is difficult to see how, under similar circumstances, the press can be wholly independent. In Nigeria, which is not unusual in being governed by a military regime, there is a degree of freedom which is greater than most other African countries; there are no censorship laws and no official ideology which has to be followed. Nevertheless, public expression of opinion is not free. Journalists know that they can be prosecuted or imprisoned under various military decrees relating to state security. As a rough general rule they know what topics to avoid (this is sometimes called self-censorship). From time to time individual journalists may slip up and are questioned by the police or temporarily shut up. Also issues of periodicals which have given offence have been seized. This activity is relatively mild, but it does represent control; the people feel that they never know precisely what is happening.

In may African countries attempts to ban individual books or particular issues of periodicals occur by fits and starts—but the absence of a large or articulate reading public may make such procedures superfluous. The situation in South Africa is wholly different, and customs officials have a very long and folish list of books which they are supposed to stop entering the country. I was personally held up at Johannesburg Airport for some time because a customs official insisted that a book called *African genesis* (about evolution) must be on the prohibited list.

The above makes brief reference only to the fact that freedom is limited in most countries of the Third World. I am adding here a list of the most common controls.

1 *Censorship laws*: Where they exist these lay down that certain types of material are liable to be seized and the publishers (and sometimes the booksellers) prosecuted. This represents censorship *after* publication, although the mere existence of the laws may inhibit publication. There are also various other statutory laws relating to sedition and/or crimes against the state. Under legislation of this kind nobody is safe, and the possibility of arbitrary arrest keeps people in line.

2 *Control of the customs*: There are often regulations which exist quite independently of other forms of censorship. Customs officers are equipped with lists of books which may not enter the country. The Irish list was notorious at one time but has now been reduced. South Africa has already been mentioned.

3 *Censorship of mail*: It is, of course, possible to seize not only published material but private letters, especially those going abroad. Such activity is often secret so that citizens are intimidated.

4 *Libel*: There is one area where the individual really needs protection against writers whether in books or periodicals. Most countries have a law of libel and in some cases writers can easily be victimised by unscrupulous persons going to law about *accidental* libels, for example unwittingly using a man's name for a character in a novel.

5 *Quasi-legal councils or boards*: Films, the press, radio and television may operate systems of self-control where they set up their own councils to check on abuses. This is often advocated as an alternative to official censorship.

6 *Pressure groups*: These are perhaps less vocal in most developing countries but everywhere one finds religious and political organisations who bring pressure to bear on individuals or institutions which publish material of which they disapprove. In extreme cases writers, cinema managers, or producers of radio or television programmes face physical violence. In other instances (as in Britain) such organisations, or even individuals, attempt to use whatever laws may exist to launch prosecutions. In can be said that if large numbers of people hold illiberal views, then freedom is impossible. Historically, most of this type of activity

has been directed against alleged obscenity, but as a political process it is even more dangerous.

7 *Expurgation*: The texts which writers hopefully produce may be tampered with by publishers for political or religious reasons, usually by omitting the offensive materials. (Some newspapers leave blank spaces as a protest against this kind of censorship.) Special 'harmless' editions of the classics are produced for children and in other cases the offending passages are indicated by dots or asterisks or printed in a foreign language; at least in such cases one knows what tampering with the text there has been. Some writers expurgate their own work when, in old age, they come to disapprove of their former selves. Widows have a tendency to destroy the work of their defunct husbands.

8 *Censorship before publication*: In the Soviet Union writers who have been branded as subversive cannot get their work published at all. Professionally, they have become 'non-persons', and unless they emigrate, can only keep silent or send their writing abroad (which invites further persecution); or their material can be circulated clandestinely. In other countries there are milder variations on this method, where writers know that they will not find a publisher or cannot print what they like. This may include items such as correspondence in the press.

9 *Physical intimidation*: As indicated above, this extreme form of oppression persists. Amnesty International has detailed evidence which governments either ignore or deny.

10 *Economic circumstances*: All the symptoms of underdevelopment such as illiteracy, language difficulties and a weak economic infrastructure are potent curbs on freedom. Foreign domination in the production of books, is likely to continue. Recording companies are mostly not indigenous and the entrenched position of the Western news agencies inhibits cultural independence. This absence of autonomy is perhaps the most pervasive and persistent of all cultural constraints.

11 *National aggrandisement*: The last of the 'methods' just mentioned refers to the absence of cultural freedom resulting from colonial activities. A somewhat neglected aspect is the historical suppression of subject cultures and associated with it, the removal of the evidence of former magnificence. One of the first acts in the long history of imperialism was the total destruction by Cortes of the literature of the Aztecs. Since then repressions have been perpetrated either by one nation on another or within their frontiers as in the suppression of cultural minorities. One characteristic of the post-colonial era is the presence in the museums and libraries of Europe and America of so much of the past of

conquered peoples. The artefacts of once living cultures are now ghostly items displayed in the mausoleums of the West.

I am not discussing whether these objects should be returned to their original homes, but simply noting that this looting still continues and includes the transfer of libraries and literatures by legitimate or often more dubious means. In order to study Africa or India one has to go to the libraries and museums of Europe, and now it is inevitably happening that many European topics can be studied only in America. Cultural transfers follow in the wake first of military conquest, and then of economic power. An extraordinary feature of the reparation conditions which were inflicted on the defeated powers in World War I was the obligatory return of art treasures and library materials to the countries from whence they originally came. No such reshuffling of past relics is likely on a global scale, and these absent witnesses to the conflicts of former times are symptoms of a parallel absence of historical freedom. That is what happened and the consequences are naturally with us still.

Conclusion: the liberal dilemma

Implicit in much of this discussion is the belief that freedom of expression is not only desirable but essential for human progress, and it is an ideal for which many throughout history have suffered and died. We betray whatever progress may have taken place if we deny the need for this continued struggle. Because of this I have found that students, in discussing these questions, state that all forms of censorship are intolerable. This does justice to their high intentions, but it emerges that when a specific (possibly hypothetical) instance is cited, they immediately insist that such a thing should not be allowed. For example, a postgraduate student who had lived in Britain, declared that films on British television which portrayed Africans as painted savages should be banned in view of the misconceptions and stereotypes so widely prevalent amongst the British people. One sees the point, but once one admits the need for such acts, then the case for total freedom is undermined.

It is a most complex issue, and in developing countries, which are necessarily trying to move in a particular direction and attempting to change the attitudes of millions of people, how can unrestricted exposure be permitted to every kind of influence, some of which are wholly inimical to development? What follows is that valid ideals can only be carried out in the light of particular circumstances. It is, for example, generally recognized that in time of war certain restrictions on individual liberty have to be imposed—those who openly side with the enemy may have to

145

be interned. The circumstances of development are not unlike those of war-time. Once this is admitted, the way is open for abuse by powerful vested interests who are concerned only with their own privileges and position. But control of unbridled power is what politics is about.

The remedies lie in appropriate political action to defend public and private liberties. For this reason, at the time of writing there has been an agitation in Nigeria to insert into the new democratic constitution a clause affirming the freedom of the press. It is not, of course, just a matter of the 'people' or the masses versus the government. Particular regimes represent or profess to represent certain classes or factions within society, and claim that their enemies cannot be allowed to agitate for their overthrow. If a monstrous tyranny is deposed, should those who benefited from its existence be allowed to campaign for its return? One must conclude that intellectual freedom is not a transcendant absolute, but a goal to be achieved. Always we must ask: freedom for whom, and for whose benefit?

9

MASS COMMUNICATIONS

Throughout this enquiry we have looked at aspects of human communication and the impediments they encounter. In this chapter attention is focused on film, radio, television and the press. We can assume that part of the success of development depends on these mass media. There is now considerable literature on communication: departments have been set up in universities and it has become part of the academic scene, an interesting example of how new subjects arise from areas which were formerly interdisciplinary. Much of the academic literature on communication is technical and I cannot hope to refer to it here. Even so, on human communication generally certain basic points need to be made.

The first is that all human communication can only be partial. Anyone who has experience of the teaching process either as teacher of learner knows how limited communications can be. In the same way interpersonal relations largely consist of passing from one misunderstanding to another. For physical and psychological reasons we are alone, and much of our time is spent trying to overcome or transcend this solitude.

In another work I have adopted the triple analysis which distinguishes three types of communication. There is a trinity consisting of our relationship with God, with other people and with ourselves. (There is no significance in the order.) The quality of anyone's life depends on how effective, how honest and how connected these three types of relationship are. In traditional society this perception is all one so that there is no clear distinction between different modes of contact or connection. In such a context the individual is not 'alone' in the sense which I have suggested, and an emphasis on aloneness is largely a symptom of modern developed civilisation. Many religious and political movements are driven by a need to overcome this isolation. We are not concerned with them but they should be part of our awareness in this investigation; otherwise we are in danger of regarding communication problems as purely technical.

A complete investigation would eventually deal with the nature of human love (including sexual love), without which true communication is impossible. This has been a major theme for the psychologists, and some modern gurus (like Eric Fromm in the USA) have stressed that if we cannot reach an accommodation with, or acceptance of, ourselves we are unlikely to communicate successfully with other people. Those who cannot trust themselves are suspicious of others. But we must return to our main theme, which is person-to-person communication.

The second basic point is that we do not have to assume that all communication is desirable. This is mentioned because much of the literature on the subject has taken it for granted that all barriers to full communication should be removed. One imagines this is how it must be in heaven, and no doubt the angels understand one another very well. But we are not yet in Paradise and earthly arrangements may require a degree of non-communication, as every happily married person appreciates. Within the marital predicament perfect communication would be intolerable and so also in most other social and political relationships.

One can deal with this matter by distinguishing between different kinds of communication; the most satisfactory form may consist of messages which do not have to be spoken. Such is the significance of silence. The most profound transmissions of meaning cannot be directly expressed in speech but must be made by other symbolic means; so it is the realm of art (especially music which is 'pure') and in religious parables that such expression is made. It is also in the sphere of prophecy and extra-sensory perception (ESP). That we are not extending our explorations so far should not lead us to imagine that this realm of discourse is not valid. It must lie behind all our discussions, which are necessarily limited to levels more amenable to rational analysis; these are, in any case, sufficiently complicated and extensive. We could for example devote all our attention to the problems of language but this alone would deal only with the country of the blind and there remains the problems of visual perception. This enquiry, then, is mainly limited to the communications we can see and hear and interpret rationally. The symbolic transmissions that we receive from poetry and music or any of the arts may also be rational and expressed in words or realistic pictures but the meanings are not in the rationality: they arise from something 'far more deeply interfused'.

Traditional societies

In the villages of the past and in some of them even now there were no 'masses' and no 'media'. We should therefore note how human intercourse

148

differed from the communication processes of a national state. The methods used were extensive, varied and effective; I have grouped them according to the means of perception:

1 *Visual*: Some communication systems like smoke signals or even drums were used to pass messages from one community to another but most were practised *within* the village and these are our main concern. Many visual means of communication are supplementary or used to provide emphasis. They included the 'body language' which is part of any culture and involves facial expressions, modes of walking and gestures of all kinds. Likewise costume and ceremonial dress are important, particularly in ceremonial masquerades, when masks are worn. These costumes often represent or embody ancestral spirits or emanations from another world, and in many cases may be taken in some sense to be 'real' rather than somebody dressed up.

Special significance used to be attached to tribal marks or scars since they usually indicated tribal (but not individual) identity. Similarly all the visual arts communicated meanings which were not just aesthetic, but could be used in many cases for magical or practical purposes. There were also private messages such as those conveyed by the tying of knots in grass. Such signs are similar to those used by hunters and travellers, and were utilised for his own purposes by Baden Powell in his prescriptions for the Boy Scouts, a movement designed to return young urbanised people to an imaginary tribal life. In the remoter past in all societies war paint was intended to frighten the enemy, just as modern cosmetics are meant to attract or to please a potential friend.

2 *Aural*: The more specific communications were of course oral and aural. Town criers were almost universal, using bells, gongs, special horns or drums. These were for important official announcements. The inherited wisdom and view of the world held by the community was expressed in artistic form in drama, folk tales, riddles, proverbs and songs. Drumming performed the same function and the so called 'talking drums' found in some countries were also concerned with specific messages. Quite apart from its usual function, singing was, and is, a constant feature in the work songs to be found all over the world. This is a special kind of communication designed to provide inspiration rather than transmit messages.

Such methods remind us of the fact that much of this traditional communication is *ritualised*; that is to say, it proceeds by ancient formulae and the content is prescribed to meet situations which constantly recur.

149

When such procedures take place there is no need for more than a slight individual contribution. But on a personal level there is still much to be said and this includes the sending of messages, naturally verbal, in a non-literate society. This brings us to ordinary conversation, the most common form of all. The varieties of talk include the sublime, the obscene, the abusive and the ridiculous; even the apparent triviality of gossip should not be overlooked. In many communities gossip is frowned upon and thought more suitable for women, who are precluded from the solemnities of public affairs. Yet not all gossip is malicious and a curiosity about others is preferable to indifference.

Finally it would be unrealistic to omit religious observances and the prevalence of prayer. The atheist would claim that this cannot be communication since there is Nobody there and no palpable response, but this is not the view of the communicators who are the people involved. Many of these methods persist into modernised societies but they now take different forms or have lost their importance. Many are profoundly modified even by the introduction of literacy.

3 *Other forms*: It is not always appreciated that activities which serve other purposes have in addition an important communication value. Markets which bring buyers and sellers from large areas around have always been news and communication centres. Festivals and annual ceremonies preserve and pass on the customs by which the past transmits its values and beliefs to the present and future. In most of these ceremonies dancing is a common feature and a powerful agent of communication—not as some have supposed simply a means of erotic discourse.

Religious activity is often regarded as a kind of social cement, binding communities together by a variety of aural and visual techniques. Witches and their enemies the doctors, oracles and sorcerers, necromancers and diviners, prophets, priests and *shamans* are all interpreters of signs and symbols, essential intermediaries between the palpable world and whatever lies beyond the veil. Many of the above manifestations are not so much methods of communication as cultural institutions which use communication techniques; in this sense culture is communication.

Such customary practices are far from simple. With regard to African greetings systems, Fafunwa (1) states that 'It is perhaps not exaggerating to say that the Africans have the most complicated verbal and physical communication system in the world and the child must master the various salutations of his own ethnic group before he reaches maturity.

Characteristics of traditional communication
As distinct from mass media the methods summarised above are interpersonal, and therein lies their strength and their significance. But a corresponding limitation was that they were restricted to the village level.

Of the three types of communication mentioned it is difficult to understand precisely what form communication with the 'self' took, since the self was not believed to exist as a separate entity. This is no doubt a gross oversimplification. Most traditional societies provided for some kind of privacy and there have always been 'marginal' people half outside the community; it is a privilege sometimes accorded to the aged (as distinct from the elders). In extreme environmental conditions such as those which exist amongst desert peoples like the Tuareg of the Sahara, communality even now is so total that conversations between individuals have to be specially arranged by wandering away from the group which is always there.

Since these personal means of contact preserved tribal identity they also served to exclude outsiders, an important part of their function. Many types of communication, including some earlier forms of literacy, were designed to preserve not only identity but also the secrecies of privilege. Even in modern societies there are various sub-cultures, including that of children, which develop their private languages.

Communications of this interpersonal kind are more effective, with regard to immediacy, than printed or written records. Recorded information persists and is no less accurate in the future than it was in the past. The limitations of oral cultures in this respect are clear. Their perceptions of the past depend on the tribal memory, which is both fallible and often deliberately falsified. Their understanding of the present is limited by the presence of secret organisations in their midst, such as those which exclude women, and by the prevalence of rumour. The repetition of verbal communications, especially those distorted by malice and hostility, results in drastic modifications to whatever truth they once contained.

In such communities everybody 'knows' everything, but what they know cannot easily be verified; knowledge resides in the person, not in the messages transmitted. I have stressed these circumstances because our critique may lead one to suppose that the mass media are wholly

151

inferior in their impact. It is now time to consider their role with particular reference to national development.

Characteristics of mass communication

1 *Who are the masses?* The use of the term 'the masses' is not clear in any context but unfortunately cannot be avoided. In older usage it was often used as a term of abuse notably by conservative thinkers. Raymond Williams notes that it can refer to 'a many-headed multitude or mob: low, ignorant, unstable', but also that it can be 'a description of the same people but now seen as a positive or potentially positive social force'. (2) The double usage can be detected in discussions of the role of the 'media' (another unfortunate word). But on the whole it is the second usage, with its revolutionary implications, which is most preferred in developing countries. It is rightly felt that somehow the masses must be mobilised for development, and radio, the cinema, the press and television are agencies for this purpose.

With regard to quantity, a 'mass audience' is inevitably a relative term. It depends on how many people can read or afford radios or can be exposed to television or films. What is implied is a very large number who are not differentiated; in fact we do not know who they are. We do not usually regard a lecture given to three hundred students as mass communications. They are not 'the masses', but students with common motives and abilities. Likewise a preacher delivering his sermon may not ask for 'any questions', but his audience has already agreed to his message or they would not be there. On the other hand the same lecture or the same sermon broadcast or televised is clearly mass communication.

The audience may run into thousands or millions who have no characteristics in common except that they have ears and eyes. A film may not have a very large audience in any one cinema but of course it is produced for any number of cinemas and therefore has a mass distribution. Newspapers and some popular periodicals have a mass circulation since they may sell in millions and are produced, not for a particular section of the community, but for everybody who can read. But most books and periodicals have a 'minority' circulation and are not usually regarded as mass media; first because their circulation is relatively small, and second, because they are produced for a defined group of people with a common interest and often a similar educational level. This obviously applies to all specialist publications. I have laboured this point because

152

some critics have included all books as mass media. According to the approach used here this is inadmissible. In the case of books and pamphlets an exception is usually made for 'bestsellers' for example, novels whose sales run into millions. This category is not relevant in our context because the reading population is not large enough to support sales of this order.

2 *Simultaneous and immediate communication*: Another concept sometimes associated with the mass media is that their messages are simultaneous in the sense that they are absorbed by a mass audience all at the same time and may not be repeated. They have therefore an immediate quality, as compared with a printed book which may be read and re-read by individuals over an indefinite period. Normally people do not read last week's newspapers except when they live in inaccessible regions. However, this distinction applied mainly to radio and television, and should not be pressed too far. Increasingly, with the use of cassettes and videotapes, programmes can be repeated for individual needs. Similarly popular music on discs which have a mass distribution can be individually owned and played at will.

3 *Lack of feedback*: Personal communication provokes responses. It is two way and reciprocal; even at the somewhat diluted level of a university lecture some reaction is always present. With smaller groups where there are opportunities for discussion and questions the element of dialogue is naturally greater. All this, in the jargon of the subject, is called 'feedback' and it is characteristic of the mass media that generally there is no immediate feedback. Angry listeners can react to radio or television programmes they dislike by switching off and in extreme cases they have been known to attack the sets or throw them out of the window. Similarly to relieve ones feelings one can tear up the newspaper, but the producers or editors are not affected by these reactions. It is well known that audience participation also occurs in the cinema, and shots have been fired at the villain (or more often at the hero) on the screen, but no-one is damaged thereby—so that the producers of a mass-media programme do not know directly whether their messages are getting through in the manner which they intended.

Nevertheless several kinds of feedback can be organised, and as we shall see such arrangements can go some way to overcome the feedback limitation. All the media have means of discovering how many people are listening to their messages; at the lowest level they thus have some idea of their popularity. Newspapers, periodicals, recorded discs and cassettes have sales and circulation figures, and cinemas the statistics of attendance; these give some indication of quantity. Beyond this, correspondence columns are an important means by which readers of journals express their reactions, and the radio provides for audience response by question-and-answer programmes. In a more immediate manner radio and television can provide for instant participation from the public by telephone. Popular music programmes on radio have long featured listeners requests, a prominent feature of the overseas broadcasting of the BBC. The degree of feedback therefore is greater than has often been supposed. It is one of the responsibilities of the media producer to discover what audience responses are.

4 *Centralisation*: The very nature of a mass procedure implies that the messages are transmitted from one centre or at the most a few regional centres—depending on the size and resources of the country. This relative degree of centralisation is dictated by technology and the fact that the expensive equipment required cannot economically be duplicated all over the place. The mass media therefore are industrial undertakings, whereas a man giving a lecture under a tree is not an industry. This economic factor has important implications in underdeveloped countries as the media industries are dependent on overseas technical and economic support just like any others.

5 *Industrial dependence*: That the mass media in economically dependent countries are not fully in control of their own policies or programmes is a major impediment to their development role. The situation is similar with all the media.

The press
Leaving aside the question of ownership where foreign interest may be involved, the main economic factors here are, first, that newspapers lack the resources to organise an effective news-gathering system within their national or even regional area and, second, that they have to rely on established international news agencies for their overseas news; they cannot afford to employ correspondents all over the world. Both these limitations are serious.

Within the nation some of the economic obstacles are outside their control, notably the absence of good communications (roads, railways, cable etc.) This means that they find it difficult, first, to collect information, and second, to distribute it when printed. In many parts of Nigeria daily newspapers may be delivered only once a week. In the matter of news-gathering journalists also may not be able to get about because of the lack of transport facilities, both private and public.

Another handicap (made much of by hostile critics of the press) is that, being in its infancy, the profession of journalism has not reached a very high standard (naturally varying from country to country). It could hardly be otherwise. In most places efforts are being made to improve training facilities for journalists, often a neglected sector of the educational system. One serious result of this neglect is not so much the inaccuracy of reporting, nor even the bias or irresponsibility of comment (which is what over-sensitive authorities complain about), but an absence of what may be called 'quality' professional journalism. Because of this, features or educational articles, so important in developing an educated or informed public, are produced either by enthusiastic unqualified amateurs, by equally unqualified academics, or reproduced often without recognition 'by a correspondent' from overseas. None of these procedures is desirable. The first person is often semi-literate; the second produces academic jargon wholly inappropriate for mass circulation, and the third represents alien influences which may or may not be suitable. The answer may come from a more educated type of journalist and from a higher degree of ideological awareness.

These handicaps are serious enough, but probably much more dangerous is the inability to obtain world news except through sources with a Western bias. (Countries within the communist orbit have different problems.) Much attention has been paid to this at an international level, and in 1977 a Unesco conference in Nairobi made proposals for a Third World news agency to overcome the distortions which undoubtedly prevail in agencies such as Reuter and United Press. These are naturally more concerned with sensational or lurid items of news (often presenting new countries in an unfavourable or ludicrous manner), than they are with the success or failure of development. The distortions are often unconscious which makes these all the more harmful. Idi Amin is always in the news; Samora Machel, the President of Mozambique, and his policies are not. By the end of 1977 the proposed new machinery had not been set up and there has been inevitable opposition on the grounds that one kind of bias would be replaced by another, so that only the official version of events drafted by governments would be made available.

In developing countries there has been an inevitable trend that the press, originally largely owned by foreign intersts, should come under government influence and control. The main consequence has been a limiation on press freedom and a degree of censorship. The situation with periodicals is somewhat different. There are for example a number of transnational English-language periodicals in Africa, like *Drum* (monthly), some of which are largely indigenous.

Newspapers are influenced or controlled either by business or government interests. The first type of ownership is often socially irresponsible and may lead to links with political factions or pressure groups as happened with the Nigerian press before military rule. The second results in a press which reflects official policies and is to that extent not free. However, in a development context, it can be argued that freedom of the press cannot be paramount—an argument that has led to grave abuses in many countries.

Literacy
The weakness of indigenous press publishing arises partly from the low level of literacy, which results in relatively small circulation figures as compared with the press in developed countries. Most newspapers in Africa probably have a circulation of less than one million, as against a figure of about twelve million for a popular newspaper in Britain.

Cinema
In Africa the film industry is the sector in which cultural imperialism most noticeably prevails. There can be no doubt that people, especially the young who have flocked to the towns, are very much influenced by the type of films they regularly see. In developed countries, we are familiar enough with the alleged evil effects of violence, sex and anti-social values on the screen. In poor countries the same allegations can be made, but there are so many additional factors to be observed that it is an entirely different situation. Obviously the available films are not concerned or even consistent with national development; this is the negative aspect. Whether they are positively harmful is not so easy to establish.

Much official concern has been expressed in Nigeria and in late 1977 the federal government announced its intention of taking steps to control the importation of foreign films. One of the main national newspapers, the *New Nigerian*, welcomed this decision with considerable fervour: 'the foreign films being shown on Nigerian screens possess no social message, contain no social worth and lack entertainment value beyond mindless violence, sex and other harmful foreign vices'. (3) (It is commonly believed in Africa that sex was invented by aliens!) The leader then referred

156

to the earlier Hollywood impact, and: 'Then came the Indian invasion, especially in the Northern parts of our country, where the amorous exploits and implausible heroisms of Shammi Kapoor, Dev Anand and Dhramendra turned them into societal legends . . . As if all these were not enough cultural pollution, we next had the breed of Hong Kong [Chinese] films with a new and alien brand of blood, death and violence . . . The situation has now deteriorated to the point where American, Indian and Hong Kong films have a stranglehold on our cultural jugular'. The editorial then proceeded to the essence of the matter, the need for indigenous enterprise, which so far has not developed: 'Not only have they obviated the need for any serious effort at establishing an indigenous film industry, their enormous monopoly power has served to ensure that all home-grown films come out either still-born or handicapped'. We noted precisely this dilemma in the case of publishing and the solution is equally hard to come by; cultural imperialism and the alienation which it produces is rooted in long-term economic realities.

Radio and television
These two media, like the cinema, have a special significance because their impact is not dependent on literacy. They are inevitably government financed and controlled and used as agencies for promoting government policies. The degree of freedom of discussion allowed and the type of programmes permitted will depend on the type of government in control. The kind of independence which is possible for corporations like the British Broadcasting Corporation is not to be expected at this stage in developing countries. As distinct from the cinema there is indigenous ownership and control but alien influences manifest themselves in the foreign programmes, including feature films, which the networks have to use.

In Nigeria at least the media often seem curiously indifferent to the ideological implications of some imported entertainment. For example, when the Soweto disturbances in South Africa were the concern of world opinion, a television film was put on showing the Boers (in about 1830 considered the 'goodies') happily slaughtering Zulu 'savages'. No doubt they have to use what is available.

The potential influence of the mass media
How can the mass media be most effectively used to promote national development? This is a question which faces all new states. In developed countries it does not arise in the same way, but their cultural role is

equally great, since it is obvious that they have an impact for which there was no parallel in former times.

Because of this importance much attention has been paid to the exact nature of mass media impact, and certain conclusions have emerged. At first it was thought that the influence of the media for mass propaganda was almost limitless. In Europe observers were perhaps misled by the apparent success of mass methods of persuasion in Nazi Germany and in two world wars (particularly the 1914-18 war) on both sides. What was overlooked was the fact that these were crisis situations, perhaps without precedent before or since, and at such times normal human responses are in abeyance. Similarly extravagant claims were once made that by using the radio, and to a lesser extent the other media, people's fundamental attitudes would be changed, and this would be the essential factor in engendering progress. The theorists of development, insisted that unless traditional attitudes which were hostile or contrary to modernisation could be eliminated, then the required social transformation could not take place.

This analysis is largely correct, but accumulated evidence has shown that by themselves, the media cannot effect such a drastic reorganisation of the human mind. If other circumstances are propitious they can help, that is all. One might think common sense would indicate that unless there is some violent social convulsion people do not change their religious beliefs, nor do they drastically modify inherited attitudes. Very well, the developers have said, the impact of modern technology does represent a convulsive change, so this is where the mass media can step in—to remodel a broken mould. The proposals once sounded plausible but it has emerged that it is one thing to break up a way of life and quite another to replace it; the remedies are so superficial as to seem absurd.

What *has* been shown is that deeply held political, social, moral or religious attitudes can be *reinforced* by the use of the media, but mass persuasion can usually go no further. Even then, in this role of reinforcement, circumstances need to be favourable, and crude methods do not work. In most developing countries one is bombarded from above with constant exhortations: 'Be honest, hard-working, punctual, loyal, tidy, respectful, conscientious, thrifty, law-abiding, frugal, modest, chaste, humble, sober . . .' and so on through the gamut of social virtues.

However, this cannot be the end of the enquiry, and other human attributes are decisively influenced. Under suitable circumstances skills and aptitudes can certainly be transmitted by the mass media and this is the educational function mentioned later.

158

Culturally even more important is the matter of taste and the subliminal impact of visual images. Far beyond the realm of exhortation we are influenced in a subtle fashion by artistic symbols and by material which is apparently only recreational and therefore unimportant or 'harmless'. Curiously little attention has been paid to this major role of the media, whether it makes its impact felt on the screen (cinema or television) or in newspaper advertisements. (This neglect of imaginative processes reflects an understandable preoccupation with science, which in the popular mind is associated with the world of solid facts.)

Here we return to the Indian and other films mentioned above. The values of Hollywood films are well known and their possible bad influence sufficiently discussed. It has been thought that images of affluence on the screen contribute to the syndrome of rising expectations and produce revolutionary attitudes. There is little evidence to support this notion, perhaps because the audience rightly perceives the world portrayed as a kind of dream world or fairyland. Illiterate people find the relation between fact and fiction difficult to grasp so that they can easily confuse historical films with news items or vice versa. Some audiences are consoled to think that all the people slaughtered on the screen are not really dead but others are annoyed; they are being deceived.

Whatever the responses they are unpredictable and would certainly surprise the film-makers. The *New Nigerian* item about the film industry, quoted above, also asserted that 'the universal language of death, sex, violence and crime are offered for this market because more "serious" foreign films would not be understood: their values are not ours and . . . their norms are often incomprehensible to the average Nigerian cinemagoer', whereas in these 'action' films one can observe 'how enthusiastically the audience applauds gun battles, sword fights, Kung Fu, shop and boat robberies. All scenes of speeches or dialogue are received with hisses and total lack of interest. The situation has become intolerable'. Perhaps the writer might have added that dialogue is not particularly relevant anyway, as it is in a foreign language, and most people cannot read the sub-titles. It is for this reason no doubt, that the acting is strong and simple (what is usually called 'ham') and in this and other respects these films have the international appeal of the old silent films.

This type of critical damnation is all very well but the stressing of the 'foreign' evades the entire issue. It overlooks the fact that 'uneducated' audiences react the same everywhere and identical audience responses can be found in the poorer parts of cities anywhere in the world. The values of serious films or literature are always impenetrable to a majority of the people; they are alien not because they come from overseas but

159

because they are sophisticated and reflect a 'civilised' way of life un-known to the dweller in a shanty town who has never been to school.

If a popular film industry ever established itself in Nigeria, or any other African country, there is no reason to suppose that its values would be any less simple or its content any more elevated. All that can be said is that indigenous fantasy could be more culturally valuable than the foreign products. (It is noteworthy that at one time the Brazilian government insisted that all cinemas should devote one evening a week to Brazilian films or pay quite a heavy fine—many cinema owners preferred to pay the fine.)

The Indian film industry is particularly interesting since India is also a developing country. It seems reasonable to suppose that the film in-dustry developed there (in spite of American domination) because the sub-continent already had a long dramatic and musical tradition of its own. This tradition included public performance, as distinct from the cultural songs and dances of the folk. (The same of course is true of Japan and China; Hong Kong is another matter, but its culture is more Asian than British.) There are serious Indian films of the highest quality but it is not these which are exported to Africa, and audiences would be unhappy if they were.

It is arguable that the popular Indian films are less harmful than those from America or even Hong Kong. There are different kinds of viol-ence in these films and the Indian kind seems relatively healthy. Neither are they erotic in the Western sense. Not only is there no active sex but no kissing either. Their romantic scenes are not likely to trigger off public orgies or even private masturbation; the eyes (heavily made up for the purpose) are the windows of the soul. The films conform to an elaborately stylised pattern, not without artistic merit and certainly with genuine musical appeal. Their audiences understand the formula and the conventions and recognize the songs. The record industry bene-fits in consequence.

There is little harm in fairyland so long as no one suggests it is real. The values of this particular sector of the mass media are wholly false and, if they have any influence at all, merely reinforce attitudes which are already present amongst the masses. The same might be said for broadcast music, which is all that many people listen to on the radio. Popular music, whether Western or traditional, is not geared to develop-ment. No doubt such entertainment helps to keep the urban masses in their proper place and for this reason the privileged members of the new élite should welcome them.

A positive role in development

So far we have stressed the negative characteristics of the mass media, since these are most prevalent, particularly in the sphere of entertainment. It remains to discuss their considerable potentialities as agencies for promoting development. They have been used for this purpose all over the world and the following conclusions can be drawn from experience:

1   Centralized programming by radio or television, in order to be effective, needs to be supplemented by local personal activity. This is called a 'two-step' process and the second step may be more difficult than the first since it involves social organisation to follow up the message as transmitted.

Farming or health projects can be launched as a regular feature by radio but for them to be carried out the people in the villages must be organized and persuaded, not from 'above', but by those who have gained their confidence. Many projects fail because the villages are suspicious of government or party agents. Military regimes find it difficult to promote development in the rural areas because they have no mass organisation to support their decrees or to carry out their policies. Traditional rulers are used for this purpose; as a link to explain national policies to the people. They mostly have the confidence of the masses but whether they are enthusiastic about modernising policies is another matter. Local government is also supposed to be responsible for community development, but it is not part of a national organisation either, and may have its own interests to attend to. Finally civil servants of the conventional sort are often unsuitable, and some extension officers do not speak the local language. (One that I knew would not even go to the village concerned because the rough road would ruin his car.)

At the root of this dilemma is the much discussed gap—which is also one of communication—between the cities and the country. As President Nyerere once said, it is easier to get to the moon that to establish good communications with the 80 per cent of the people who live in the rural areas. In consequence the masses cannot be mobilised.

2   Many innovations or reforms have failed, even when supported by the mass media, because of quite simple mistakes on the part of those who devise the programmes. They usually arise from an inability to understand the mental world of illiterate people or the nature of their perceptions. (This may affect the success or otherwise of pictorial material such as posters.) Many of these mistakes cause the people to disbelieve the messages, owing to suspicion about their motivation or their

161

authenticity. The most famous example is probably the 'giant louse' on the screen, which was treated with derision because a louse is not that size. An agricultural film showing white labourers was also treated with contempt by its audience, since in their experience white men do not work on the land. It follows from all this that mass communication work must be highly professional; there can be no doubt that many radio programmes are simply not understood solely for language reasons.

3 We need not labour the economic and technical difficulties. In most countries, for obvious reasons, the number of television sets and even radios is limited. Even more decisive is the absence of electricity. In some parts of the world it has been policy to install village generators but this has not been done much in Africa. Perhaps the invention with the most far-reaching consequences is the transistor radio, which seems to make McLuhan's 'global village' a reality at last. This small machine has abolished the empty spaces and the trackless desert so that nobody need be totally isolated again. Its importance is, of course, limited by the manner of its use and the type of programmes it carries.

4 Finally, mention should be made of the use of mass media, especially television, for formal education purposes. Where there is a shortage of teachers closed-circuit television may be considered economical. (In Saudi Arabia, where women may not be taught by men, male teachers are allowed to appear on closed-circuit screens provided their faces are not shown.) In some francophone African countries extensive use has been made of television for education.

Conclusion

In most underdeveloped countries use of the mass media for educational or development purposes is still largely potential. Governments which claim to be revolutionary have used the media with remarkable success, notably in China, where the citizens never escape from one or several of the media. (In this endeavour they are attempting to recover the communality of the tribe on a national scale.) There are radios in public places which never cease their uplifting messages, but to what extent the people are really uplifted or persuaded it is difficult to tell. The more educated or sophisticated the people become the more subtle such propaganda has to be. It seems likely that the Russian masses no longer believe all their messages, but they are relatively helpless because alternative voices are not available. In most other countries there may be foreign newspapers or at least contrary information from radio networks outside. Such governments do not make the mistake of underrating

162

recreational programmes and these too are controlled; rock music has been excluded.

Elsewhere recreational material is less affected by ideology but the media nevertheless play an important role in cultural life. In the cities television (preferably in colour) has become a status symbol along with the car and the refrigerator. Already social life has been modified as it has been in the West. Also voices are being raised about possible harmful effects, such as those which have been analysed in developing countries.

In our context I have not considered this an important factor at the present time. Neither have I taken seriously the claims of those who (like McLuhan) have insisted that because of the mass media literacy has been downgraded or bypassed. The same obstacles which impede and hamper universal literacy also inhibit the use of the media, so that it is improbable that they could replace the printed word.

Becoming literate, as we have seen, can be a revolutionary process for the individual mind; it is doubtful whether constant exposure to radio or cinema or television could have the same effect. It remains true that illiterate people may achieve only a limited understanding of the messages sent out. Apart from other difficulties their educational background may be so meagre that programmes are not intelligible.

All the world can now listen to music of some sort. As Caliban observed, 'the isle is full of noises, sounds and sweet airs'. This has always been so; traditional folk created their own music. Now 'sometimes a thousand twangling instruments will hum about our ears and sometimes voices'. But what the new voices say is not easy to understand.

REFERENCES
1 Fafunwa, A B, *History of education in Nigeria* Allen and Unwin, 1974, 25.
2 Williams, Raymond, *Keywords: a vocabulary of culture and society* Fontana, 1976, 158.
3 *New Nigerian* 27 December 1977, 28 December 1977.

10

BOOK PRODUCTION

Without the multiple duplication of words the modern state could not function and without their daily distribution its citizens could not survive. They can survive without potatoes and yams since there are substitutes (let them eat rice) but there are no substitutes yet for paper and print. The new methods of mass communication eventually reach us all, yet they too depend on printing and are still mainly supplementary.

We do not have to bring out the evidence; the importance of this industry is established. Also well known is the fact that there are a number of peculiar features which make it different from all other production processes—let me briefly review them.

What publishing, bookselling and printing all have in common is that they belong not only to the world of profit and loss but to the arts and to technology as well. Their finished products are sold like other products but the people who create and distribute them can claim that they are not *just* manufacturers and businessmen. When they put out their messages they are directed to the human mind and spirit, and furthermore their productions have a physical form which can be a work of art. The publishing industry employs typographers, illustrators, designers, binders and other creative people who together combine to make the finished article appropriate, attractive and in some cases even beautiful. They are involved not only with aesthetic principles but with intellectual processes. The publisher employs people who have to read and assess the material before it is published; they are the readers and editors. Many of the basic procedures, particularly with regard to printing, are highly technical and subject to constant change.

All these stages follow on from the work of the writers—this is where it all begins. As Achebe says: 'This process is not akin to the cloth trade or the beer trade . . . when I read somebody is talking to me; and when I write I am talking to somebody. It is a personal, even intimate, relationship'. (1)

165

On the margins of all this, but equally necessary, the publishing industry helps to support a whole army of supplementary people such as critics, reviewers, bibliographers, translators and adapters. Lurking in the background there are censors whose job it is to try to regulate the morals and the ideas of their fellow citizens.

In view of these multiple activities, which require people of so many different skills, one can appreciate how sophisticated the industry has to be. It is for this reason amongst others that publishers (particularly in England) were traditionally 'gentlemen' as well as businessmen. (In the old days gentlemen did not go in for trade at all.) This claim was often valid in the past when publishing firms were small and intimate; it is less so now when large publishing houses behave like any other commercial combine. As we shall see, in the case of British publishing companies in Africa there is some doubt as to whether they have exported the qualities of gentility along with their books. In Nigeria indigenous publishers and booksellers are businessmen above all, which has been used to explain some of the deficiencies of the industry.

Another distinctive characteristic of book production is that although any one published item may be reproduced a million times (as with other manufactures) once the million copies are gone that is the end of the matter, at least until there is a new impression or edition. In the case of beer any bottle made by the same brewer is the same as another one and he can go on producing it forever.

These special features are characteristic of publishing and book-selling everywhere but there are great differences between countries. Obviously publishing as a private enterprise business is carried out only in capitalist countries.

In the Soviet Union and the countries within its orbit publishing is a planned state activity like any other. In Third World countries the industry is underdeveloped, although in this respect Asia is more advanced than Africa. In some new nations there is little or no indigenous publishing and this is our main theme in this chapter. I have taken Nigeria as a model, although most other African countries are in a less favoured position. It is remarkable how the industry's problems illustrate the realities of neo-colonialism and how entrenched the system has become. The economic similarities to other industries requiring transfer of technology, the creation of capital and management 'know-how' are very close.

There is in addition another dimension—the production of print is a process which has a direct bearing on the intellectual, cultural and ideological life of a nation. It is wholly involved with cultural freedom, and underdevelopment in this area is a most serious obstacle to the establishment of the true independence which is a state of mind. The simple fact that many people, both indigenous and foreign, are quite unaware of this dilemma is an indication of its gravity.

Ideas and values are of course international, but in order to become real they must be made to feel at home; imagination grows out of the soil. True internationalism (for example African unity) can only come to pass if nations have developed their own cultural identity in the first place; the alternative is 'cosmopolis', a world without roots. Or, more precisely, the alternative is a collection of peoples who (however wealthy some of them may become) will continue to be mentally deprived and psychologically dependent on the advanced regions of the world. It is these matters which we shall pursue.

Publishing: adverse factors

The foreign-based publishers: It is convenient to summarise some of the factors which have adversely affected publishing, with special reference to the need for an indigenous industry.

British firms have built up a trade on which African countries are dependent; this is the key factor we have to consider. After World War II a curious agreement was made between American and British publishers —an agreement which survived until 1977, when its demise was negotiated. It was a thirty-year protocol whereby British publishers received as an exclusive market all the countries that had been part of the British Empire in 1947. As stated in *The economist* the forces of the market place around the world had been piling up against its antique trading agreement for years'. (2)

What is significant for us is the way that the 'forces of the market place' can divide up the capitalist world much as in the old days of territorial Empire it was divided politically. It was not necessary to consult the nations who happened to be the markets; if they need the books (which they do) does it matter where they come from? We shall try to answer that question.

The British have been most successful in providing textbooks for Africa, in many cases specially produced for the African market. In Nigeria a large proportion of the trade is shared by two firms, Macmillan and the Oxford University Press. Recently, because of the oil boom, and the resultant scheme for Universal Primary Education (UPE), there has been a considerable expansion which has probably increased demand two or three times over.

Behind these figures lies a success story of thirty years. Now that the firms which established themselves have become partly indigenised (OUP, Longmans, Macmillan, Heinemann, and Evans all have Nigerian subsidiaries), the majority of their staff at all levels is Nigerian, and according to law they have a local shareholding of over 50 per cent.

It has been said that these ventures have been of inestimable benefit to the recipient countries; ultimately a technology will be transferred and a flourishing local industry established. This claim must be taken seriously. The argument is that the overseas-based publishers have been able to meet a need which is vital for educational development and which could not be met by indigenous publishing. Furthermore the existence of these firms has enabled people from all branches of the industry to be trained either locally or in Britain; this will eventually lead to the establishment of successful and wholly indigenous firms. The subsidiaries are already Nigerianised, and many of their textbooks are specially produced for the African market.

The case for the defence, then, seems quite formidable but it does not impress the prosecution. Nigerian and other critics have pointed out that the mere existence of the companies has prevented the growth of the domestic industry. Onibonoje, for example, has complained that 'their attitude towards the indigenous publisher, which varies from open ridicule and a patronising tolerance to outright threats and open hostility, can only be explained as panic and fear of competition'. (3) He goes on to accuse the indigenous power élite of having 'no voice of their own' and quotes Freire, the apostle of cultural liberation: 'What is called underdevelopment is at its deepest root a prostration of the spirit'. Such radical views do not normally come from businessmen; they are an indication of the gravity of these problems.

Similar arguments are used by analysts of neo-colonialism in other fields. Always behind the subsidiaries producing drugs, detergents, biscuits or cosmetics, there are the transnational parent companies supporting them from beyond the seas with all their resources, so that competing local firms cannot survive. It is held further that publishing, being involved with ideas rather than objects should not be influenced by alien companies in this way.

The objections which can be made relate not so much to what has been published as to what has not. With such a set-up material which ought to be essential for national development is not produced. The titles in Heinemann's admirable African Writers Series are written and selected partly with a foreign readership in mind. It is possible also that controversial works might be avoided in order not to offend the authorities.

As for the training of Africans by foreign-based firms, it may well be that their allegiance becomes confused and their attitudes alien to the true interests of their own people. This is the allegation usually made against the new élites. These arguments cannot lightly be dismissed.

Just as education in its full sense suffers because it is constricted by the straitjacket of formal education structures, so cultural development is impoverished by a lack of literature outside the textbook field. The economic factor is that there is insufficient demand, but if indigenous publishers were not excluded from textbook publishing they could more easily subsidise the less lucrative literature which is needed for development. Such material, for example adult education literature, including vernacular publications, cannot be produced overseas. The only possible alternative is to produce 'cram' books of the question and answer type for which there is a local market. This is what Onibonoje has been doing, and he hopes to use this trade to help publish other material of national importance.

We can conclude by agreeing that the localisation of British firms has benefited Nigeria to some degree, but although the staff of the subsidiaries may be largely local it is open to doubt whether they control the policies of the firm; some vital processes are still carried on outside the country. Having granted that the subsidiary publishers have a case, there is still no evidence that they will eventually become wholly indigenous, nor is there evidence that local publishers can grow as a result of their presence. They are, after all competitors and business is not mutual aid.

However, the calls which are heard from time to time demanding the expulsion or the complete nationalisation of foreign firms are not realistic. As usual, local entrepreneurs are not likely to produce the goods even if their foreign competitors are removed. Such realities are rooted in the economic structures of the world; these have been built up over the centuries and will not be dismantled overnight.

Other obstacles: If the existence of foreign-based firms is a major factor, it is also necessary to summarise the other circumstances which have impeded growth.

1   The conditions which operate against local publishers are the same as those limiting other capitalist enterprises, in particular the lack of capital and credit facilities. Businessmen do not find publishing a safe

or lucrative investment as the rewards are long-term and there is no immediate or substantial return. In the uncertain context of post-traditional societies there are better investment rewards elsewhere.

2   The small size of the local reading market, outside the textbook field, has already been discussed. If indigenous publishing takes over the primary school sector, as is possible, then there will be new opportunities. Beyond this, as illiteracy diminishes, the demand for other types of literature will increase, particularly at a popular level. The development of public libraries will have the same result.

3   Book distribution is inadequate, so the people are not exposed to literature and do not know what reading matter is available or how it could help them.

4   Similarly the lack of public library facilities at present means, firstly, that library demand itself is not there, and secondly that the reading habit is not stimulated.

5   Publishers are handicapped because local printing firms do not meet their requirements. Many of these difficulties are technical and are discussed below.

6   There is a shortage of skilled manpower and expertise. Booksellers can operate after a fashion even when workers know little about books, but lack of trained staff makes publishing difficult and printing impossible.

7   In most countries state assistance or state intervention has either been unsatisfactory or non-existent. There are further possibilities here, some of which are being explored in Nigeria.

8   Finally we come to the writers themselves, on whom all else depends. Under existing circumstances, one cannot blame them for preferring overseas publishers—that is where the market is. Even with periodical articles there is little incentive to publish in local journals, whose circulation is small and appearance unpredictable. University presses will expand but they are mostly still in their infancy. Appeals to the patriotism of writers are often made, but if high motives cannot be rewarded such appeals may fall on deaf ears.

These are the problems for writers who have produced manuscripts. What is to be done where the desired local literature has not even been written and Miltons remain mute and inglorious? Expatriates continue to provide the bulk of children's literature; this is a specialised field discussed in the chapter on reading. Also specialised is the writing of textbooks, and there have been many calls for more local writers. It is sometimes overlooked that within an expanding education system teachers may be too overworked to write textbooks. In Nigeria this situation is improving, with particular reference to the primary level.

International concern
Inevitably there has been international activity, and publishing matters fall within Unesco's responsibilities. There were Unesco conferences in Tokyo (1966), Accra (1968) and Bogota (1969). Another conference at Ife in Nigeria (not organised by Unesco) was held in 1973 to follow up the Accra proposals.

Much of the information in this chapter has been taken from the various papers given at the Ife conference and subsequently published. These meetings all analysed the problems of publishing in developing countries and made proposals. The papers described the situation as outlined in this chapter. The recommendations were necessarily of a fairly general kind and included proposals for the setting up of Book Development Councils and 'long-term low interest loans to assist in the creation and strengthening of domestic publishing'. They also stressed the urgency of training programmes and the need for publications in African languages. The various papers presented were indeed valuable in providing information and drawing attention to the predicament of African book production.

Beyond this necessary foundation work it should be realised that such conferences cannot make any decisive contribution, and we should not expect Unesco or any other international body to have much practical impact on the symptoms of underdevelopment. The deliberations of international gatherings—as we shall see in the case of libraries—may, when national circumstances are propitious, point the way forward for specific advances, but that is all. Their role is diplomatic and they are prevented by their structure and membership from making drastic proposals. Because of this their recommendations may seem to be more no than pious hopes. Onibonoje, in addition to his criticism of the British has made a scathing attack on such meetings and the futility of their proceedings. But how could it be otherwise?

There have also been contributions from other nations and organisations with similar goals. The Franklin Book Program was established in 1952 to strengthen the indigenous book trade in developing countries. There are conferences and publications but the Program made little impact in Nigeria, possibly because of the operation of British vested interests. There was also a conference at Airlie House, Washington DC, in 1964, which was to provide 'policy and program guidelines' for AID activities.

171

When they are not a cloak for outside business interests these international projects are of considerable value, provided that one appreciates the limits of their influence. They have the funds to bring together people with similar problems who would not otherwise meet. It is a role which can easily be underestimated, but naturally their functions are mainly advisory.

Methods of publishing

Private enterprises: The special circumstances which made possible the Onitsha 'market literature' no longer exist; they were tragically brought to an end by the civil war. It is possible that glossy popular magazines have replaced the pamphlets to some extent. The publishing and printing of Onitsha literature is important because the enterprise was wholly indigenous. As Obiechina says: 'Onitsha attracted the printing presses because of its importance as a trade and educational centre . . . printing and publishing became a highly lucrative business and so popular . . . that along New Market Road, more than half the front-houses contained printing presses or bookstores selling the products of the local presses'. (4)

In view of our discussions on the alleged lack of demand for literature it is noteworthy that some sales were high, sometimes in the region of 40-60,000 copies. There were hundreds of titles and many are still to be found on the book stalls and kiosks. There are also currently similar productions from other quarters, but this small-scale industry does not have the same importance that once it had. In some respects it illustrates the possibilities and characteristics of an intermediate technology. It is true that the presses must originally have been imported but they were largely old second-hand machines which had been sold at knock-down prices.

Apart from the output from these presses there are other pamphlets on the market, mostly published by their authors. They have been called 'vanity publishers'. This method of publication takes place on a substantial level and Omotoso mentions that out of six books by one Lagos press (Di Nigra Press), five are by its owner. (5)

Publishing abroad: Other Nigerian publishers have gone abroad to establish themselves, sometimes with the intention of returning. For example, the Third Press was founded in 1970 in the USA and is now the largest black-owned book publisher there; subsequently Third Press Africa has now established itself in Nigeria as a separate company.

172

Subsidies from abroad: Cultural bodies have made some contribution by providing assistance. Presence Africaine was established in Paris as early as 1947 and is the oldest African publishing house still in operation. Its cultural influence has been considerable and a high standard has been maintained, particularly by the journal with the same title which carried the early contributions of the apostles of negritude.

Black Orpheus, a literary journal now issued from the University of Lagos, was founded by the Mbari Press, which was originally an artists' and writers' club founded in 1956 and associated with Nigerian creative writing (notably Soyinka and John Pepper Clark). It was never a business organisation and was at one time assisted by the Paris-based Congress for Cultural Freedom. The Nigerian Civil War was a factor in its demise.

Under this heading *Transition*, the most successful and important of all African English-language cultural journals, should receive mention. Its history is symptomatic of the hazards of African periodical publication. Its founder and editor Rajat Neogy was imprisoned by Dr Obote, at that time President of Uganda. After much international agitation he was subsequently released and moved the editorial offices to Ghana. Later in 1976 Wole Soyinka became editor and the journal is now established in Nigeria. *Transition*, in the early stages, also received assistance from the Congress for Cultural Freedom and it subsequently emerged that unbeknown to its editor CIA funds were involved.

Indigenous capital: The most successful of Nigerian publishing firms is that of Onibonoje. Having built up the business with popular educational aids and Yoruba books for schools he announced in 1977 that he would begin publication of an African Literature Series. In his own words this was 'a giant step forward . . . What we have now is not truly African because the European audience was borne in mind before most of the books were written'.

Another significant venture was that of the British publisher Andre Deutsch, who set up in Lagos the African Universities Press, with Nigerian capital; this was taken over by Pilgrim Books during the civil war. He also, in 1965, set up the East African Publishing House in Nairobi, Kenya. *African Report* desribed this as 'Perhaps Africa's most enterprising publisher with an extensive list including original fiction, numerous academic titles . . . conference reports and general books on East Africa'. (6) Deutsch is no longer associated with the company.

There are a few other Nigerian commercial publishers of note, such as Nwamije (Enugu), but their contribution is still small.

The missionary contribution

The Christian missionary endeavours were of course the pioneer publishers in Africa; they continue to publish both in English and in the vernacular languages. Complete Bibles have been published in 138 languages, the whole of the New Testament in 310 languages and the Gospels in 561. In addition to Bibles, catechisms, prayer and hymn books, they have published material on development subjects such as intermediate technology or the problems of unemployment; they also publish general secular literature, usually of a 'wholesome' kind. Yet they have not altogether neglected local literature; in quite early days D O Fagunwa's Yoruba novels were published by a missionary press, and as long ago as 1875 the Basel Mission in Ghana published work on the Ashanti and Fante languages.

Most of the printing is still done abroad, but there are missionary presses in Malawi, Egypt and Madagascar. Their success can be attributed first to religious commitment; second, to heavy subsidy from the funds of Bible societies; and third, to an effective distribution system. Theirs seem to be the only organisations which are capable of distributing books from one part of Africa to another.

The largest Christian publishing house in Africa is the Evangel Publishing House, a non-denominational organisation founded in 1964 in Kenya, which has its own printing press. Their large number of tracts include vernacular languages, for example Hausa. The best known Christian publisher in Nigeria is Daystar which is historically important.

In francophone Africa the largest organisation is in Yaounde (Cameroon)—the Centre de Litterature Evangelique. CLE was founded by protestant churches of French-speaking African countries, with Dutch and German assistance. Its aims were defined as 'promoting, developing and disseminating the African cultural patrimony and Christian thinking by Africans in Africa'. The firm is significant because it has successfully published general literature including popular series. A large proportion of their writers are African and about half are Cameroonian. It is unfortunate that governments have not been able to sponsor projects of this kind; they indicate that when publishing is subsidised it can overcome the other obstacles, of which the higher import duties on printing equipment has been found to be the most formidable.

Vernacular publishing

Various references have already been made to the use of the vernacular, with particular reference to reading (see chapter 6) and to religious publishing. It is one of the areas where one would expect a state contribution, for several reasons. First, governments have a responsibility to preserve traditional culture which is based on language; second, it has become official policy everywhere to stress adult education and literacy programmes which use the vernacular; third, it is often policy to use the vernacular for primary education. Finally, such programmes are not economic and need to be subsidised. In spite of these aims it cannot be said that the practical implications have been fully explored. The problems can be summarised as follows:

1   There are a great many languages in most African countries (395 in Nigeria alone), and often those used by the smaller ethnic groups have no orthography. (The missions provided many transliterated versions.) One remedy for this is to concentrate on the major languages in each country (say half-a-dozen in Nigeria), or alternatively to introduce a national language to replace the European languages as a *lingua franca.* In Nigeria this would be politically improbable, but, as already noted, Swahili may eventually be so used in three countries in East Africa; there is now a considerable amount of literature in that language and it has become the official policy of the Union of African Writers to advocate the use of Swahili for other parts of Africa. In Nigeria possibly forty million people speak Hausa but the rest do not.

2   There are reading difficulties even for those who are fully literate in English; they may have to learn to read their own languages. Amongst the Ibos there are a great many dialects and although a standard or 'central' language has been adopted it may have to be learnt, especially in the written form.

3   Many of the languages, unless more words are invented, can only be used at a fairly simple level. One alternative very noticeable in Yoruba speech is to use a liberal sprinkling of English words, but this seems less desirable in print.

4   Most of the languages are tonal, with the result that the same printed word may have at least four quite different meanings. If diacritical signs are not used the reading process is slowed up, since readers have to use the general context to get the meaning of the word. If they are used there is extra trouble and expense. With some publications these marks have to be inserted by hand.

At various times and places enthusiasm for learning to read in the vernacular has not been noticeable because the people want to learn to read English as the language of social advancement. The French colonialists encouraged the use of their own language, but the British efforts,

175

especially through the Literature Bureaux, to publish vernacular literature, a policy which was often opposed by nationalists who felt that it
would perpetuate the subservient position of the people. In more recent
years the new leaders have changed their line and have at least announced
intentions to promote the vernacular. We shall see that the people will
not want to read their language unless it can be of some use to them.

Another cultural factor which still may limit official zeal is that if the
languages are not national they may be seen as divisive. In Africa a major
effort has been required in the new countries to create a national consciousness; unity within the nation has been the watchword. To concentrate on local languages (necessarily tribal or ethnic) may not help in this
process. Such a view could be short-sighted, since oppression of local
cultures may serve to strengthen them.

In view of these factors it is perhaps not surprising that vernacular
publishing, at least in West Africa, has made little headway except with
regard to newspapers. (In Nigeria now there are newspapers in Hausa,
Yoruba, Ibo, Efik, Tiv and Ijaw and the creation of new states may provide a further stimulus.) The old Northern Literature Bureau started by
the British for the Hausa language was discontinued in 1968 when the
Northern Nigerian Publishing Company was set up, with 41 per cent of
the shares held by Macmillan and 51 per cent by the Gaskiya Corporation. This is a relatively small organisation and is not a government-
owned company. It publishes vernacular literature, mainly educational
and religious, in Hausa, Fulani, Tiv and some Arabic. The proportion of
Hausa titles is increasing. The Ghana Literature Bureau does little more
than survive. On the other hand, for reasons already discussed, the East
African Literature Bureau has made an important contribution. In
Sierra Leone there is a Provincial Literature Bureau which is a co-operative
venture between the government and the United Christian Council. It is
under-capitalised and functions on a small scale.

The wide range of vernacular publishing by Christian missions has been
noted above, so that all that remains is to mention the activities of the
foreign-based publishers in Nigeria. Several have expressed an interest
in vernacular publishing for educational purposes. Already the Oxford
University Press publishes some material in Hausa, Efik, Ibo and Yoruba.
Macmillan publishes in these languages together with Eddo and Igala,
and the firm has declared an intention to expand its vernacular programme.

We may conclude that, except where it is intended that the vernacular
should become the national language, the future of this type of publishing

may be limited to primary school readers, newspapers, popular booklets such as already exist in Hausa and bread-and-butter manuals, again at a popular level. There is also a need for more texts for semi-literates who have attended literacy classes. Many of these programmes may be subsidised by religious or official bodies, but it appears that providing for the primary school market could be an economic proposition for indigenous publishing.

The university presses

Publishing done by universities in Africa is in its infancy, but this is one field where local ownership and control is guaranteed. These presses will play a bigger role in future, but meanwhile their contribution is limited; their special purpose is of course to publish material by and for the academic community. Already they are important in Nigeria as a means of subsidising professional and academic journals, for example *Savannah*, and others in fields such as economics, education, geography, history, engineering, agriculture, and Islamic studies.

The university presses encounter the difficulties experienced by other indigenous publishers. One authority observed some time ago that, 'The fledgling university presses are hopelessly hamstrung by the smallness of the local market and the absence of funds for expansion'. (7) At the present time the more pressing problems which tend to occur are as follows:

1 A lengthy decision-making process which may cause potential writers to prefer an overseas publisher, so that indigenous presses may be landed largely with material that writers cannot place anywhere else. Selection of manuscripts by a committee of academic staff, assisted by at least two outside readers, takes a long time. Academic staff do not always appreciate that work which is submitted for a doctoral thesis is usually not suited for publication as it stands; they are then reluctant to make the necessary modifications or take a long time doing so; sometimes revision has to be done by the editorial staff, which is again a lengthy process.

2 Next in importance to the factor of delay (and contributing to it) there are the usual difficulties with indigenous printers. (It has been known for one book to be sent to three printers in succession, ending up overseas.)

3 Output is likely to remain small for some time. Since its inception in 1976 the ABU Press, founded in October 1977, has actually published only one book, although a further seven have been sent to the printer.

Another ten are in progress, making a total of eighteen. This is quite a sound record for a new press.

4   They have no distribution facilities and usually rely on foreign distributors, who may prefer to concentrate on their own publications. Sometimes they co-operate with commercial publishers in the publishing of particular items, as is done by Ibadan University Press.

The other difficulties are similar to those discussed for publishers generally. With regard to the limitations of the university publishing sector it may be supposed that policy is not likely to be very adventurous; a committee after all has no soul, and controversial or unorthodox material might face rejection.

In view of the fact that indigenous publishing experiences the difficulties we have observed, it is surely appropriate to discuss whether the university presses should not extend their role and their range to undertake tasks which in more advanced countries are carried out by the trade. Ruby Essien Udom is on record as stating that 'There has tended to be a certain stunting of growth among the university presses largely because the dynamic potential of a university press has not been recognized'. (8)

In developing countries, we are constantly informed (quite rightly), the universities have a special role to play in national development— one which does not arise in the same way with older universities and older countries. If this is so, and universities are trying to link their work more closely to their environment, should not the role of these presses be re-examined? One can envisage the university presses publishing indigenous imaginative literature, or even general educational material by local writers who need not be connected with the universities. Or experiments could be made in fields which are not economic for commercial publishers.

A parallel could be drawn with state publishing, which is advocated because indigenous firms are under-capitalised. This would involve abandoning the minority market and producing instead for a wider demand, which would doubtless require a change in the organisation to suite its new function. Such a change of direction would also mean that a publications committee would have to draw up a more positive policy and identify areas where publication is thought to be needed.

It will be objected that at present these presses are not in a position to consider such explorations and this may well be true. Nevertheless one feels that it should at least be considered in relation to future policy. As publishers the university presses are potentially much more important than those in developed countries, where it is not so apparent that they are even necessary. (The Oxford and Cambridge university presses should be regarded as normal commercial publishers.)

State publishing
Faced with the inability of indigenous commercial publishing to meet the needs of the new countries in Africa, international gatherings have recommended state assistance, perhaps in the form of subsidies to individual firms. Usually they have not proposed that governments should take over full responsibility, either because they have represented interests which would suffer from such a policy or because they have not been able to see how this could be done.

This particular proposal, at least in Africa, has met with little or no response, and it appears that subsidisation is improbable for various political reasons. What has happened, however, is that various forms of mixed or joint enterprise have come into being, and these should be reviewed. Behind all these endeavours is the reality that states can supply capital but they cannot provide skills or expertise; this has come either from expatriate firms or, in one or two cases, from religious organisations. The several forms of state participation are as follows:

1   The most significant ventures in English-speaking Africa have taken the form of state enterprise in conjunction with British firms, notably Macmillan. The arrangements have been different in each case. Probably the best known and most ambitious has been the Ghana Publishing Corporation, where the government had 51 per cent participation and provided the capital, while Macmillan provided the technical and professional know how. The project also included a printing press which experienced technical difficulties and there were consequent delays. The history of the Corporation was so troubled that a commission of enquiry had to be set up. Professor Kotei notes 'It is on record that financial mismanagement, under-utilisation of equipment, stagnation, corruption, nepotism, equivocal policies and, most pernicious of all, political interference, have interfered with progress'. (9)

Kotei has also suggested that experience indicates that state publishing is likely to fail in Africa. Other commentators hold that this is an unwarranted conclusion and that a decisive factor was the controversial nature of the agreement made with Macmillan. Irele contends that the corporation got off to a bad start 'due largely to the indefensible arrangements it was made to enter into with a British commercial publishing house'. (10)

Other similar projects have tried to avoid these pitfalls. For example, in Zambia (1964) the Kenneth Kaunda Foundation set up two publishing companies—one for textbooks and the other for educational material by and for Zambians. This company, NECZAM (The National Education Company of Zambia), was set up in conjunction with Macmillan, whose shareholding was a minority one and confined to five years only. The Foundation was also assisted with international funds, so that altogether the arrangement was less open to objection that that in Ghana. Simon Allison records that for the first four years there was no dividend and afterwards (after 1973) the Macmillan connection 'withered away'. (11)

Allison claims the advantages of such an arrangement to be: first, that the overseas publisher provides professional and technical advice and training; second, financial assistance is found; and third, it is possible to get some word done overseas, notably colour printing. The government's support was not financial but consisted of the commissioning of books for schools; such an arrangement lessens the possibility of state interference. (Certainly one of the adverse factors in Ghana was that textbooks were not commissioned as much as had been hoped.) A different organisation was used for the Tanzanian Publishing House.

The Ethiope Publishing Corporation has been one of the most suffessful local publishing ventures in Nigeria. This was set up by the former Mid-Western State in Benin in 1970 and is now supported by Bendel State. The significant factor is that it is run on commercial lines; it has a close relationship with the Bendel State Library Board. The Ethiope Bookshops were established to solve the distribution problem. This pioneer project may well lead to a complete change in the bookselling pattern in Nigeria.

These three variations on a joint enterprise pattern do not of course exhaust the possibilities of state publishing. It may well be that in future some governments may be able to assume total responsibility for large-scale ventures. Such a possibility exists with the new states in Nigeria, and already large modern presses have been set up (as in Jos) for newspaper printing. Once this is done the range can be extended to other types of material, particularly in the vernacular.

We have already noticed the work of the Literature Bureaux, which are of course government sponsored; the publishing of textbooks, particularly at primary level, may also become official. Outside the scope of this discussion there exist the state documents which all governments publish as part of their functions. Those who object to state publishing often forget that in the advanced countries (notably in Britain) the government publishes a wide range of material not directly relating to government business. Admittedly this in no way constitutes a monopoly and the commercial publishers are well enough established. Finally we should mention state publishing in the Soviet Union and other communist countries, but we have not discussed it here as its relevance to Africa is difficult to establish.

In conclusion we should note the alleged disadvantages and advantages of state publishing, bearing in mind that African countries differ so much from each other that a list of pros and cons is difficult to apply. For example, the size of a country—and hence its potential market—is a decisive factor. Zambia, with its population of only four million, has quite different problems from Nigeria, where official publishing may be done at state rather than federal level. The following points do not refer to joint enterprise but to state publishing in the more exact sense:

Advantages:

1   As indigenous publishing is undeveloped, state participation becomes essential, especially in small countries. The alternative is either to rely on foreign-based firms, or to wait until domestic publishers establish themselves, or to subsidise private enterprise. None of these alternatives is attractive and the last is open to the objection that the government may have no control over policy or guarantees against failure.

2   'Safe' publishing, for example textbooks, can be used to subsidise less economic publications including those in the vernacular. This point is important because of the small size of the market outside the textbook range.

3   State involvement guarantees financial support and the creation of an indigenous industry which can concentrate on national development needs.

Disadvantages:

1   If the state enterprise constitutes a monopoly (as it might often be in existing circumstances) it may result in high prices, low standards and stagnation. These are the evils which competition should avoid.

2   There is a possibility of government control or censorship. This seems to me a great danger and most indesirable. However, it should be pointed out that publishing can be controlled by governments even if they are not the publishers themselves.

3   State activity may mean that private entrepreneurs, whether foreign or national, cannot establish themselves or survive. Those who favour a mixed economy will deplore such an outcome. Because in many countries it is the foreign-based firms which are established already, it is

most likely that the indigenous sector would suffer. How much this would matter is debatable.

4   There remain the problems of production and distribution which exist where there are no overseas connections; this particularly applies to printing. Most of the successful existing presses in Africa do have overseas links.

Other objections that have been made seem to me less valid. References have been made to corruption, nepotism and so on, but these evils do not flourish only in state organisations, although they may be especially prevalent there.

Finally one should repeat that there are various other government policies which could assist publishing. These include the relaxing of financial controls, for example the reduction of import duties on equipment and paper. Also recommended by the Ife conference were Book Development Councils, to consist of an advisory body representing all parts of the book trade including publishers, printers, booksellers, and librarians. The Nigerian one was set up in 1973, but little has been heard of it since. If the various components of the trade are not themselves well developed —and furthermore not always on good terms with each other—one may have doubts about the success of such bodies.

Book distribution
The absence of satisfactory book distribution channels is perhaps the weakest link in the entire chain from publisher to reader. The reasons can be summed up as follows:

1   The decisive factor is lack of demand and an inability to stimulate it. The market for textbooks is supplied partly directly from publishers to education authorities; university bookshops provide for the needs of higher education and a multitude of small shops dealing with stationery sell educational books for other readers, particularly those studying for examinations. As we shall see there are some other 'proper' bookshops, but this bookselling activity is mainly urban; there is nothing to provoke a response in the rural areas. People will not ask for items they have never heard of or learn to enjoy what is not available. Advertising and publicity are necessary to sell anything and by such means demand is created, but the resources are not available for such an effort.

2   The publishers are not happy about the efforts of the booksellers and vice versa. Booksellers complain of not getting enough support from publishers because of ungenerous discounts, lack of returns

182

facilities and downright competition through direct sales to the public, which destroys what should be a complementary relationship benefiting both parties. The reference to 'returns facilities' concerns the procedure for sending back unsold books to the publisher. University booksellers have made the same complaint. On the other hand, one publisher's difficulty is the lack of warehouse facilities.

With regard to direct sales the question which we must ask is 'Why not?' If booksellers have not reached the standards which are found in some countries, are they really necessary at all? Could not distribution be done by some other means? These are rhetorical questions but not irrelevant. In Britain the book trade is governed by a net book agreement which provides that publishers do not sell direct to the public and lays down what discount the bookseller should receive. It also controls price reduction, so that booksellers cannot reduce prices until after a certain period.

Anyone unfamiliar with these proceedings might well ask whether they are necessary or desirable in the circumstances of other countries. Selling books in multiple stores or drugstores (as in the United States) is not what we mean by bookselling here, although this trend exists in the new countries also. Such stores, which sell books like shirts or anything else, do stimulate some demand in the towns, but that is all. What other organisation is required? It is hoped that possible answers might emerge before the end of this section.

3   The reason why the small booksellers do not have to develop special skills is that the bulk of the trade at present involves textbooks only. It is possible to sell other books also, particularly in the slack times between seasonal sales of textbooks, but how these are selected or obtained is somewhat mysterious. An examination of these small establishments reveals collections which are diverting, but not to be taken seriously within the solemn context of national development. 'The danger of not learning to actively sell general books is already being seen in the panic which grips the book trade whenever a government decides to operate textbook distribution'. (12) If publishers find that their books are not promoted they may turn to direct selling or the state may intervene.

4   Another important factor is that the library market has so far been negligible. The result is that when new library services are set up the booksellers are not geared to meet the demand.

5   Finally there is an absence of adequate bibliographical information at every level. Newspapers carry occasional book notices but there is

183

nothing systematic and the educated readership is too small to support cultural reviews. Even libraries may have to rely on overseas sources for information about new books of local relevance. Within the trade there have been calls for more bookselling and publishing journals and for more frequent trade fairs.

At this point it is worthwhile to draw attention to two special services which try to deal with the lack of information. The first is Publishers' Information Cards Services Ltd (PICS). This British-based firm issues a card service, listing new titles as they come into print, to libraries around the world on behalf of the publishers who subscribe to the service. There is an additional service which informs university faculty and departmental libraries and other specialist libraries. For the publishers it is an inexpensive way of informing the library market.

The second is International Book Information Services (IBIS), a London-based company which specialises in developing mailing lists for people publishing academic and other specialist books. There is available on a computer in London a list of names of 400,000 individuals and institutions around the world. IBIS works closely with an American company which has a similar American list. This means that publishers, at a cost of £20 for one thousand addresses, can buy a list of those interested in specialist subjects. Another firm is Mail Communication Ltd, which specialises in mail campaigns for the publishing industry. These organisations are mentioned because they may help publishers and libraries to overcome the lack of bibliographical information; they were amalgamated in 1978.

6   The bookshops lack trained staff. At the present time, in most countries, it is difficult to see how training could be organised except in university bookshops.

Types of bookselling
Existing forms of distribution can be summarised, using Nigeria as an example, as follows:

Missionary endeavours: Historically the Christian bookshops are important, and they now extend their provision into the realms of secular publishing. As one observer has noted: 'These shops are some of the best bookshops in Africa—second only to university bookshops . . . they are responsible for the distribution of the largest share of the pre-university educational and general books sold and read in Africa'. (13)

184

In Nigeria the Sudan Interior Mission (SIM) has from 20-30 shops now known as Challenge Bookshops; the Church and School Supplies (CSS) has over 30 and the Sudan United Mission about 15 shops in Northern Nigeria. Their contribution to book distribution has not ended there, and they have shown that much can be done in spite of the alleged lack of demand. Just as the Salvation Army has taken its journal *War cry* into pubs and open places, and the Jehovah's Witnesses have distributed their *Watch tower* from door to door, so the missions have used unorthodox methods to carry the Word into remote and unexpected regions. Itinerant vendors called 'colporteurs' have travelled through rural areas in various parts of Africa. In Liberia the Christian Literature Crusade has used mobile book shops which visit the 'pay grounds' on pay day, and schools and country markets. There are already kiosks and Christian reading rooms and it should not be forgotten that long before these times the Muslim traveller (who in one person combined trader, scholar and missionary) carried Arabic manuscripts throughout West Africa.

This is the kind of activity which librarians could emulate. There are mobile libraries in several African countries but their impact is still small. Prophetic voices have called for 'barefoot librarians'—there is even a book with that title, but an examination of its contents reveals a total absence of bare feet. The missions are evangelical and their significance mainly religious, but cultural missionaries if they existed (publishers, librarians, booksellers, adult educationists) could do the same. Alas, such zeal on behalf of secular causes is not often to be found. The consequence is that beer (when it is available) or some alternative when it is not can be found in the remotest villages of Africa but not the printed word.

University bookselling: University bookshops are naturally free from many of the limitations we have discussed, although they have special troubles of their own, particularly with regard to the wider range of material which we have considered to be necessary for development. They are usually under-capitalised, and have been under pressure to expand in a manner which may be economically disastrous. Foreign exchange problems are a constant cause of delays in payments. It has been claimed that in Nigeria, for example, the Central Bank may delay money transfers abroad by up to twelve months in some cases. In consequence they frequently have not been able to meet their bills and some overseas distributors have stopped supplies. As has often been observed, overseas publishers do not appreciate the 'excruciating circumstances' under which university booksellers must operate.

There are also problems peculiar to this sector which arise in trying to meet the demands of university departments (for example over-ordering). Frustrations for students and staff can lead to direct ordering, by various dubious means which include that strange organisation the Crown Agents. Local channels may be bypassed, and this does not help towards indigenous enterprise. The provision of periodicals exemplifies some of these obstacles. Books may be obtained on the 'pay later' system but not periodicals. Subscriptions must be paid before they are sent, which, because of regulations, often cannot be done. How such difficulties can be overcome is outside the scope of this chapter.

However, this established sector of the trade will at least continue to grow. Their influence and services extend in the absence of other good bookshops beyond the universities, and they could become growth points for the trade generally; this could include the training of staff who might eventually set up elsewhere.

State distribution: State distribution of reading materials has frequently been recommended, and this could be a further development both with regard to textbook provision and other types of reading. The Book Centre of Bendel State, set up in Benin in the former Mid-Western State as part of the Library Service, is of great importance as a pioneer project. It has succeeded in distributing books to schools and has also extended its activities to serve other libraries and the general public by using the mobile library service. The use of what could be in effect mobile bookshops seems to be one of the most practical methods of distributing literature in areas where it is unlikely that book stores could be established.

The Bendel State services are of particular interest because it coordinates publishing (the former Ethiope Press), printing and library services. There seems to be no reason why such services should not be set up elsewhere. Commercial booksellers, if this should happen, would be the losers, but so far they have not established that they could meet what will be, as literacy grows, an increasing need.

Other channels: Finally we should not omit to mention that beyond whatever bookshop walls exist there have always been and no doubt always will be the teeming markets in the towns of Africa, where miscellaneous literature may be found mixed up with curious objects from the ends of the earth. Thus in the *Sabon Gari* (foreign quarters) in the Hausa-Fulani cities of Northern Nigeria one may find the thoughts of Chairman Mao jostling the grim dicta of Lenin and the comforting messages of Christian tracts.

Printing
In many respects the technical problems which arise in an emergent printing trade are the most formidable of all the obstacles we have noted. Printers who are caught up in the toils of technical transfer often cannot meet the requirements of indigenous publishers. Their main difficulties are as follows:

1   Printers complain that publishers do not co-operate with them and lack understanding of their problems. For example 'publishers tend to think that the problems or requirements of a Nigerian printer are the same as those of a European printing firm'. (14) On the other side, the publishers object that prices are too high.

2   Printers are faced with heavy duties on imported machinery and even heavier ones on paper. Also, because of exchange controls, they cannot pay on delivery. This affects prices because delays in payment incur interest charges. One answer might be to have more indigenous paper mills. (In Nigeria there is one at Jebba.) What is also required is research into local products which could be used for various book production processes including paper-making; for example, alternatives to imported wood (normally tropical wood is too hard).

3   The lack of trained labour cannot quickly be remedied, especially as there are many innovations to keep up with (particularly developments in electronics). One answer is to build up printing departments in technical colleges; at present it is alleged that they are inadequate and that in some cases they teach only letterpress printing. 'Our printing graduates do not even know the machines which they are supposed to handle.' (14) Also students who go to Britain get little opportunity for practical experience; they are shut out by union regulations.

4   Various other technical difficulties all add up to an inability to keep to a firm schedule. 'All the printers in Nigeria are limited in the kind of work they can undertake. They have a restricted range of typefaces and untrained staff are unable to follow specifications which their editor has marked.' (14)

With such a complicated industry as printing this situation is only to be expected. For example, in Nigeria new printing equipment has been introduced for the printing of newspapers and the local workers are not familiar with them. But as more work is done locally the possibilities should improve. Meanwhile growing pains continue.

Conclusion

Now that this discussion is concluded I should make it clear that it would be possible to give a descriptive survey of the book trade in Africa which would be quite different from the above account. In accordance with the theme of this work what I have emphasised is the characteristics of and the possibilities for the indigenous book industry, using Nigeria as an example.

REFERENCES
1 Achebe, Chinua, 'Publishing in Africa: a writer's view' *in* Oluwasanmi, E, and others (ed), *Publishing in Africa in the seventies* University of Ife Press, 1975, 41.
2 *The economist* 11 June 1977.
3 Onibonoje, G O, 'Wanted! a cultural revolution, not a dialogue' *in* Oluwasanmi, E and others (ed), *op cit*, 268.
4 Obiechina, E N, *Onitsha market literature* Heinemann, 1972, 7.
5 Omotoso, Kole, 'The missing apex; a search for the audience' *in* Oluwasanmi, E, and others (ed), *op cit*, 254.
6 Onibonoje, G O, as reported in the Nigerian Press, 1977.
7 Collings, Rex, 'Publishing in Africa, an industry emerges' *Africa report* Vol 15 (s) 1970, 31-33.
8 Udom, Ruby Essien, *The university press in Africa* Ethiope Publishing Corporation, 1972, 2)-25.
9 Kotei, S J A, 'Some cultural and social factors of book reading and publishing in Africa' *in* Oluwasanmi, E, and others (ed), *op cit*, 201.
10 Irele, Abiola, 'The Ethiope experience' *in* Oluwasanmi, E, and others (ed), *op cit*, l43.
11 Allison, Simon D, 'State participation in publishing: the Zambian experience' *in* Oluwasanmi, E, and others (ed), *op cit*, 63.
12 Oduyoye, Modupe, 'The role of Christian publishing houses in Africa today' *in* Oluwasanmi, E, and others (ed), *op cit*, 215.
13 *Ibid*, 213.
14 Idris-Animashaun, Alade, 'Some reflections on the problems of establishing a modern book printing industry in Nigeria' *in* Oluwasanmi, E, and others (ed), *op cit*, 70.

PART IV

LIBRARIES

11

LIBRARIES AND INFORMATION

Scope
By implication, the use and organisation of information is treated throughout this work. It remains to examine information processes more precisely,
with reference to how they operate in developing countries.

In the case of technology we suggested that there is a *perception* difficulty which causes the meaning of technology to elude our understanding. The same happens with the use of the word 'information' and for
the same reasons. One of them is that the meaning seems to be obvious
and is therefore taken for granted. Another reason is that information,
as distinct from bits of information, is a process which includes both a
personal and a social component. For example, if a document should lie
(as many of them do) quite lost in some attic, can this be regarded as information? It is *unused* information; once it is discovered or retrieved it
can be of value. But the meaning lies in the use. You may call a spade a
spade but if it is being wielded as a weapon rather than employed for dig-
ging, does it not have a different significance? We must assume that a
document does not contain information for illiterate persons. Similarly,
if it is written in a lost language, it becomes a scrap of paper.

We are suggesting, therefore, that the meaning of the information concept cannot be understood without reference to its social function. There
is a formal meaning such as may be found in a dictionary definition but
if one stops at this level a distortion of reality arises which is usually
called formalism.

The role of information
The question we have to ask first is, what is the role of information in
different kinds of society and what forms can it take?

In 1959 I wrote a book which attempted to analyse these matters with
reference to the various social agencies which pass on information or
channels which allow it to flow through. I still consider that this approach

191

is essential and is a form of systems analysis. What I was attempting to discover was the extent of society's need for information and how this may be met with regard to types of published reference material. This relationship is elusive, partly because information retrieval is rarely studied in this way.

Students of librarianship are usually presented with sources of information and retrieval methods which they then learn. The textbooks proceed in this manner because it is a necessary practical approach, at least for librarians in those countries where the information is generated. But I shall suggest that the method is *not* practical for countries who immport that information. Vickery, for example, starts his investigation by noting that 'Modern society incessantly produces and uses information'. (1) He goes on to say that the social role of information is 'to bring people together'. This is the crux of the matter and a concept which Illich has developed in his proposals for *personal* links between people who have common interests. Vickery then continues, 'To deal with this subject . . . would lead us into the organisation of technical activity as a whole'. Quite rightly, in his own context, he declines to be led into temptation.

Yovits and Ernest state that the 'flow of information is defined by what we have called the basic information system, which is a naturally occurring phenomenon and about which little is yet known'; they continue, 'a clear and definable concept of information is yet to emerge'. (2)

My own feeling is that the concept will never emerge if it is regarded as something which occurs 'naturally'. There is a mystification here, since the social context of information processes can be traced even if at present the linkages are not very clear. It is not difficult, for example, to illustrate how all the major printed reference sources produced in the English language were brought out in response to the needs not just of society generally, but of particularl classes or social groups, especially those who were becoming dominant as specific times. The Oxford English Dictionary was precisely a reflection of British imperial power, as was the Dictionary of National Biography. In *every* case it could be shown that various information sources were created to meet particular social needs. This is clear enough in the case of Emily Post on etiquette but less obvious with quotation sources, some of which are democratic and some are not. We have discovered that even after students have studied encyclopedias and other compendia and factual compilations, they are unaware of an ethnocentric bias which is naturally undeclared and not always intentional.

I discussed the role of reference material in national culture in a former work with reference to Britain: 'many reference works achieve the status of symbolic institutions. The elaborate structure of our society is reflected precisly by the regular appearance of *Whitaker's almanack*, *Who's who*, *Crockford* and the *Annual register*. Historians of the future will find much evidence for a picture of our times in the *Stock Exchange year book*, in the *Wisden Cricketers' almanac* and in *Debrett* . . . A civilisation is only as good as its reference literature. In times of trouble, the year books become irregular and the *Almanach de Gotha* ceases to appear at all'. (3)

In addition to this direct social symbolic function there is also an indirect one which relates to status, rather than immediate practical use. Private libraries have often been collected mainly for a status value. In this sense a book is no different from an automobile or a television set; which of these brings the higher status depends on various social factors which vary according to the society. A data bank, no doubt, brings prestige to the banker, and those who control computerised information systems have their own non-informational rewards.

But this is not all. It has been pointed out by many critics that in post-industrial societies both 'objective' knowledge and/or information are now being fed into a process which is called 'decision-making'. To quote Illich again, 'The world does not contain any information. It is as it is. Information about it is created in the organism through its interaction with the world. To speak about storage of information outside the human body is to fall into a semantic trap. Books or computers are part of the world. They can yield information when they are looked upon. We move the problem of learning and of cognition nicely into the blind spot of our intellectual vision if we confuse vehicles for potential information with information itself. We do the same when we confuse data for potential decision with decision itself'. (4) This passage indicates his main theme, which is that the institutionalisation of knowledge makes people dependent on having their knowledge produced for them and leads to a paralysis of the moral and political imagination. We shall not pursue these matters because they are more concerned with the information needs of advanced countries. We have discussed the knowledge industry centred on the universities in those countries. There is an information industry also, and we are faced once more with the questions: can such an industry be transferred, or is there any reason why it should be? That is the theme of this chapter and that is where the librarians come in.

193

Traditional societies

With the exceptions already noted, non-literate African societies did not require written records. Elsewhere, in the past, information was usually recorded in the first instance in response to the needs of a ruling or priestly caste. (Taxation without using records is a tricky business.) But where there has been no writing and when information had to be stored the source has been human memory.

Scientists inform us that the organ responsible for memory in the human brain is called the 'hippocampus', because it resembles that strange vertical little creature, the sea horse. The hippocampus performs prodigious feats but it can exist only within the individual brain. It is a storage system of a peculiar kind, since at any given time its reliability depends on personal mortality, human fallibility and social stability. When societies decayed or disintegrated or were destroyed by wars, the hippocampus became deranged or ineffective; in the terminology of modern retrieval, it started to produce 'noise'. However, information transmitted by memory has usually survived in some form, whereas recorded information (also fallible because it has a human source) can be destroyed.

There are other records, of course, such as fossils in the rocks or artefacts like houses and pots, most of which in Africa the termites have eaten; they have returned to dust.

We must conclude that insofar as information has to be preserved, the requirements of non-literate societies were of a different order. In the traditional past research certainly existed. For example, it has been observed that 'where scientific procedure is different amongst the Yoruba is, among other things, the reluctance to make discoveries public. Knowledge cannot therefore be cumulative or advanced. Insofar as the Yoruba did not traditionally have an accepted procedure for patenting such discoveries, this action can be understood if not appreciated'. (5) It is true that the patent system is an important part of the modern capitalist organisation of knowledge and is one of the barriers to the easy transfer of scientific information. Our main concern is with this modern situation.

Literate transitional societies

Pre-industrial literate societies which preserved records were not concerned with 'bringing people together', and their rulers were consciously engaged in making sure that information was not made generally available. This was done at government level; information did not 'flow' throughout society because it would have been a disruptive force.

194

Peasant societies have always been secretive. Under subsistence conditions and in a world of scarce resources the national or even local communality implied by the sharing of information is not possible; it is also precluded by the existence of ethnic or class divisions. I emphasise this because such conditions still prevail in transitional or modernising societies; the use, misuse or perversion of information is a social weapon.

We have already quoted Vickery—'Modern society incessantly produces and uses information'. But the societies we are discussing are by definition not modern and do not produce or use information in that manner. The sources have not grown up in response to some indigenous need; they have been transplanted from another place. In this respect an information source is no different from a washing machine and neither is politically neutral.

We are now in a position to look at the information scene more carefully. The main point is that in underdeveloped countries there is a prevalence of secrecy, especially at an official level. Where suspicion and distrust are endemic, individuals, as a matter of habit and self preservation, do not pass on information—except within closed networks. Such restricted structures include the family, which may be extended to embrace at least a hundred persons. There is then, quite distinct from official channels, a social flow of information.

The local centres for this type of network have usually been provided by drinking establishments. Much has been written about the cultural role of coffee houses in eighteenth-century Britain, and some attention has been paid to traditional African markets as communication centres, but the role of pubs or bars has been seriously neglected. In most places official library literature has regarded them as an undersirable alternative to libraries, which it was claimed (without much evidence) would help to moderate drinking habits. But the bars were not thought of as information centres in themselves, perhaps because bibliophilic missionaries considered it the wrong kind of information.

The fact remains that quite distinct from the establishment of national networks for information, there have always been channels where the information flow is inspired by the presence of alcohol or some less malignant drug such as cannabis. This is not a frivolous point, since in secretive societies where people's lips are sealed they may be unsealed by such means. In many African towns and villages where there is no electricity the drinking establishments are the only social information sources, with the important exception of religious organisations. We are not suggesting that they are sufficient, because they do not contribute information for

195

development; they do not lead to action but function rather as a kind of social lubricant.

In many communities a similarly serious claim could be made for the not unrelated institution of prostitution. The vulgar mind tends to associate these ladies solely with sex, whereas they have other social functions including a role as an important link in local information structures. This is particularly so in some polygamous societies where Purdah (the seclusion of women) is practised amongst the wealthier classes. Because they are not shut away the so called 'free' women are more articulate and well informed, not only about routine local gossip, but also about matters of social significance. At a national and international level they are part of official espionage systems.

Bureaucracy

In terms of political power we have to consider various forms of bureaucracy. One feature of bureaucracies is that 'knowledge', or the possession of certain kinds of information, endows its owners with power over other people. (Traditionally seers, necromancers, prophets and witch-doctors derive their powers from their real or imagined connections with supernormal forces.) We instinctively fear policemen or other official representatives because they are equipped with special information and it may be about *us*. In countries where social mobility both upward and downward is the rule, and people grow rich and then poor again almost overnight—where, in the words of a mammy wagon slogan, 'no condition is permanent'—a degree of insecurity must prevail. Inevitably therefore people are obsessed with power relations.

Wherever the power struggle goes on, the maintenance of superiority over others requires that information should be withheld. The economic value of information for the individual requires that it should be ir-retrievable except to privileged minorities. In most places people have experienced a bureaucratic situation where an official has refused to supply information for no apparent reason. One can therefore only conclude that he is either mercenary, or subject to obstructive psychological drives, or both. Where money is required for the information the remedy is at hand; it is a simple haggling process similar to what happens in the market place. If you fail to pay the required amount, you will receive inadequate or false information—a natural economic response. However, it is the second of these possible motivations which is more likely and more difficult to deal with. Those who are driven by demonic forces are not easily moved.

196

The same tendency can be observed with regard to education. Fadipe observes: 'the general result of education on the Yoruba was not to give him a critical attitude towards existing customs and practices but to provide him with a position of privilege in relation to those who did not have formal education'. (6) It is fair to add that such attitudes are not confined to the Yoruba; they are symptomatic of societies at a particular stage of development.

Secret societies
In West Africa and elsewhere secret societies have been a central element in traditional social life—they preserve the purity of the tribe and provide a feeling of identity and a social reality for their members, who are usually but not always all male.

Fear of women has been partly responsible for the setting up of secret male organisations. As Fadipe notes in the case of some Yoruba communities, 'the Ogboni fraternity in every community felt the need of an expeditious and vigorous handling of certain classes of offences, disorders and crimes in the community, free of the paralysing and distracting mysteries of the womenfolk'. (7) From this point of view such associations are counter-mysteries; they **have** also helped to keep alive the universal belief in the reality of witchcraft. Amongst other things the institution of witchcraft was a formidable device for the control of women, an aspect which has been curiously neglected by authorities.

It is apparent that the functions of these societies are now no longer administrative but social and cultural, a significant example of the survival of the traditional in another form. Yet in a modernising state such societies begin to take on the sinister overtones that have surrounded such secret bodies as the Freemasons. In Nigeria and elsewhere they have also played a political role in supporting particular political parties such as the former Action Group. These consequences are not our concern, but their role as an information network indicates the presence of closed systems which do not facilitate a national information flow.

The librarian's role
Modern libraries are information centres above all. Since the industrial revolution the nature and scope of librarianship has been profoundly changed and extended by the growth of information centres and libraries in special subject fields. This development took place in all industrial countries and the specialised activities made a decisive impact on general library practice and theory. But in underdeveloped countries special

197

libraries have not come into existence in this manner, so that their influence on general librarianship has been limited. The significant libraries are those concerned with scientific and industrial research and they have not been required in poor countries because large-scale production and research takes place elsewhere, mainly in the metropolitan centres of the developed world.

This helps to keep the level of information service down, not only in specialised institutions but in general libraries as well; the importance of information is not apparent and the status of information workers remains correspondingly low. As Cavan McCarthy notes, in the case of one Latin American country which is more advanced than most, 'Brazilian special libraries tend to be set up under universities or ministries because the other branches of the field, notably industrial librarianship, are underdeveloped. This is not simply a reflection of the low status of the library, it is more connected with the stage of development of the industry. Foreign-based firms tend not to need libraries; their research and development is done in the mother coutnry and technical innovations are not read in journals but brought in by foreign engineers posted to Brazil for a tour of duty. Brazilian firms are run on an entrepreneurial rather than technological basis'. (8)   This is a situation typical of developing countries, except that the indigenous businessmen in Brazil are probably more capable of competing with foreign combines than those in Africa.

The above reference is to individual industrial firms and their non-use of information. There remains the possibility of national centralised documentation centres, either specialising in particular fields or covering general science and technology. Certainly they have been set up in many countries—for instance, in Brazil itself, in the case of medicine. There are national documentation centres in India and Indonesia. Some have benefited from foreign aid; some are primarily prestige projects whose use may not match their status value. In Nigeria under the current development plan, there are proposals for a National Scientific and Technological Research Centre; in Ghana a network of research units exists and is centred on a national centre. But the presence of such organisations is not an indication of their use.

To return to general library service, the absence of the habit of producing and distributing information is partly respobsible for the level of activity. There are, of course, other contributory factors such as a lack of subject knowledge or bibliographical expertise. But the service motivation remains weak, since librarians cannot be expected to have attitudes which are different from everybody else. To many ears, the very word 'service' has a menial ring and is instinctively associated with domestic service or other demeaning activities: why should one provide information to persons who exist on a lower salary grade? Such attitudes are not always conscious but they are, none the less, present and deeply ingrained. There should be no need to add that there are naturally exceptions to these generalisations.

There is also the question of supply and demand. The would-be information officer may well find that nobody seems to want his services. Certainly in former times the small public reference libraries in rural Britain were very little used, for similar reasons. The use of organised information is particularly associated with the existence of an urban middle class. It is possible to claim that the need for information exists in any type of community but the point is that it is not a felt need. This is a development problem and something which librarians and information officers have to understand, since part of their job is to identify needs and translate them into a conscious system. Otherwise people in the villages will try to find out what to do by asking their friends, their kinsfolk or their traditional rulers, or even by writing to the newspapers, and none of these may be able to supply what is required. These needs are very much present in illiterate communities but the villagers either have no questions or if they do, they will not ask.

So far we have not considered the more obvious control of information which happens under modern authoritarian regimes, partly because it is discussed in Chapter 8. Free information networks exist only in democratic communities, as distinct from the controlled systems found in the Soviet Union and elsewhere. In such countries the information that should 'bring people together' helps to keep them apart because it is doctored or 'laundered'; it is a means of manipulation. In these industrialised countries it is possible to have highly efficient information retrieval systems but they also are closed circuits and often the members of the network are privileged persons. For example, anti-Soviet literature is available in some libraries in the Soviet Union but only to a limited number of 'specialists'. This ideological control is a deliberate policy, whereas in the countries under discussion the obstacles I have mentioned are not overt; they are culturally embedded, as it were, and not planned.

Information storage
There are difficulties associated with the *collection* of official information. Modern states cannot function properly, for example, without reliable

199

statistics. These may not be available because false figures may be deliberately or accidentally supplied.

Census figures are notoriously politically 'sensitive' and the Nigerian government found it necessary to withdraw the 1973 national census figures altogether. M C Smith, in his work on Zaria, in Nigeria, refers to the fact that the British colonialists, on the evidence of figures collected, became convinced that the Hausa population was infertile, whereas the population was simply 'under-represented'. The British had 'for long been concerned with the apparent failure of population in these Fulani emirates to increase in accordance with their expectations. During 1929/30 an elaborate investigation was conducted into the reason for low Hausa fertility. Diet was blamed, on the curious ground that rats fed with Hausa staples tended to lose their powers of reproduction. Actually Hausa are highly fertile'. (9)

One of the early attempts to set up Universal Primary Education in the then Western State of Nigeria partially failed because there were more children than had been anticipated. In fact, education statistics are notoriously unreliable. As Myrdal notes, 'the educational statistics are probably even less satisfactory than statistics in almost every other field'. (10) And furthermore, 'there are opportunistic interests best served by having the actual situation unrevealed or at least presented in a way that does not raise thoughts about the need for a radical change of educational policy'. Likewise in fields such as health or labour the statistics required for planning have not been collected. In such cases information cannot be retrieved because it has not yet come into existence. 'The world does not contain any information', and in the Third World those who interact with the world politically may have good reasons for not creating it.

This state of affairs causes problems for the institutionalised social scientists, who believe that politicians should not act unless they have sufficient information provided for them to make predictions possible. The pedlars of pseudo-science are in consequence faced with a grave dilemma in Third World countries. As one of them notes: 'since we know so little it is wiser to act towards goals that are relatively proximate and therefore relatively calculable, than towards goals that are so broad and remote that all calculations break down. *It is easier to save a village than to save the world*' [My italics]. That is precisely what the colonialists used to believe in their plans for community development. The implication seems to be that we cannot 'save the world' (meaning carry out national development) since there is not enough information.

It is suggested by Berger that in making development policy we should apply 'some variant of cost/benefit analysis' and try to build up a calculus of the probable results in terms of human suffering and human values. It is a bleak and wholly reactionary doctrine which I believe rests on a fundamental misunderstanding of the political process, especially in countries which have to be mobilised for development. The suggestion is that 'absolutist', religious or ideological beliefs are dangerous because those who hold them fail to appreciate the limits of action and their own limitations. It is not the *amount* of available information which should determine policy, but how it is used to modify theory which has to be tested in practice. (Similarly a well researched book is not necessarily a good one.) Information is not a thing but the result of human activity, and information is not available in the Third World precisely because most human activities are underdeveloped. Like illiteracy, overpopulation, or epidemics, the absence of reliable information is a *symptom* of under-development, which exists not because the required research is too costly or time-consuming (although that may be the case) but for the reasons mentioned above. What is produced is not information but misinformation or lies or rumours or finally *silence.*

The transfer of bibliographical information
Librarians in new countries commonly believe that the latest techniques should be introduced as soon as possible. The automation of library processes can certainly be introduced and is being introduced in developing countries. In the case of **charging systems** or internal cataloguing and other recording processes there are advantages which may well lead to their adoption. However, in this section we are concerned not with these systems but with the possible transfer of bibliographical information. One possible type of transfer is through the use of overseas bibliographical services such as the MEDLARS or the MARC projects. Foreign countries can import either the computer generated lists these agencies produce or they can import tapes to be handled by their own computers. Some of the possible difficulties are as follows:

1   Although external data bases take over clerical tasks and may alleviate a shortage of skilled staff at one level, professional skills are still required for selection and acquisition work. Indeed, improved skills may be necessary.

2   Difficulties obviously arise with the use of computers in places where electricity services are intermittent or fluctuating; this applies to any type of automation. (The usual response to this criticism is that the

electricity services will eventually improve and that the objection is not therefore valid.)

3 Many libraries in developing countries are too small for automatic processes to be economic.

4 The selection of machines causes many problems; projects may be initiated too early or systems may be outmoded before they are put into operation.

5 Data bases produced abroad such as the MARC system, which includes all the entries in the current British and American national bibliographies, contain a very large number of items. When one considers the probable lack of demand in developing countries for so many titles it might be difficult to justify the cost of importing and maintaining these systems.

I have stressed the MARC principle because it is an excellent example of the problems of transfer, even when the data base remains external. Scholars have dreamt of a universal bibliography for centuries. Technology has now made this possible, but is it practical for transfer? Most of the objections to importing these processes to developing countries fall under a single rubric, which is that neither the infrastructure (communications) nor the level of library service is sufficiently developed to support them. For example, co-operation between libraries is hardly possible, so there is an immediate limitation.

Retrieval systems
In addition to these basic recording procedures, information science now uses highly sophisticated electronic and transistorised devices for the storage and retrieval of every kind of information. Much of the work hitherto done by the human brain is being taken over.

These latest developments have widened the technological gap between the rich and the poor countries even further. It is not practical to take about catching up because the *current level of social development cannot support such systems*; they do not exist in a vacuum. To insist on this point is likely to make one unpopular, and the accusation will be made that there is a plot to keep the developing countries down. One can only repeat that the natural tendency to want the best and latest technology may be an obstacle to development and part of a refusal to understand the social situation. We are back with the question of relevance.

Many instances could be quoted but two should suffice. Public library services in anglophone West Africa were naturally patterned on those in

Britain or America. This is quite understandable since some model has to be adopted, but it has led to a neglect of the fact that public needs and reading habits are not the same.

One requirement is that large reading rooms should be set up in all urban centres to provide for those who are simply studying for their examinations using their own textbooks. Because these students are not using the book collection but only the building they have been 'frowned upon' (a common expression), and until quite recently at the Kaduna State library a notice informed the public that they must not take their own books into the reference library. Such rooms are not provided because they would not constitute a 'proper' library. The consequence is that in Lagos and other cities where reference libraries on a British pattern have been built, an overflow of young people occupies every available horizontal place—a pathetic sight: They are defined as 'drop-outs' and regarded as a nuisance, yet they are the citizens who need the library most.

In the same way the illiterates and neo-literates in the rural areas are considered troublesome because they cannot read. Clearly the readers are expected to exist for the sake of the library instead of the other way round. The library, to be good in an 'international' sense, requires suitable readers, and if they are not there then they ought to be and the librarians should behave as if they were!

A second example of irrelevance can be found in the practice of *over-cataloguing*. McCarthy mentions these practices in Brazil, where the librarians use foreign codes with all their detailed ramifications: 'Librarians in developing countries would be better advised to follow the spirit of our librarianship, rather than our cataloguing rules, but the spirit is not codified in the same way as the rules, nor is it so easily transmitted via cold printed text'. (11) One result of this is that 'Brazilian libraries have vast backlogs of uncatalogued books. The most famous example of this is the National LIbrary, which in 1971 had 2.5 million items, of which half a million, or 20 per cent, were uncatalogued and therefore unavailable to readers; it was taking an average of six years to process books'. He also mentions that in some Brazilian library schools as much as one half of the lectures may be devoted to classification and cataloguing. 'It is very difficult for the foreign librarian to know what attitude to take'.

I do not find it difficult at all; the 'spirit' of librarianship cannot be transferred because it is part of a democratic process which is not present. All that can be transmitted is an obsession with routines which is noticeable elsewhere in libraries. Neither the theory nor the practice of

cataloguing and classification are reactionary or bureaucratic in themselves; they are simply misused in a land where, to misquote 'Ranganathan's law', books are not for use.

Methods or means have become divorced from ends. Means become
ends in themselves and cease to have meaning; this substitution is a well
known characteristic of nihilisms. Are we suggesting that all these conscientious librarians are barbarians? Only in the sense that when the active
barbarians are at the gate it is the passive ones who let them in.

What then should be done?

At this point I should make it clear that I am not suggesting that modern
information techniques and systems should not be adopted. As in other
areas there can be no going back; somehow the transfers must be made.
There are appropriate metaphors for the processes involved. Are they
similar to transplanting, or is it grafting on to a different plant already
there, or should one start again and import the seed? Meanwhile there
is the stony ground and the tropical sun.

In spite of what has just been said it is now time to assert that information services are of quite fundamental importance if national development or any form of modernisation is to continue. A comparable need
was noted in the case of mass communication, since these agencies constitute one of the means by which information is transmitted. The information which libraries contain is dead or stillborn unless it can be organised for use.

The essential element in this process is not the methodology—not the
elaboration of techniques—but *personal* activity. Some old-fashioned
librarians were sometimes referred to as 'walking catalogues'; obviously
their modern equivalents need other attributes, but without their services
the retrieval systems are so much useless ironmongery. Live information
will begin to flow when the right persons are installed at key points
throughout society. Such informational growth points will include
national documentation centres (in both general and special subject areas)
nespaper offices, radio and television stations, industrial firms, commercial
organisations such as banks, welfare institutions, government departments,
archival agencies, museums, and national institutes of sound and visual
records. They will also include, above all, the village information centre
which will link the villagers—literate and non-literate alike—with the
ends of the earth. This list sounds Utopian and is meant to be, since
both national development and the provision of information to assist it
are still largely *potential*.

The history of the Sahelian drought of the early 1970s illustrates very clearly how the use of information is determined by social, political and economic factors. In six very poor nations a prolonged drought led to the disappearance of almost all livestock. The consequence was mass famine and the destruction of an ancient culture.

At one of the many conferences which subsequently discussed the drought it was recommended that a documentation centre should be set up to provide information, particularly on the causes of the disaster and on what preventative measures should be taken in the future; this was not done and the need remains. However, it was not lack of information which rendered the people helpless in the face of what is often alleged to be simply an Act of God. Furthermore it was not lack of information which prevented the governments of several countries (notably Ethiopia) from revealing the severity of the crisis to the rest of the world until it was too late. Finally it was not lack of information which caused national and international aid to become ineffective and insufficient. On the contrary, the decisive obstacles were political. The nomadic peoples had survived prolonged drought before and what they have to contend with today is an additional factor called 'development'. As one authority has noted, 'It is widely agreed that a crucial cause of the events in the Sahel in 1972 and 1973 was the inappropriate and destructive development programmes which had taken place in the preceding ten years.' (12) The provision of wells and vaccination programmes had led to seriously overstocked Sahelian pastures and training in new techniques amounted to little more than ignorant interference with a subtle local economy'. The Secretary of the Permanent Inter-State Committee for Drought Control in the Sahel is on record as having said (1973) 'We have to discipline these people, and to control their grazing and their movements. Their liberty is too expensive for us. This disaster is our opportunity.'

This last quotation has the merit of being an honest statement of what modernisation may involve. I have cited it in order to indicate how development policies can affect the course of events. The 'information' which may or may not become available is determined in the same way; it does not exist without reference to its use.

REFERENCES

1 Vickery, B C, *Techniques of information retrieval* Butterworth, 1970, I.
2 Yovits, M C and Ernest, R L, 'Centralised information systems' *in People and information* (ed) by H B Pepinsky, Pergamon, 1970, 7.

3 Benge, R C, *Bibliography and the provision of books* AAL, 1963, 117.
4 Illich, Ivan, *Tools for conviviality* Fontana, 1975, 101.
5 Okedidiji, F O and Okedidiji, O O, *in* Introduction to Fadipe, N A, *The sociology of the Yoruba* Ibadan University Press, 1970, 15.
6 Fadipe, N A, *op cit*
7 Fadipe, N A, *op cit*, 249.
8 McCarthy, Cavan, *Developing libraries in Brazil* Scarecrow Press, 1975, 126.
9 Smith, M G, *Government in Zazzau, 1800-1950* OUP, 1960, 282.
10 Myrdal, Gunnar, *The challenge of world poverty* Pelican, 1971, 170.
11 McCarthy, Cavan, *op cit*, Chapter 6.
12 Marnham, Patrick, *Nomads of the Sahel* Minority Rights Group Report No 33, 1977, 12.

12

THE LIBRARY PROFESSION AND LIBRARY EDUCATION

Discussions on the characteristics of professions and whether librarianship meets all the requirements are by now sufficiently familiar; they need
not be repeated here except as a list to serve as a basis for what is relevant
for these present explorations. It is usually agreed that professional groups
can be distinguished by the following:

1 An effective professional organisation.
2 An adequate structure of professional education.
3 Personal service and code of ethics.
4 A coherent and established body of knowledge.
5 A degree of independence.
6 Status or public recognition.

I am concerned with these characteristics only is so far as they are present
or not in the countries we are discussing.

Library associations
Professional organisations are likely to be weak because numbers are
small; as compared with teachers, doctors, or lawyers, librarians represent
a new profession. Accordingly, unless outside subsidies are forthcoming
(which is unlikely in most cases) there will be a shaky financial base.
Quite apart from the lack of money, there are not enough members to do
what is required. In any country only about a quarter or less of the qualified professionals are likely to be active members, so that where numbers
are small to begin with, the activists will be few indeed.

Another point is that when libraries are in their infancy individuals
have to be highly competitive, and in consequence do not co-operate well
for the common good. In some countries this lack of a mutual correspondence of interest is intensified by ethnic rivalries which are none the
less real for being submerged.

Where countries are large (as is the case with Nigeria) communication difficulties are a major obstacle to the activities of councils and committees. It may be possible for members to gather together for annual conferences but the vital work done by elected officials is hampered by the distance between places and their relative isolation. The work of associations is also limited by the non-existence of an official headquarters or of paid officers. Indeed it is safe to say that without this material structure a professional body cannot be fully effective.

Another factor which may operate against high motivation is that taking part in the work of the organised profession may not be essential for advancement or promotion. When library systems are still being created the jobs are readily available.

I have stressed these inherent limitations because associations are often unfairly criticised for their lack of impact. It could hardly be otherwise; no library associations have been able to exert much influence in their early days.

Independence and personal service

Librarians everywhere are not usually autonomous as individuals—unlike doctors or lawyers they cannot go into private practice. In new countries they are mostly civil servants, and some authorities have gone so far as to suggest that those who are employed by the state cannot be regarded as truly professional because they lack independence.

It is necessary to look most carefully at this particular requirement because such autonomy may help to bring professions into disrepute. To whom should loyalty be given? The professional person owes an allegiance to himself and his family, to his profession, to his employers, and to the people whom he is supposed to serve—which in the case of librarians is the reading public. Which of these loyalties should be paramount? We cannot assume that the demands made by these various groups will never clash. If a professional body concentrates mainly or solely on the interests of its members it becomes a trade union and no more. If librarians simply go along with the erratic political policies of state organisations they become civil servants and nothing else. The conclusion can only be that demands for professional independence are not admissible unless they co-exist with a sense of responsibility towards a clientele.

This is the service ethic which we have already discussed, particularly in the chapter on information. In underdeveloped countries the service ethic cannot be taken for granted and frequently it is not there. It is

208

possible, for example, for doctors to go on strike, and they have often
done so, mainly to protect their own interests (which are then labelled
'selfish' by an angry government).

Ghana is one of the few African countries where there is something
approaching a middle class. In 1977 professional organisations cour-
ageously opposed the policies of their government, which was severely
shaken. In this instance the middle-class elements were not simply concerned with their own interests, but the significant political factor was
that they had little contact or support from 'the masses' (they were of
course backed up by the students). Ever since the nationalists first
started agitations against the colonialists there has been that lack of involvement with the mass of the people; a truly national allegiance has
been absent.

I have brought in these wider issues since the political parallel resides
in the nature of élitism. From the point of view intended by those who
drew up these abstractions an élitist profession cannot be truly professional. It is in this sense that professionalism may be not in the interests
of national development. It should not therefore be assumed that the
only requirement is to build up a strong profession. For example, it can
be seriously doubted whether the American Medical Association has been
wholly concerned with the health requirements of the American people.
Capitalism breeds its own type of professional; for such a person independence based on a responsibility to and for those he serves then becomes
a secondary consideration. In communist countries the professional is
subservient to the state apparatus and has neither economic nor intellectual autonomy.

Status

So much ink has been spilt on the alleged lack of status of librarians that
only a few observations should be necessary. The first is that in most
undeveloped countries the status of librarians compares favourably with
that of their colleagues in industrialised countries. This is because they
are members of a small class who are socially separated from the majority
of the people. They often have cause to complain that their expectations
or rewards may compare unfavourably with the other members of that
class, for example, army officers or academics, but otherwise their position
is assured.

In the old countries it is customary to compare the lot of librarians
with that of teachers, often to the disadvantage of the former. If the
same comparison is made in our context it will usually be found that the

status of librarians is higher than that of teachers. Perhaps it is a comparison which should not be made in these circumstances, and we should place more emphasis on other criteria. First, we can say that from a salary and conditions-of-service point of view matters are usually satisfactory. It is in this context perhaps fortunate that in most new countries local government authorities were never financially strong enough to support libraries.

There remains the question of public recognition and here the equation is clearly different. Amongst the mass of the people the librarian has status like any other member of the fully educated class: in this respect he is in a stronger position than a librarian in the older countries where such a person is not respected just because he is educated and literate. The unlettered masses may not know or care what a library is for but they recognise a 'big man' when they see one. So far so good; where the library worker is less secure is in relation to his peers amongst the educated. He finds that they do not appreciate the importance of library or information services often because they have played little part in their own lives. Even when they do appreciate the uses of reading it may only be for themselves. It does not follow that they feel (whatever they may say) that everybody has a need or a right to such advantages. It follows that the librarian has to struggle for recognition and support. However, this fight against indifference has happened everywhere, except in the communist countries, where official support has always been forthcoming for ideological reasons. It is therefore only a matter of degree, and we can conclude that librarians probably receive the status they deserve.

At a deeper level and without reference to particular countries it has to be recognised that there is something inherent in library and information work which renders it less urgent or vital than the activities of doctors or lawyers, or even priests. The significance of a librarian is not usually that he is suddenly required in time of crisis or dismay but that he is there all the time like the weather; he is part of the foundation of a civilised life whereas neither doctor nor lawyer nor soldier are needed all the time. Like teachers, librarians are embedded in the foundations of the cultural process; their tragedy is that they ought to be most noticeable when they are not there, but in many countries this does not happen.

Education
As libraries are set up, sooner or later an indigenous system of professional education has to be introduced to meet their staffing needs. Exactly when this should happen varies according to national circumstances and resources.

At this time a discussion of the advantages or otherwise of this process is not necessary. From the point of view of national development and the position taken throughout this book, local library schools should be set up as soon as possible. Students should also be able to go overseas for study purposes at some stage, but preferably not until after they are qualified. This means that an indigenous school (necessarily a university department in most countries) should be able to offer degrees up to the highest level. If it does not do this, the national school cannot develop as an educational institution. It is not until staff and students begin to be involved with the right kind of research that a department can grow. This is particularly important in countries where the profession is new because it is at the higher degree level that a beginning can be made in the investigation of local circumstances. However, it has to be said that often there is no easy answer to the problem since indigenous library schools frequently do not have the type of staff or the research resources which are essential. In one case a student doing research in his own country cannot find all the literature he needs; in another the literature in foreign countries with good library services is available but the researcher's supervisors do not understand his problems. The alternative is to conduct research in subjects which have no relevance to his own country, which is clearly undesirable.

In view of the disagreements which have existed, some reference should be made to the type of education programme which should be set up. For Nigeria the development of library education has been attended by controversies which have arisen because two different types of basic programme were established—one postgraduate programme at Ibadan and one undergraduate at Zaria. Some conclusions may be drawn which have wider reference.

American and other experience has shown that undergraduate or first degree programmes for the education of librarians become necessary in any country where there is a rapid expansion of library development and where a large number of library staff are required. Relying on a postgraduate programme alone usually does not produce sufficient numbers rapidly enough. (The assumption here is that, if this is an expanding economy, there will be a demand for university graduates in every field. It may or may not be a permanent condition so that university programmes have to be flexible enough to allow for change.) This was the situation in Nigeria in 1978, and the two fully established library schools could not provide enough recruits, so three or four more schools are likely to be set up. The type of programme to be introduced will be largely determined by factors which are not strictly academic and this is how it should be.

In 1967, at the University of Ghana, I introduced an undergraduate programme (which was later abandoned for reasons which are superficially obscure) and there are underlying social considerations which need to be discussed. In the first place the requirement mentioned above was not there; at that time the economy was not expanding and there was not a pressing demand for librarians. (Whether the programme subsequently established met later requirements is not the point here.) In working for such a programme I had been influenced by other factors and at that time believed that an undergraduate programme was most appropriate for developing countries. It now seems to me that I did not sufficiently allow for the élitist bias which is built into both the academic institution and society generally (in Ghana and in other ex-colonies). This takes the form of an over-evaluation of academic qualifications, so that a person with two degrees feels automatically that he is superior to another person with one. In the context of competitive career structures whether this is a false value or not is irrelevant; that is the way it is.

The theoretical answer to this problem is of course to provide for both an undergraduate and a graduate programme (as is now done in Zaria) but this raises further questions in turn. One of these is that there will be two possible qualifications for librarians, and in the context of development we have to consider whether this is advisable.

It is of some significance that Nigerian students always assume that two qualification structures are wholly undesirable—and the are not impressed by the fact that in Britain or the USA there are a number of different degrees. This instinctive reaction should be taken seriously, as it springs from their own experience of a very competitive society. In this respect Nigeria is not typical because it is sufficiently large and diverse ultimately to accommodate idfferent types of qualification which may reflect various local circumstances.

What is important is not so much the qualifications which are established as *when* they are set up. A qualification is recognised when there are enough people to hold it and defend themselves; a degree inevitably becomes a vested interest to be supported against others. It may well be that this kind of competiton is healthy. In the long run the educational standards which are present in institutions must have some effect irrespective of the type of programme. My tentative conclusion therefore is that a variety of qualifications may not be against the best interests of the library profession once the library situation has developed beyond a rudimentary level.

212

Indigenisation

I have discussed the need for a radical approach to this problem in another chapter. It remains to apply some of these conclusions to library education.

Already noted is the fact that it is the approach, not just the content, which is of vital importance. We are concerned with cultural liberation and a modification of consciousness which is what education for national development should be about. This is not achieved by tinkering or tacking bits on to syllabuses which have emerged in other places. For is it simply a matter of adding courses with local colour or including in examination questions the formula 'with special reference' to whatever it is. What often happens now in librarianship courses is that a body of knowledge is assumed to be universal and then an attempt is made to apply it to individual local circumstances. If neither the theory nor the practice fits the environment then it is to be hoped that one day they will all correspond—for example, that all the people will become literate. But 'knowledge' is not universal but a social construct so that one should begin at the place where one happens to be; the individual should be at the centre of his world. This is not a moral or normative prescription concerning what ought to be done but a matter of perception.

A consequence of cultural dependence is that perceptions are blocked or distorted so that people are *prevented from seeing their own world*; they are using borrowed coloured spectacles. With regard to education for librarians this causes the unfortunate students to concentrate on non-problems and provide answers to questions which should not have been asked. It is of course true that the textbooks are inappropriate, but that is partially true of all textbooks; the teacher's task is one of interpretation and eventually to provide his own text. Must we therefore place the balme or the responsibility squarely on the teachers? At this point we return to the malign influences of the education systems as already discussed. It may well be that both students and teachers have already been thoroughly brainwashed. All that one can hope for is that these mental structures can somehow be dismantled. This situation is best illustrated by examples.

Library history

When we consider the history of libraries it is difficult to persuade students that there is not a *thing* called history. They therefore conclude that we can achieve local relevance by increasing the number of details about their own history and by limiting the amount of time to be spent

213

on the rest; that is not what we mean by indigenisation. The history of libraries in Babylonia, ancient Rome, Greece, in the European Middle Ages, or in the present-day USA or USSR is relevant not because we can learn lessons about what should be done—we can only learn from our own mistakes.

These far away times and places can become 'real' only when we work out what significance they may have for us wherever we happen to be. As always in higher education this is not a matter of truth but of *meaning*—a quite different thing. The study of history therefore is not in the first instance a guide to action but a key to understanding both the universal past and the present—our indigenous present.

Library management

I have already suggested that 'scientific' management in both the East and the West has been used as a collection of techniques for exploiting the workers. What I wish to explore here is that even if we accept that the theories of scientific management as they have been developed, for example in Britain and the USA, should be applied in new countries, then difficulties emerge which are commonly ignored.

Management theories are ethnocentric and when applied to developing countries simply obscure social realities—yet another example of inappropriate transfer. I am not simply stressing that industrial societies are different from those which are not; that is obvious enough. I wish rather to draw attention to one particular manifestation of that difference. One of the alleged characteristics of modern societies is the existence of efficient bureaucracies. In developing countries it is a matter of common experience that the official bureaucratic machinery does not function properly. The implications for management are quite fundamental. Yet institutions *do* work because there is almost invariably a double system. The official structures have been set up for stated purposes but they can only function if there is also a parallel unofficial way of doing things which supports them.

This state of affairs is commonly deplored as 'corruption' but these condemnations miss the point that under the circumstances of underdevelopment a double system is *essential*, otherwise nothing would work at all. That these symptoms are universal in the Third World is an indication of their inevitability. (Singapore has been claimed to be an exception but I am not competent to pronounce on this.) Evidence for the need for these methods is available from Brazil where the second system has been fully institutionalised (as distinct from being condemned

214

or winked at). Agencies exist as intermediaries between the individual citizen and the bureaucracies and you pay them for their services. It may well be objected that these procedures are characteristic of government departments but that they do not necessarily operate in other organisations. The evidence is, however, that the double system operates *in some form* in all institutions.

All that I wish to establish here is that orthodox theories of management make no provision for such conditions, and this is only one example. The 'principles' proceed from invalid assumptions which are not part of management theory but derive from social conditions in other countries. As in the case of economic 'laws', the principles when transformed to a different environment are not wrong but irrelevant, and education which ignores these differences in social reality has not been indigenised; it serves to promote further mystifications.

Book selection

Most curricula in library schools in developing countries quite rightly include book selection as a subject. In this field it is probable that *all* the various factors involved are wholly different from those in the industrialised countries. It will be at once apparent that in developing countries these differences should add up to an altogether new theoretical structure. Some of the relevant factors are: the nature of demand, the supply situation, bookselling and publishing, the availability of bibliographical services, the existence of library co-operation, the accumulations of materials from the past, and so on.

Vital to book selection theory is the question of value. On what grounds (apart from demand) do we assess individual items? Is this a 'good' book or periodical or film *for us*? The answers may be various and complicated but they are not the same as those which have to be made in different societies. One requirement which should arise concerns the items which are essential for national development in the broadest sense. What is this literature and where is it? Often it is not easily found. Meanwhile the existing textbooks cannot help and students do not have to answer this vital question.

Co-operation

The examples I have quoted indicate approaches which are commonly omitted. There are also the sins of commission; a notable one is the theme of library co-operation. It is a curious fact that students (and others) in countries where library services are just beginning display a

215

fervent interest in library co-operation, presumably based on accounts of such systems in Western Europe and the USA. Nobody seems to have pointed out that in most cases the prerequisites for effective library co-operation are not present because, *inter alia*, individual libraries have not reached a level of development where such co-operation is possible. Also in most countries the necessary infrastructure, such as a good transport and telephone system, is not present.

The illusion that co-operation has some kind of primary or central significance presumably derives from British and American experience and the literature about it. The 'theory' as it appears in this literature is based on the concept not of a national library system but on isolated individual libraries such as used to exist in Britain. In that country, because in the past there was no national system, co-operation was the only way to meet readers' requirements. But in new countries libraries, if they are going to develop at all, have to be part of a national development plan. The individual units co-operate because they are part of the same system. In this context library co-operation between all types of library in a national network is of course important, but it is another problem, so that a wholly different theoretical approach is required to correspond. Meanwhile students at all levels think in alien terms.

Relevance versus international standards
We have suggested that the alleged opposition between local relevance and excellence is a false one. Also illusory is the concept that excellence is somehow bound up with a mythical international standard. A knowledge of library theory and practice as it exists in other countries is of course necessary for both theoretical and practical purposes, but this does not mean that foreign models can be used as anything but a guide. Such knowledge is also required when government officials have to be convinced about the importance of good library services. But an imaginary international standard should not be adopted as an educational approach, nor can the literature about conditions in other countries be used as it stands. This may sound too obvious, but the fact remains that students are constantly and perhaps inevitably misled by the literature. One example should suffice.

Research in library studies
From personal experience I have found that unless they are properly warned, students doing any kind of research, whether at an undergraduate or higher degree level, will be led astray by foreign systems. This happens

216

even at the beginning when students are choosing their field of investigation; they are influenced by the topics chosen elsewhere.

In American universities research for the most part is primarily valuable as *an academic exercise*; its value in exploring library situations is probably secondary, if only because most areas have already been investigated. A large body of knowledge about every kind of library and bibliographical activity already exists for developed countries; this foundation is absent in developing countries so that national library development requires that many topics need to be investigated for the first time. Yet the teaching is such that students, influenced by exotic example, choose subjects which have no central significance for the indigenous environment. For example, one student wanted to investigate prison libraries in Nigeria when he was fully aware that none are evident! To take another instance, many potential librarians are fascinated by the possibilities of *bibliometrics*. With some reluctance I am prepared to admit that these studies, if properly carried out, have some value in mature bibliographical situations, but their relevance to national development in new countries is surely minimal; they represent a typical neo-colonial preoccupation.

The psychological drive behind these choices is that they are 'advanced'— even esoteric—areas which therefore must bring status and prestige. Also, in this manner, it is possible to evade the social and cultural predicament both at a personal and professional level. One does not need to be committed to bibliometrics except as an academic ploy. (I should make it clear that I am using this topic simply as one example among many to illustrate the prevalence of certain attitudes.) In this discussion I have not gone beyond a choice of subject; the pitfalls that await the hapless student when he comes to use the appropriate literature are even now calamitous. He may be able to allow for that part of the literature which is wholly or partially irrelevant, but what most often escapes his attention is the assumptions on which the texts are based. It is these which he may subconsciously absorb as he has probably done throughout his education; that is how mimic men are created.

Leadership

There remains one vital matter which is of particular concern in our context. In all developing countries students are frequently told that they are the leaders of tomorrow and the word in this case is used literally and not figuratively. In a rapidly developing situation it is not unusual for a person with no library experience to be a student one day and the next day head of a state library system. It follows that educational and training institutions have a special responsibility.

This much is established but to what extent education can produce leaders is problematic in the extreme. Leadership qualities, once they are present, can be developed by a suitable environment or they can be stunted or misdirected by an unfavourable one. To that degree the methods and content of a professional course can be important. However, differing social situations require different types of leaders and in conformist societies individuals with marked individuality may not succeed. It is likely that in most developing countries there is a very considerable wastage of human potential partly because of the nature of the education system, and also because of authoritarian structures which stifle personal initiative. By the time students reach university level (if they arrive there at all) they may have been trained for social roles which are more appropriate for some other society. This is the failure of the education system which we have already discussed.

It is true therefore that something can be done to foster leadership qualities, but only within the limits indicated above. It is my personal view (one that is not universally shared) that in the countries we are considering, a general ideological foundation is more important than the acquisition of professional knowledge or the mastery of techniques. This ideological education, which can be called decolonisation of the mind or cultural liberation, can awaken a political consciousness even when it has not been present before university education. I am claiming that if this element is not present there can be no real leadership, whatever other qualities people may possess. In rapidly changing circumstances the first requirement is to know where you are going and why.

In advanced societies which are more static this ideological base perhaps matters less, and persons without radical inclinations or interests wider than professional ones may make wholly successful librarians. In transitional societies the foundations have shifted and a wider understanding is required.

Conclusions
I have selected only those professional topics which are relevant to the theme of this work. Some of the implications are considered in the remaining chapters.

13

THE PLANNING OF A NATIONAL LIBRARY SERVICE

In the thirty odd years of Unesco's existence it has been concerned, amongst its other library activities, with the planning of national library and bibliographical services; this has required a strategy to transfer material and intellectual resources from the developed countries to the less developed ones so that they could be stimulated to build up their own library services. My intention here is to examine certain ideological manifestations and this will involve some reference to library literature generally and to the programmes of professional international bodies.

Foundations
Stephen Parker has produced a comprehensive and well documented survey which traces the emergence of the current Unesco concept of a planned centralised national library system. (1) I propose to summarise some of the findings here although the conclusions drawn are naturally not his, but my own.

Parker shows how Unesco's work in this field was rooted in the pioneer labour of a few individuals, both between the wars and after Unesco had been set up. With regard to public library development, due recognition is paid to the foundation work of bodies such as Carnegie United Kingdom Trust and the Carnegie Corporation of New York. These two bodies closely influenced the development of public libraries in Africa, the West Indies, Australia, New Zealand and Canada. As early as 1928 a Carnegie Corporation-sponsored expert had made proposals for a nation-wide library service in Kenya and similar recommendations had been made elsewhere. There was an important pioneer scheme launched by the Corporation in the Eastern Caribbean and this work was taken over by the British Council in 1945. The Council also made a significant contribution in several African countries, notably in Ghana and East Africa. Arising from this experience a few individuals, mainly British and American, acquired the experience which was to become so useful for later developments. Several of them were employed by international and other agencies, and eventually by the new emergent countries, both as advisers and in several cases (notably in Ghana and in the West Indies) as directors of the new library systems.

The British contribution included many years of activity undertaken by librarians who became well known for their work in this field, notably Edward Sydney, Lionel McColvin, Frank Gardner, Eve Evans, Sydney Hocke Harold Bonny, and Sydney Horrocks. Mainly as a result of their expertise, principles for the planning of library services were put forward at Unesco's early international gatherings of librarians. So it was that the pervasive influence for Unesco's library policies came from the Anglo-American tradition. In view of world history between the wars, it can now be seen that this role was inevitable. It reflected the last stages of the British colonial tradition and later the increasing American role in international affiars. In consequence it was to be expected that the Unesco Public Library Manifesto was originally drafted by an American, Emerson Greenaway. It is also not surprising that Lionel McColvin's ideas had a significant influence on the initial formulation of Unesco's libraries programme. (These ideas naturally reflected the British situation where McColvin had made his own proposals for a national library service and where it had long been apparent to all except the most blinkered members of the profession that a national system would eventually have to be set up.)

It is also worthy of note that Julian Huxley (Unesco's first Director) himself epitomised liberal dilemmas. It was said of him that, with equal fervour, he simultaneously embraced a large number of contradictory ideas and ideals. He wanted to synthesise the two opposing ideologies of East and West which, as he said differ essentially on one central point, namely the relation between the individual and the community. This forlorn attempt at a synthesis naturally continues to occupy the attention of international agencies and lies behind current formulations in the field of library services. Meanwhile Huxley was well aware that Unesco's cultural policies were then based on one tradition alone, the Anglo-American one. The Soviet Union did not join Unesco until 1954 and was originally hostile to its policies including those for libraries, regarding them as a form of cultural imperialism. Scandinavian influence was also limited although Denmark, for example, had possessed a State Library Commission since 1909.

It is only in this fashion that we can understand why the Unesco concepts of national library services failed to take account of experience in the USSR, where a national system had been set up by Lenin himself in 1920, and where during the 1930s successive five-year plans had included an integrated programme for libraries.

Ideological consequences
The most important immediate policy result was a preference for pilot projects which would demonstrate to an indifferent world the value of the public library contribution. As noted in the Library Association Record of 1952, 'The Public Library Service in the West is a record of development by demonstration'. (The writer failed to note that British libraries might have developed much more rapidly if the public libraries Acts had *not* been permissive and dependent on local initiative.) It was thought therefore that if model public libraries were created in one particular city in a developing country the government concerned would proceed to set up libraries in other places. It is established that the projects set up in Delhi in 1950, Medellin in 1954, Enugu in 1958, and Abidjan in 1963 were all most successful with regard to the development of their own services, but as demonstration models they were, at least in the short run, relative failures. There is naturally a vast gap between the resources need for one project and those required for nation-wide undertakings. This is not to deny the obvious value of these experiments and the fact that the experience gained was important in relation to future policies both nationally and internationally.

It was during the seminar that developed from these projects that ethnocentric assumptions often emerged; the participants were naturally conditioned by their own experience. For example, at Delhi it was suggested that public library services would not develop unless there was first an indigenous book industry; second, a fairly high literacy rate; and and third, a viable local government structure. These preconditions had been present in Britain, America and Scandinavia but not, be it noted, in Eastern Europe. The dilemma is plain.

Similar influences were apparent in the Sharr report (not of course a Unesco document) on public libraries in Northern Nigeria (1968), where it was recommended that local government units should partly support library services and further that libraries should concentrate on services for the literate and neo-literate minority of the population. (2) Another transferred assumption notable in the earlier years of pilot projects was the emphasis on the need to encourage the reading of imaginative literature (especially novels) and a preference for not supplying textbooks; also it was often felt that 'light literature' should not be provided. The

221

background of reading habits which we have discussed was known but more often deplored than explored. I should make it clear that I am not here criticising the use of overseas models for starting library services; one had to begin somewhere. What is relevant for our purposes is the complex of assumptions which when transferred became central for library policies.

The second phase
Following this experience with pilot projects, Unesco continued to hold a series of meetings of experts in the planning of library services during the 1960s and early 1970s. Between 1960 and 1965 there were seven meetings at Delhi, Mexico City, Bogota, Enugu, Mendoza, Cairo and Manila.

By this time the lessons of earlier experience had been absorbed and macro-planning had arrived. Penna's book which summarised these developments and these ideas had been published. (3) It had at last been accepted that centralised planning was necessary for developing countries. (During the last ten years there have been further meetings at Quito in 1966, Colombia in 1967, Kampala in 1970 and Cairo in 1974.) An agreed policy had been achieved which on the face of it did much to overcome the divergence between the library systems of East and West. Allegiance was still given to libertarian ideals, while at the same time it was agreed that centralised planning was essential for new countries and that the plan for libraries must be integrated with the overall development plan. It had also become increasingly felt that public library systems could not be considered separately from other types of library service, and that the circumstances of new countries required a library network which could somehow embrace all types of library as formerly understood. At the same time, and as a result of the work of other Unesco bodies, the same need for national co-ordination had been felt in scientific and technical information and also sound recommendations had been made for national bibliographical services. The time had arrived for all these proposals to be seen as part of one global endeavour.

The concept of national information services
In the 1970s this work culminated in the creation of NATIS which had followed the information proposals for science and technology generally UNISIST (1970) and in particular fields, for example INIS (nuclear information) and AGRIS (agriculture). The significance of this development was that it had become recognised, first, that all library and information

services within a country must be considered as one system and, second, that they must operate on a global basis.

Technological developments in bibliography, particularly the MARC project, had made it technically possible to link all bibliographical services together, including those of the developing countries. Yet fundamentally the situation with regard to the latter remained as it had always been, that is to say, the question remained—how could these rudimentary services be plugged in to the global network that was to be created? Already it had been alleged that the earliest UNISIST proposals did not make sufficient allowance for the needs of the less developed countries.

The basic NATIS concept is that NATIS should provide an 'umbrella-like framework' for the voluntary co-ordination of information services and provide governments with a set of guidelines so that they can draw up national information plans which will tie in with one another and with internation units. One such unit is the Universal Bibliographical Control clearing house in London, established by IFLA.

Unesco's responsibility is to assist member states, especially developing countries, to develop national infrastructures for information. Accordingly in 1974 there was a Unesco/IFLA 'Intergovernmental Conference on the planning of national documentation library and archives infrastructures'. The *Final report* of the Intergovernmental Conference was issued by Unesco in 1975 and clearly sets out the concept of National Information Systems: 'The precise form and character of the national information system (NATIS) composed of a number of sub-systems will vary in different countries but co-ordination of all elements must be the goal . . . The task of NATIS is to ensure that all engaged in political, economic, scientific, educational, social or cultural activities receive the necessary information enabling them to render their fullest contribution to the whole community'.

Objectives for 'National Action' are then set out; they include a national information policy promotion of the reading habit, assessment of users' needs, analysis of existing information resources, analysis of manpower resources, and recommendations for planning.

Finally UBC is considered in relation to NATIS and certain objectives for international (as distinct from nationa) action laid down. These future policies include: assistance to member states mentioning 'the elaboration of methodologies', the application of information technology to documentation, and a revised programme for the education and training of information manpower. A further objective is the promotion of UBC, which naturally depends on national programmes. The London

centre could 'play an important role in the development of the bibliographic aspects of libraries and documentation services in developing
countries'. This, then, is the culmination of Unesco's work in the field,
and an impressive achievement it is. It now remains to examine some of
the implications.

What difference does it all make?
There can be no doubt that the proposals are sound, but naturally they
remain simply recommendations. I emphasise this point because some
students (and also lecturers) of library science behave as if these national
information systems already exist whereas this 'umbrella' is still largely
an abstract notion.

With regard to underdeveloped countries the situation remains as it
was, and there is no firm evidence that the umbrella will become effective. The contingent factors are of course the usual political and social
ones. This has always been recognised, and it has been assumed that they
lie outside the control of librarians; therefore if they cannot be ignored
they can at least be left to the politicians whose concern they must be.

There are many warnings in the literature . For example, in an early
Unesco document quoted by Burckhardt, 'The basic point upon which
emphasis has to be laid is that the decisions taken in respect of library
development are fundamentally of a political nature. The first step in
the planning of library services is the identification of the objectives of
the service'. (4) It is these *objectives* which have to be political.

Such factors were usually referred to quite correctly as prerequisites
or preconditions which were stressed; for example, the need for legislation, a guarantee of funds, an expert director and so on. Later it became more apparent that it was the social preconditions which were more
basic. Thus Penna noted in his manual that the influence of early plans
was limited because they were not integrated with national development
plans as a whole. Sometimes the political issues emerge by stealth. For
example, Shepard states: 'Two decades have been a long gestation period
for library planning in Latin America. Difficulties to be overcome include:
a characteristic desire for autonomous individual action; an unwilling-
ness to form wider units of library service'. (5) How could it be otherwise? (Shepard was in charge of the Library Development programme of
the Organisation of American States [OAS] a body whose political record she fortunately does not have to discuss.) Similarly, dealing with
Ecuador, one writer notes that 'There is nevertheless an obstacle to
success. This obstacle is the socio-economic condition of Ecuador which

will there, as in all developing countries, influence the character of library development'. (6) Perhaps the mistake in Ecuador, as elsewhere, is to *start* with the plan and then to consider the social conditions as obstacles. If these conditions exist, as they do everywhere, then the plan must either be scrapped for the time being or a different kind of plan will have to be introduced. It is this possibility we should now discuss.

It is clear, for example, that if a high level of illiteracy is to continue (as seems likely in most countries) the role of libraries will have to be different from that in developed countries—unless a decision is made to serve only the literates and neo-literates, who live mainly in the towns. Most students can draw up a different kind of programme and regularly do but the implementation of such policies is outside a librarian's control and often beyond his understanding. The implications of the foregoing chapters have been that unless and until general development takes place (as distinct from economic growth or changes which take place only in the cities) then library development on a national scale can only be spasmodic, partial, and limited by the presence of social conditions such as those brought about by extreme poverty. This does not mean that library systems cannot otherwise progress but it does mean that national plans drawn up by outside experts will remain on the drawing boards. For example, we can easily envisage a possible role for a libray service for illiterate people, but the same factors which prevent the elimination of illiteracy will render all such projects abortive; the existing services are mostly not geared to national development.

Strategies of mystification
It remains to note that our hypothetical student is very likely to be misled by the literature on national library development. It is true that great progress has been made and that if there are several traditions representing the main contending power blocs of a divided world, official cultural recommendations contrive to strike a balance somewhere in the middle.

In the case of the proposals of Unesco, which must carry on in spite of global conflict, a balancing act is essential, and Penna's book, quoted above, meets every requirement when one considers that he has to leave out the politics. However, not all the English language literature on library development needs to be inhibited in this way, even though most of the experts who produce it have been conditioned by their experience at cosmopolitan meetings.

A minor indication of the tensions involved can be seen even in the Unesco manifesto for public libraries which (originally produced in 1946)

225

was revised in 1973. The changes are few and the almost Rotarian ideal-ism of its original contents remain. The only addition seems to be a reference to 'new forms of record' such as audio-visual aids. But it was thought appropriate to leave in the reference to public libraries as 'a pro-duct of modern democracy' since the word has different meanings accord-ing to where one lives. In any case the liberal elements can safely remain unheeded, as they do in the official constitution of the Soviety Union. With regard to liberty there is a little watering down, since the injunction 'to maintain freedom of expression' has disappeared so also has the phrase 'It [the public library] should not tell people what to think but it should help them to decide what to think about'—perhaps the only thought in the original version which borders on the subversive. Otherwise the mani-festo is harmless enough

Turning to non-official literature, an important recent work is *National library and information services: a handbook for planners*, edited by C V Penna, D J Foskett and P H Sewell, who all have unrivalled experience in this field. (7) Yet the difficulty here would appear to be that it is a composite work with many collaborators, both non-communist and com-munist. Perhaps because of this we encounter the device which so often pervades the new literature, and which aims to be 'scientific'. What these experts have in common is a new international language, so that beliefs and purposes and ideology can be safely set aside. The contrasts between the USA and USSR are here described as contrasts in 'organisational patterns'. The living issues are dispensed with and the influence is not really scientific but technical.

National library and information services is the work of technocrats and this kind of literature derives from the field of engineering in parti-cular, as well as from public administration and so-called scientific manage-ment. By using the terminology of systems (systems science, systems de-sign and so on) it is possible to claim that national planning is on the march without reference to what kind of planning it is or what it is for. The political factor is of course that planning in Eastern Europe is different, not only in intent but also as a method, from what happens in Britain or the United States. The planning which is possible in most developing countries is quite different again. All that can be hoped for is that there may be some similarity in certain methodological processes.

It is admitted that planning must have a policy but an international unit like NATIS cannot recommend a particular policy. Needham notes that the expression *'bibliographical control'* is confusing because control is often considered as the *purpose* of the library, whereas it is simply a

226

process. 'To suppose that purposes can be born within the world of documents and documentation is a fundamental error. This is the world of functions. Nothing we do as bibliographers can have any significance in itself, but only insofar as it serves a purpose beyond itself'. (8) Bibliographers were often political idiots; perhaps they had every right to be. But librarians who show themselves to be aware that the world exists perpetuate similar confusions. For instance, one writer states that 'we might also take heart from the fact that in a world increasingly fractionated along ideological, linguistic, political and even religious lines, there is a demonstrable forward surge of library unity. Through out humble efforts to support the universality and integration of knowledge we may at least help to bind up the world's wounds. Perhaps the universal language of the future will be MARC'. (9) One supposes that statements of this kind (reminiscent of similar claims about comparative librarianship) derive from an evasion of the reality of the 'world's wounds' and a consequent absorption in a small professional coterie.

In view of the enormous amount of time, money, energy and mutual hospitality devoted to the cosmopolitan gatherings of library development experts, it is disappointing that their work should be partly invalidated by inauthentic attitudes. In Stephen Parker's valuable thesis, already quoted it is evident that he is aware of these dilemmas, yet he closes his survey as follows: 'If . . the influence of the Anglo-American tradition on library development in the Third World is weakening in the face of the greater involvement in the development of libraries from other traditions this should be no cause for regret but should rather be welcomed as perhaps another step along the road to a truly international concept of library development and library service'. (10) I have tried to suggest that this 'truly international concept' is either a mirage or a mechanism without much significance.

Our last example should come from a country of the Third World. Joyce Robinson, who has directed a dynamic library system in Jamaica (which in 1978 had a progressive government), insists that the librarian must be concerned with a wider social purpose. Having mentioned population growth, illiteracy, education, limited human and technical resources, she goes on: 'the librarian's analysis and understanding of these problems is a prerequisite to library planning in each country'—she is a committed person. (11) Yet having absorbed the Anglo-American tradition in these matters she feels obliged to say (in the same paper) that we must preserve 'the neutrality and objectivity cherished by the profession'. Can we be neutral about illiteracy or objective about disease? It is because the profession is so often neutral that it has sometimes made little impact.

Conclusion

Faced with these circumstances, which at the present time limit the possibilities of library development, what should the librarian do? He can become a social revolutionary, which may take him out of the library altogether. Or he can pretend that the social conditions around him do not exist or are not his concern (a common response). Or within the circumstances in which he finds himself he will do what he can (not a heroic role but an honest one). All that I am suggesting is that his first responsibility particularly as a student is to *understand*. That is the proper limit of my responsibilities as a teacher.

REFERENCES

1 Parker, J S, *A comparative study of the diffusion and application in developing countries of the concept of integrated national planning of library services with special reference to the work of Unesco* FLA thesis, 1978.

2 Sharr, F A, *The library needs of Northern Nigeria: a report* Ministry of Information, Kaduna, 1963.

3 Penna, C V and others, *National library and information services: a handbook for planners* 3rd edition, Butterworth, 1977.

4 Burckhardt, F, *National library planning in the United States* National Commission on Libraries and Information Science. Ch 3.

5 Shepard, Marietta Daniele, 'National planning for library services in Latin America' *in* Penna, C V, *The planning of library and documentation services* 2nd edition, Paris, Unesco, 1970, 143.

6 *Meeting of experts on the national planning of library services in Latin America*, Paris, Unesco, 1966, 10.

7 Penna, C V and others, *op cit*.

8 Needham, C, *in* New, P G, *Education for librarianship* Bingley, 1978.

9 Vosper, Robert and Newkirk, L J (eds), *National and international library planning* Munich Verlag Dokumentation, 1976, 14.

10 Parker, J S, *op cit*.

11 Robinson, Joyce L, 'National planning for libraries in developing countries: the Jamaican situation' *in* Vosper, Robert and Newkirk, L J (eds), *op cit*, 69.

14

INTERNATIONAL AND COMPARATIVE LIBRARY STUDIES

In the previous chapter we considerd international programmes on behalf of national library services. It remains to examine other international professional activity, with particular reference to its literature. In so doing it will be necessary to indicate its value and limitations.

International librarianship
The study of library development beyond national frontiers reflects the situation since World War II, when for the first time global preoccupations became central and not peripheral. To tribal societies like those of the Old Testament, 'the eyes of the fool are fixed on the ends of the earth', but in our time the fools are those who ignore them. Current library developments also constitute a response to the challenge of a changed international power structure and the emergence of the Third World.

The literature dealing with these events is necessarily, in the first instance, largely descriptive and a record of what is happening both in individual countries and in their relations with each other; much of it is an account of the work of professional associations, national and international. I have stressed that we are dealing mainly with the literature because there is a curious tendency to consider the documentation (much of it official and therefore highly suspect) as if it were reality, or rather as if it were the *only* reality. There is also a quite unnecessary amount of mystification and many arcane problems have been invented so that academics can validate their existence and provide elaborate mysteries for the edification of their students. These are dealt with in the last part of this chapter, and before entering this murky arena, it might help if we enumerate some of the library activities which can be called international —a full description of these is outside the scope of this enquiry.

International activities
1   International organisations promote library development in individual countries and attempt to set up those standards which can be transferred

(for example, with regard to statistics). Unesco, as a specialised agency of the United Nations, represents national co-operation, as distinct from IFLA and FID which organise the national organisations on a professional basis. This distinction is of some significance as it gives the work of Unesco an added dimension. There is also now an association representing the library profession in the countries of the British Commonwealth (the Commonwealth Library Association, COMLA). The current trend is for these bodies to co-operate more closely with each other in joint ventures as with the NATIS project (Unesco and IFLA).

2   Capitalist philanthropic agencies such as the Carnegie trusts and the Rockefeller Foundation have had a decisive impact on library development in individual countries of the Third World. All foreign aid involves strings, but in the cultural and educational field these are usually not directly economic but ideological in a subliminal way. For example, advisers come from the donor countries or students are sent to study there. Recipients are not expected to be grateful but the cultural influence is naturally felt.

3   For the English-speaking world the national information services particularly USIS (the United States Information Service) have set up libraries which, in addition to providing information and propaganda on behalf of their governments, may serve as model libraries.

4   Cultural bodies like the Alliance Francaise, and especially the British Council, have made a very substantial contribution to library development in many countries and also provide libraries which can be regarded as model services. In many ex-colonial countries the British Council has pioneered the public library system and has continued to provide assistance of various kinds. I have separated this kind of cultural work from direct propaganda of national information services because the distinction is often not understood.

5   Library associations in the developed countries have undertaken various useful activities in the less developed world; notably the American Library Association, as one would expect from US global interests and responsibilities.

6   Some governments, notably those of Britain, the USA and Canada, provide opportunities for young people to go abroad to assist national development by working in libraries. The value of the contribution made depends on the quality of the individuals sent and how they are employed. The American Peace Corps volunteers have been suspect in some countries as possible agents of the CIA, probably an unfair suspicion. Volunteers are sometimes exploited by the host countries and given too much or the

wrong kind of work. No survey of their contribution has been made but it is likely to be out of all proportion to the numbers involved. Many teachers who have worked under these schemes have also helped considerably in building up school libraries.

7   There are various types of educational programmes, run by national and international agencies, including assistance for students to study overseas. These may take the form of a basic professional education, the provision of opportunities for higher studies, special international courses such as those run by the British Council or the College of Librarianship, Wales, or of educational tours. Not all of this training is foreign aided, as individual governments provide grants for their own students.

8   Individual advisers or 'experts' sponsored by a variety of agencies including those mentioned above have played a significant role throughout the Third World. The value of their contribution derives not so much from their expertise (which may be no greater than that of some people on the spot) but from the fact that they are outsiders who are not involved in local power struggles. Whether their reports or their recommendations are even implemented naturally depends on the social forces in operation at the time. All over the world, in half-forgotten files, their reports have accumulated, but here and there, when times are propitious, they are taken out and dusted and even acted upon. The functions of these temporary advisers should, of course, be distinguished from those of foreigners who actually work in the countries concerned.

9   Many librarians and some library school lecturers have worked in a senior capacity, often as pioneers, in countries not their own. Here we are concerned only with those who have been employed by developing countries. The time is approaching when a comprehensive and accurate evaluation of their contribution would be most useful. In most cases an accurate or balanced account of the expatriate contribution has not been forthcoming, partly because indigenous librarians find it difficult officially to give due recognition for the work their foreign colleagues have done. (Their private responses are another matter.) Many of these expatriates started as employees of the foreign agencies we have listed, and then have continued to spend their entire careers in one or several Third World countries. I am referring particularly to individuals from the industrialised countries, but there are now also a number of senior librarians from underdeveloped regions, for example India and Pakistan, who have taken up posts elsewhere.

10   All of the above activities are reflected in the literature, which I am here mentioning separately in order not to confuse the records with

231

what they attempt to describe. The literature on international librarianship includes the reports of international conferences and the accounts to be found in the journals of international scope such as the *Unesco bulletin for libraries*, *Libri*, and the *International journal of librarianship*. Much of this documentation is 'international' in the sense either that it is describing the development of particular library services *for* the benefit of foreign librarians or that it is a description of these same library services *by* foreigners. We are justified in regarding such literature as having an international significance in a peculiar sense because in each case there is a foreign impact. A report intended for domestic consumption obviously should be different from one written for an international or even a foreign journal. Similarly accounts produced by outsiders, whether they are detailed or impressionistic, are quite different from indigenous literature. As we shall see such documentation, necessarily descriptive, cannot be regarded as fully comparative, but it constitutes the raw material for such studies; it is produced for a different purpose. A comparative element may be present (often not explicit) because at a rudimentary level all thinking is comparative.

The above outline is presented with special reference to the impact of developed systems on those which are not. There is, of course, an influence in reverse and the writer of these words is a living witness. All I can do here is to mention such interaction, since it is outside the scope of this chapter.

Cultural independence
In other chapters we have tried to indicate how the power structures of the world cause a lack of independence which is not simply material, but also cultural and ideological. This is the legacy of European expansion, which still operates even in Latin America, where individual countries have been nominally independent for a very long time.

One can use expressions like 'cultural imperialism' but they are not very helpful and may be misleading if they are interpreted to imply some kind of conscious continuing process. On the contrary, the lack of cultural freedom is built into the historical circumstances; it is not a concept or a political programme which can easily be formulated or defined. One would naturally not expect that librarianship (the practice) or library science (the theory) could be immune from such factors, and we should now refer to some of them. We can take it for granted that while the positive value of a foreign impact, whether it is practical or theoretical, is relatively obvious, the limitations are not and are less likely to be discussed. All international relations have to include diplomacy. As one writer on comparative librarianship has observed, 'There is, in fact, a very real--albeit unstated--compromise with the whole truth'. (1) In other and less academic words, a lot of people have been telling lies.

Neo-colonial attitudes

We have already considered the reasons why the de-colonisation of the mind is so difficult that a conscious effort is required to undertake it. (I am here referring of course to the indigenous peoples of the Third World.) In the first instance the forces of nationalism begin this process, but there it often stops. Religious influences, when they run counter to the religion of the former colonial powers, also begin to shake the old foundations. This has been the role of Islam in the Middle East and elsewhere, but nationalist or religious movements often look to the past rather than the future and represent the only break with a colonial present.

In education, and therefore in library development also, a neo-colonial cultural attitude causes an inability to achieve the new perceptions that national development requires; the tinted spectacles which provide a particular view of the world cannot easily be exchanged. With regard to the new elites, a central driving force for individuals has always been that they should get away from a past symbolised by mud huts and the ubiquitous 'bush'. That is on a material level; the word 'bush' is also used in Africa to indicate a traditional state of mind and it is this mental condition which has to be discarded. When Western education comes along, it removes people from the bush for ever and in so doing catches them in a trap. This is a theme commonplace in much of African literature.

It is generally agreed that the key to any form of national development is to be found in the villages, whether it is water, electric light, roads, schools, or libraries. But the new Western-educated man, for good reasons, does not want to work in the rural areas. He prefers, again for good reasons, not to think about them. Why not concentrate therefore on library development in the towns? One is obliged to reply, 'Why not?'

The existence of foreign influence has tended to reinforce these attitudes. With regard to the setting up of libraries, foreign models had to be used in the first place, foreign advisers gave their advice and expatriates were more often employed to run library services in the earlier years. Their achievements were often outstanding, but if we are to judge by their published statements, they were not aware of the ideological problems I have concentrated upon. On the other hand, they came to understand their adopted countries well, and if they had not, would not have been so successful. It is difficult to see what else they could have done, especially in the immediate post-independence years. All that I am suggesting is that most of these foreigners and expatriates could not help in the de-colonising process except at the practical level, for example in the training of staff ultimately to take over from them. Meanwhile, the indigenous librarians could only discover new attitudes for themselves

But international activity in library development may serve to reinforce the traditional external infleunces and inhibit truly indigenous responses. A colleague has suggested that the international library network has produced a new human species which can be called IFLAman, comparable only to the Venus of Willendorf or the man on the Clapham bus. Such a man will not assist the de-colonising process; on the contrary, the indigenous librarian may become an IFLAman himself.

There has grown up, then, a kind of overhead horizontal cosmopolitan network (symbolised by the jet plane) which is preoccupied with alleged international standards and elitist concepts On an intellectual level there is a correspondence with the role of the new Third World business and professional classes generally. Their interests have united internationally in a manner which has never been achieved by the workers of the world. Expressed in this fashion this may sound like a simplistic conspiracy theory, which it is not. What I am suggesting (or repeating) is that development can only grow out of particular national circumstances and that international activities can supplement such growth. But when national development is not there, overhead 'umbrellas' may be at best irrelevant or at worst positively harmful. It should not be necessary to add that for a librarian who is often working in relative isolation and adverse conditions these international contacts can be of immense personal value.

Lastly, mention should be made of the expatriates who are involved in international library activities, whether as advisers conference participants or contributors to the literature. They are usually people (like most librarians) of great good will, but limited becuase they are too nice and too well-intentioned. Anxious (quite rightly) to avoid the superiority myths of colonial times, they gloss over deficiencies and play down the inherent conditions I have described. In some cases beneath their diplomatic behaviour one can detect attitudes which are both cynical and opportunist, as indicated by such common saws of practical wisdom as, 'It is not our place to criticise' or 'These are the stages we went through twenty [or 'five hundred'] years ago'. It is possible that such approaches can be defended in the context of professional politics, but they do not help the processes of national development or the people who have to struggle with them.

Comparative librarianship

At the beginning of this chapter we noted that there has been some confusion about comparative librarianship as an academic study. While some sceptics have doubted whether there can be such a discipline at all, the protagonists of the subject have spent much time discussing what it is not; they have argued interminably about definitions. Why is this?

Part of the answer must be that all new areas of study require some mapping out; also they have to be shown to be academically respectable. The drive to institutionalise the subject has inevitably led to the usual scientific pretensions. Some of our academic colleagues have become specialists and call themselves 'comparativists'. Yet in spite of all this methodological activity some disagreements remain and may well continue to remain.

The study of comparative education (which is often taken as a model) has been in existence for a long time but the situation is similar. As one authority notes, 'There is a curious phenomenon about comparative education. We all know that it exists. But in spite of that, the specialised teachers who have twice met under the auspices of Unesco have not succeeded in agreeing upon a definition of it'. (2) I am inclined to believe that such difficulties have always been inherent in library studies generally and I doubt whether anybody outside the academic world is much disturbed. Beyond the university walls does it really matter where one subject begins and another ends? They all represent different approaches to the same thing; it is the reality which should be our concern, not academic structures.

However, several matters which seem to me to be straightforward have been inflated (or reduced) to a quite extraordinary degree of obfuscation; theories have proliferated like jungle weeds. Is it the function of library educationists to bring chaos out of order or to complicate simplicities? A most satisfactory summary of the subject, its scope and value, can be found in Dorothy Collings' article in the *Encyclopedia of library and information science*. There is little to quarrel with there except that some of the alleged uses of comparative librarianship need not be taken too seriously.

Amongst such values most writers have been unable to resist making claims about the peace of the world: some of these have already been quoted. If the reduction of international tensions depends on comparative librarianship then Armageddon must surely be at hand.

Students who wish to examine a comprehensive overview of this field will turn to J Peram Danton's *The dimensions of comparative librarianship*, which has been called the Bible of comparative librarianship. (3) If this has become so, a little serious irreverence is called for. I am sure Danton would make no such supernatural claims except as a high priest of the academic industry. He begins his survey by noting that there is general agreement that comparative librarianship is primarily a *method* or an approach to the international library scene and I am sure this is correct. He goes on to state, however, that it is not only a method, and the rest of the book consists of a thorough exploration of what else it might be.

One of the main themes is that comparative librarianship must be guided by the work which has already been done in other comparative studies, notably in education. One can accept this without agreeing that it must be modelled on them precisely. Mainly because of this alleged necessity, he claims that comparisons should not normally be made *within* national boundaries but only across them. For example, 'the entire concept of comparative studies is violated on the point of logic, common sense, dictionary definitions and the findings, experience and development of other disciplines, when we include within their sphere and accept as such, books or projects limited to a specific country or cultural milieu. Those who would maintain other wise must be required to defend their position'. (4)

It is not however a difficult position to defend, particularly as Danton later on admits that some countries, such as Togo, Switzerland, and Canada, include more than one culture within their boundaries. This admission makes his own position untenable and curiously ethnocentric. Obviously 'cross-national' and 'cross-cultural' studies are not necessarily identical. Is it forbidden to compare Welsh culture or librarianship with that of England because they are both British? In most African countries (not just the small one he quotes) national boundaries are recent and artificial. It is useful therefore to compare, for example, one part or one state of Nigeria with another. The cultures and the languages are different. It is also worth mentioning that library systems, because they are often recent, are less likely to be of national scope than those of education or law. In consequence there may be wide and interesting variations within a nation which need to be studied comparatively. Such variations may be caused by geography or religion as well as by the decisive language factor. We must conclude, therefore, that this insistence on the significance of national frontiers is largely irrelevant.

A second unnecessary confusion which remains is that between international and comparative librarianship. It seems to me that Danton does not clarify this issue either. Many courses in library science regard the former as part of the latter or vice versa, and surely either approach can work because the conceptual distinction is clear eve if there are overlapping areas. International librarianship is largely descriptive, where comparative studies are more analytical and comparative. What else could they be? The descriptive accounts are the raw material for comparison, dealing with the same phenomena but on a different level.

In the more primitive days of library education in Britain most eaching of librarianship was descriptive. As studies progressed a greater element of analysis and even, by implication, comparison, became necessary. The approach or method, therefore, is now similar to that used in comparative librarianship, except that with the latter there is the cross-cultural requirement. It is perhaps for this reason that some critics have denied that comparative librarianship is a separate discipline at all. Certainly the distinctions are not clear-cut, and all studies of other cultures and even of one's own involve some degree of comparison, otherwise it is not possible even to think.

I suggest therefore that because the difference is mainly on of horizontal levels, rather than a vertical division between subjects, it is difficult precisely to define the boundaries of the discipline. Danton also stresses these differences between description and comparison and suggests that the second is on a higher level because it should involve research. He claims in effect that there are two academic activities and that the comparative one involves 'more scholarly investigation and research'. This is a similar analysis but I would not consider research as usually conducted to be necessarily a 'higher' activity; on the contrary. What is happening here is a concentration on *the type of academic activity involved* rather than on the reality with which it should deal. In the first instance, the workers in the knowledge industry are writing for each other and as agents of the academic process. It should not therefore cause surprise if somebody should claim that there is a gap between theory and practice. In fact this criticism has often been made, for example, 'As it stands, comparative librarianship runs the risk of encouraging superficial and bogus research based on the love of international comparison'. (5) The same writer mentions 'the questionable and highly theoretical research orientation displayed in the literature'.

Because of his insistence on properly organised academic research Danton does not consider that Asheim's book *Librarianship in developing countries* can be called a comparative study. The book was the result of an official tour and records impressions which are of great interest and importance. I would consider therefore that for librarians in developing countries, it is a comparative work of significance. Much of it is superficial and is intended to be; such reports have their place and are at least readable—which cannot often be said for the results of more academic investigations.

It seems to me that to regard such work as somehow falling below the requirements of true comparative standards is to over-value one kind of research. Academics regularly forget that the results of experience are forms of evidence which have their own value. I have found that students, for example, have been so misled by an emphasis on documents that they are unable to use their own experience of life in order to arrive at conclusions. It is possible that this is due to a misunderstanding of what research should be, but it is nevertheless a potent inhibiting factor; they come to the belief that no academic work can be valid unless it is backed up by a string of references to literature which lists other literature. If this is held to be merely an abuse of true academic work, then there is a great deal of abuse around.

The value of Asheim's book, bearing in mind that hardly anything else has been published on this subject, is that it provides a starting point. Many of his generalisations do not apply to African countries but are more applicable to the Middle East; similarly he had not visited communist countries at all, a severe handicap to the validity of his impressions. Also I have found that students become indignant about many of his statements, not so much because they are not accurate as because they do not explain why there are differences between library practices in America and the Third World. (This is what I have tried to do in some of the foregoing chapters.) Finally, he exhibits a degree of liberal confusion with regard to which American policies could or should be transferred without falling into neo-colonial practices. He believes in the 'building of bridges' between advanced and developing countries, a notion which I regard as dangerous and misleading.

Another common area of controversy concerns (once again) the place of value judgments in what is alleged to be a social science. Danton mentions Foskett's article in *Progress in library science* with general approval, but then quotes his statement that, 'What we are trying to do is to unravel the strands that go to make up a certain pattern, to assess these strands against those that make up other, different patterns and to try to *form estimates of the relative value of each*'. (6) My italics indicate the phrase to which Danton objects. He continues, 'Value judgments, in the strict meaning of the phrase, at any rate have no place in comparative studies'. (7) This is the positivist tradition of value-free sociology which we have already discussed.

Mrs Simsova takes the same line, except that her scientific model tends to be biological and not behavioural: 'Value judgments can be mentioned in the context of interpretation though they contribute little to an objective investigation as they reflect the investigators' value system'. (8) The key word here is 'mentioned'; one has to defer to values as if they were things or facts. The important point that the most powerful value systems may not be conscious or explicit is obscured. The implication seems to be that if, for example, one were to compare segregated libraries (sexual apartheid in Saudi Arabia or racial apartheid in South Africa) with libraries in other places where no such separations occur, then it would be unscientific to draw any moral conclusions.

We must agree with Danton's insistence throughout his study that the ultimate aim of comparative librarianship must consist of 'trying to arrive at valid generalisations and principles'. Yet it would appear that he is referring to *scientific* principles, and I am at a loss to understand what these might be; doubtless the answer to such a query would be that very little research of the right kind has yet been done. Presumably what would *not* be acceptable as 'principles' are Ranganathan's Laws of Library Science. As Ranganathan freely admitted in a personal letter to me in 1965, his 'laws' are not scientific but ethical principles. They are normative judgments disguised as 'laws'—for example, the law that 'books are for all' is wholly inoperative in most parts of the world but it is at least given lip service almost everywhere.

Conclusion

For the countries of the Third World the topics discussed in this and the previous chapter obviously have a special significance. Students from those countries will need an approach which meets their special requirements. At the present time the required literature is not yet available. What it will stress is that they should not begin by studying international umbrellas, nor the library systems of other countries, nor even with their own. They should start at the exact geographical location where they happen to be, whether libraries are to be found in such a place or not. The important thing is that they should exist as individuals (and not just as librarians) within their own environment, which should therefore be the centre of the world.

REFERENCES

1 Burnett, A D, *in* Burnett, A D, Gupta, R K and Simsova, S, *Studies in comparative librarianship: three essays presented for the Svensma prize 1971* Library Association, 1973, 7.
2 Rosello, Pedro, 'Comparative education as an instrument of planning' *in* Foskett, D J, *Reader in comparative librarianship* Information Handling Services, Colorado, 1976, 121.
3 Danton, J Peram, *The dimensions of comparative librarianship* Chicago, American Library Association, 1973.
4 *Ibid*, 4.
5 Jayakara, K S, 'Comparative librarianship, subject or research method?' *in Library Association Record* 76 (May 1974), 91-92.
6 Foskett, D J, 'Progress in library science, 1965' quoted in Danton, J Peram, *op cit*, 67.
7 Danton, J Peram, *op cit*, 67.
8 Simsova, Mrs S, 'Comparative librarianship as an academic subject' *in* Foskett, D J, *Reader in comparative librarianship* , *op cit*, 50.

15

CONCLUSION

We have now explored characteristics of underdevelopment which seem to me to have cultural importance. Some of the implications for library services have been noted but I have not pursued the matter as far as may be required for students: one hopes that others may do so. In 1968 Hassendorfer wrote 'what is still needed is a fuller analysis of the connexions between the political, economic, social and cultural factors in the evolution of societies and the development of public libraries':(1) this need remains for any type of library. However, I have hoped that in many cases these 'connections' become obvious once these political, social and cultural factors have been examined. Certainly it does become clear what connections should not be made.

Some examples may help to illustrate how important this is: two of them arise from comments made by Foskett. He has noted that 'If we believe that a society's traditions by and large embody and perpetuate what that society has found to be good and valuable for itself, are not campaigns to encourage reading, though highly esteemed in literate communities, likely to do more harm than good? What course then should a librarian advocate?' (2) This is a fair question and I suggest that the analysis of the foregoing chapters supplies the answer; this is, that in a context of national development, campaigns to encourage reading are essential. He also mentions that the library systems of Eastern Europe seem to be more appropriate as models for developing countries than those of capitalist states. On one level this is true: he then goes on to speculate whether such systems can be introduced only in communist societies. All the available evidence (some of which we have considered) suggests that in non-communist countries the social and political pre-requisites for transplanting these models are not present. You can have a national health service in a mixed economy like Britain and this represents a form of planning but the countries under consideration are not economies of that sort. It follows that the communist library systems cannot be transferred nor can a modified version be installed since half a plan is a contradiction in terms. All that one can hope for, in consequence, is that these same goals may be achieved by some other means. It is the goals that are important and much progress will have been made if these can receive not only passive acceptance but positive belief.

Our third example is of a different order. It is well known that in the nineteenth century Britain the pioneer advocates of public library services used to insist that setting up libraries would take people off the streets and out of the gin shops. Indeed a statement of this belief is to be found in the 'Report of the Select Committee on Inquiry into Drunkenness' as early as 1834. In retrospect this approach may seem a little odd yet in developing countries now we often encounter the same argument being used to advance the library cause. One Nigerian research student (3) has devoted an entire chapter of his thesis on reading to a study of drinking habits and there is an assumption in his work that if libraries existed fewer people would be in the bars. This, of course, cannot be proven either way yet the analysis indicates an awareness of the real social situation and therefore must be taken seriously. What he is saying in effect is that the circumstances which cause drinking to become a way of life must be eradicated before library services can be relevant. When social action is taken to create a new environment, then libraries will be a necessary part of it. An examination of these background factors may supply many answers of this kind and I have found that students are quite capable of drawing their own conclusions. For instance, with regard to Chapter 7 on culture, the implications are clear that librarians have certain responsibilities; first to understand the predicament; second to make their own contribution to the preservation of the past; and third to foster the cultural activities of the present. Or again, in the case of all forms of communication, education and information, the role of libraries can easily be understood even if it may not be fully appreciated in official quarters.

With regard to technological transfers, the implication has been that in librarianship as elsewhere they must be introduced wherever they are practical but that they should not be regarded as a yardstick for success since they do not *by themselves* constitute progress. The criteria which are central for evaluating development are not technological but human. If individual resources or qualities are absent or inadequate, sophisticated techniques become irrelevant. It is a matter, not of knowing how to operate machines but of understanding what to

242

use them for and when. Further it is a question not just of the possession of abilities but of a drive to harness them for a social purpose.

Implicit in these discussions has been a concentration on the service principle. This sounds like simple personal ethics such as we encounter in St. Paul's epistle to the Corinthians or in the other great religions of the world. The type of concern we are stressing here certainly includes individual ethics but it cannot be confined there. Everybody knows how we should behave in order to be good even if we refrain from becoming so. There are numerous immoral societies where most people are moral on a personal level: that is not the point. I have tried to show that professional ideals should not be just personal nor even social but profoundly political. This type of commitment includes not only an act of choice or will but also an effort to understand. (The type of stupidity which arises from a refusal to understand is rightly considered to be a sign of moral and intellectual turpitude.)

Students, I have discovered, can list the kind of professional activities which might be undertaken but they do not, on the other hand, fully appreciate why such endeavours may be impractical. It is paradoxical that it is their own background which they cannot comprehend partly because it is changing so rapidly and partly because the prevalent mystifications inhibit their understanding. As I have tried to show, the official education systems do little to dispel this fog: on the contrary they are fog making machines themselves. In consequence young people have an ignorance about the modern world which is truly monumental. It can be objected with some justification that this lack of awareness is also common in countries like Britain. This is, of course true, but it matters less for several reasons, one of which is that the average student at secondary or university level in Britain is not destined to lead his people into the promised land. He is not automatically part of a minority élite and if there is a promised land he does not believe in it. But in the new countries that is precisely the Moses role which the young people will have to play. In consequence their need for suitable armour against fate and for intellectual equipment to moderate their destiny is that much the greater. The conclusion has to be, therefore, that an examination of the social context is more important than similar studies in more developed circumstances: that was always the rationale behind the demand for 'general studies' in new universities.

Those who are directly involved with Library Science (by which I mean the study as distinct from the practices of librarianship) have to start with these basic elements in their situation without which their studies become meaningless. If this is not done they will continue an insidious neo-colonial tradition which consists of a cynical pretence that such conditions do not exist. It cannot be denied that the present obstacles to development are formidable. In all the preceding chapters the examination of these obstructive factors produces a negative impression and an apparent list of woes. Yet this is where one has to begin and in every case I have tried to show, that in spite of these barriers, the potentialities are there and the possibilities of human advance are infinite. In most cases the evidence points to the conclusion that these potentialities will be fully realised only when the revolution comes.

REFERENCES
1 Hassendorfer, J, 'Comparative studies and the development of public libraries' *Unesco bulletin for libraries* 22, Jan-Feb 1968, 13-18.
2 Foskett, D J, 'Comparative librarianship as a field of study: definitions and dimensions', in *Reader in comparative librarianship* op cit, 7.
3 Fashagba, Steven O, *Library possibility in traditional areas: case study, Kabba* (unpublished MLS thesis), Ahmadu Bello University, 1978, Ch 4.

BASIC BIBLIOGRAPHY

Part One of this list consists of works which I consulted. In Part Two I have added other items which are important, particularly in relation to development.

The sources I have listed constitute a small selection from a vast literature and are simply those which I found useful for my purposes: many of them were intended for the general reader and those who require a comprehensive bibliography on their topics will need to search elsewhere.

PART ONE
Altbach, Philip G and Smith, Keith, eds, 'Publishing in the third world' *Library trends*, Spring 1978.

Anderson, Dorothy, *Universal bibliographic control* Verlag Dokumentation, 1974.

Asheim, Lester, *Librarianship in the developing countries* University of Illinois Press, 1966.

Batten, T R, *Communities and their development* OUP, 1957.

Beeby, C E, *The quality of education in developing countries* Harvard University Press, 1966.

Bell, Daniel, *The coming of post-industrial society* Basic Books, 1973.

Benge, Ronald C, *Bibliography and the provision of books* ALA 1963 reprinted by University Microfilms Ltd for College of Librarianship Wales, 1971.

Benge, Ronald C, *Communication and identity* Bingley, 1972.

Benge, Ronald C, *Libraries and cultural change* Bingley, 1970.

Berger, Peter L, *Invitation to sociology* Pelican, 1966.

Berger, Peter L, *Pyramids of sacrifice: political ethics and social change* Pelican, 1977.

Berger, Peter L *and others, The homeless mind* Pelican, 1974.

Black, C E, *The dynamics of modernisation* Harper and Row, 1966.

Burnett, A P, *and others, Studies in comparative librarianship* Library Association for IFLA, 1973.

Castle, E B, *Education for self help: new strategies for developing countries* OUP, 1972.

Coombs, Philip, *The world education crisis: a systems analysis* OUP, 1968.

Curle, Adam, *Educational strategy for developing societies* 2nd ed Tavistock Publications, 1970.

Danton, J P, *The dimensions of comparative librarianship* ALA, 1973.

Davidson, Basil, *The Africans: an entry to cultural history* Penguin, 1973.

DeKadt, Emanuel, and Williams, Gavin, *Sociology and development* Tavistock Publications, 1974.

Dickson, David, *Alternative technology and the politics of technical change* Fontana: Collins, 1974.

Dim, Peter T, *Current state of printing and publishing in Nigeria* BLS research project, Ahmadu Bello University, 1976 (unpublished).

Dore, Ronald, *The diploma disease: education, qualification and development* Allen and Unwin, 1976.

Dumont, Rene, *False start in Africa* Deutsch, 1966.

Fadipe, N A, *The sociology of the Yoruba* Ibadan University Press, 1970.

Fafunwa, A Babs, *History of education in Nigeria* Allen and Unwin, 1974.

Fanon, Frantz, *The wretched of the earth* Penguin, 1963.

Foskett, D J, *Reader in comparative librarianship* Information handling services, Colorado, 1976.

Frank, Andre Gander, *Capitalism and underdevelopment in Latin America* Pelican, 1971.

Freire, Paulo, *Cultural action for freedom* Penguin, 1972.

Freire, Paulo, *Pedagogy of the oppressed* Penguin, 1972.

Gellner, Ernest, *Words and things* Pelican, 1968.

George, Susan, *How the other half dies; the real reason for world hunger* Penguin, 1976.

Hayter, T, *And as imperialism* Penguin, 1971.

Harvey, J F, *Comparative and international library science* Scarecrow Press, 1977.

Horowitz, Irving L, *The new sociology* OUP, 1964.

Horton, Robin, and Finnegan, Ruth, eds, *Modes of thought: essays on thinking in western and non-western societies* Faber, 1973.

Hunter, Guy, *The best of both worlds* (Institute of Race Relations) OUP, 1967.

Hunter, G, *Modernising peasant societies: a comparative study in Africa and Asia* OUP, 1967.

Ike, Vincent C, *University development in Africa: the Nigerian experience* OUP (Ibadan), 1976.

Illieh, Ivan D, *Deschooling society* Calder and Boyars, 1971.

Illich, Ivan, *Tools for conviviality* Fontana: Collins, 1973.

Jeffries, Richard, *Class, power and ideology in Ghana: the railwaymen of Sekondi* Cambridge University Press, 1978.

Lerner, Daniel, *The passing of traditional society: modernising the Middle East* Glencoe Free Press, 1958.

Levy, Marion J, *Modernization and the structure of societies, a setting for international affairs* Princeton University Press, 1966.

Leys, Colin, ed, *Politics and change in developing countries: studies in the theory and practice of development* CUP, 1969.

Lindgvist, Sven, *The shadow: Latin America faces the seventies* Penguin, 1972.

McCarthy, Cavan, *Developing libraries in Brazil* Scarecrow Press, 1975.

May, Rollo, *Love and will* Collins: Fontana, 1972.

Myrdal, G, *Asian drama: an enquiry into the wealth of nations* Penguin, 1968.

Myrdal, Gunnar, *The challenge of world poverty* Pelican, 1971.

Myrdal, Gunnar, *Objectivity in social research* Duckworth, 1970.

Nduka, Otoni, *Western education and the Nigerian cultural background* OUP (Ibadan), 1964.

Nyerere, Julius N, *Education for self reliance* Dar-es-Salaam, Government Printer, 1967.

Nyerere, Julius N, *Man and development* OUP, 1974.

Nyerere, Julius N, *Ujamaa; essays on socialism* OUP, 1970.

Obiechina, Emmanuel N, *Onitsha market literature* Heinemann, 1972.

Obiechina, E N, *An African popular literature: a study of Onitsha market pamphlets* CUP, 1973.

Oluwasanmi, Edwina, *and others, Publishing in the seventies.* Proceedings of an international conference held at the University of Ife, 1973.

Oxaal, Ivor, *and others, Beyond the sociology of development* Routledge, 1975.

Parrinder, Geoffrey, *African traditional religion*, 3rd ed Sheldon Press, 1974.

247

Penna, C V, *The planning of library and documentation services* 2nd ed, revised by P H Sewell and Herman Liebaers, Unesco, 1970.

Penna, C V, *and others, National library and information services: a handbook for planners* Butterworth, 1977.

Polanyi, Michael, *Personal knowledge* Routledge and Kegan Paul, 1961.

Rodinson, Maxime, *Islam and capitalism* Penguin, 1977.

Sharwood-Smith, *Sir B, But always as friends: northern Nigeria and the Cameroons: 1921-1957* Government Printer, Kaduna, 1964.

Schumacher, E F, *Small is beautiful* Blond and Briggs, 1973.

Seers, Dudley and Joy, Leonard, eds, *Development in a divided world* Penguin, 1971.

Turnbull, Colin M, *Man in Africa* David and Charles, 1976.

Van Rensburg, Patrick, *Report from Swaneng Hill: education and employment in an African country* Dag Hammarskjold Foundation, Almquist and Wiksell, Stockholm, 1974.

Vosper, Robert, and Newkirk, Leone J, eds, *National and international library planning* Verlag Dokumentation, Munich, 1976.

Wallenius, A B, ed, *Libraries in East Africa* Scandinavian Institute of African Studies, Uppsala, 1971.

Weiner, Myron, ed, *Modernization: the dynamics of growth* Basic Books, 1966.

Williams, Raymond, *Keywords: a vocabulary of culture and society* Fontana: Collins, 1976.

Worsley, Peter, *The third world* Weidenfeld and Nicholson, 1964.

PART TWO

Baran, Paul A, *The political economy of growth* Penguin, 1973.

Berger, P P, and Luckman, T, *The social constructions of reality* Penguin, 1967.

Bernstein, H, ed, *Underdevelopment and development: the third world today*. Selected readings. Penguin, 1973.

Brown, Lester R, *Seeds of change* Praeger, 1970.

DeWilde, J C, *Experiences in agricultural development in Africa* Johns Hopkins, 1967.

Donaldson, Peter, *Worlds apart* Penguin, 1973.

Finer, S E, *The man on horseback* 2nd ed Pall Mall, 1978.

Frank, Andre Gunder, *Sociology of development and underdevelopment of sociology* 1971.

Garaudy, Roger, *The alternative future: a vision of Christian marxism* Penguin, 1976.

Geerz, C, ed, *Old societies and new states* Free Press, 1963.

Habermas, Jurgen, *Knowledge and human interests* 1972.

Illich, Ivan, *Celebration of awareness* 1971.

Jolly, Richard, *Planning education for African development* East African Publishing House, Nairobi, 1969.

Leibenstein, H, *Economic backwardness and economic growth* Wiley, 1963.

NAME INDEX

SUBJECT INDEX

Adult education 83 et seq
  adverse factors 92; Europe 91;
  functional 87; illiteracy 83 et seq;
  Nigeria 92 et seq; vocational 97;
  women 93
Agriculture 22, 42
  education 66; mass media of
  communication 161
Alliance Française 230
American Peace Corps 230
Arabic manuscripts 185
Arabic script 95
Archives 204
Art
  Africa 131
Argentina 141
Aztecs 144

Bendel State Library Board 180
Bible 111, 124, 125
  publishing 174
Bibliography 227
  automation 201; book trade 183;
  universal bibliographical control
  (UBC) 223
Bibliometrics 217
Black Orpheus 173
Blasphemy 139
Book development councils 171, 182
Bookselling 182
  Arabic manuscripts 185; adverse
  factors 182, 187; Christian mis-
  sionaries 184; relations with
  publishers 187; state services 186;
  university bookselling 185
Boy Scout movement 149
Brazil 88, 160, 198, 203
British Council
  library programmes 219, 231
Bureaucracy
  information 196; modernisation 17

Cameroons 174
Carnegie Corporation of New York 219
Carnegie United Kingdom Trust 219

Censorship 135 et seq
  Britain 138; Nigeria 142
Centre de Littérature Evangélique
  (CLE) Cameroons 174
Children's literature 111
China 15, 24, 37, 46, 104, 136,
  140, 162
Christianity 59, 111, 133
  missions 59, 91, 174, 184
Clitoridectomy 126
Cinema *see* Film
College of Librarianship Wales 231
Commonwealth Library Association
  (COMLA) 230
Communication 147 et seq
  personal 147, 148; traditional 148
Comparative education 235
Comparative librarianship 229 et seq,
  232, 235
Consciousness 23, 38, 121
Corruption 182, 214
Cuba 43, 100
Culture 121 et seq
  costume 132; definitions 121;
  liberation 76, 118, 167, 213;
  oral 105, 131; revivals 132;
  survivals 129; traditional 125

Dancing
  Africa 131
Daystar 174
Decolonisation 89, 213
Denmark 220
Development 9 et seq, 13 et seq
  Africa 9; human rights 145; mass
  media of communication 157, 161;
  Nigeria 14, 22; status 43; Sudan 23;
  technology 40; terminology 11
Drinking establishments 195, 241
Drought, Sahel region 36, 205
Drums 149

East African literature bureau 176
East African Publishing House 173
Economic growth 13, 15

252

253